$\mathscr{P}$EACE
AND
HARMONY
IN
DAILY LIVING

FACING LIFE MOMENT TO MOMENT,
BEING ANCHORED IN TRANQUILITY

RAMESH S. BALSEKAR

$\mathscr{P}$EACE
AND
HARMONY
IN
DAILY LIVING

FACING LIFE MOMENT TO MOMENT,
BEING ANCHORED IN TRANQUILITY

Edited by
Susan Waterman

Yogi Impressions

Yogi Impressions

PEACE AND HARMONY
IN DAILY LIVING

First published in India in 2003 by
Yogi Impressions Books Pvt. Ltd.
61, Anjali, Minoo Desai Road, Colaba,
Mumbai 400 005, India.
Website: www.yogiimpressions.com

First Edition, February 2003
Second reprint, March 2004

ISBN 81-901059-8-1

Printed at Thomson Press, New Delhi

Dedicated to
Göran Ekdahl
of Sweden
with whom a talk triggered
the happening of this book.

"I had money, I had fame, I had the good health
to enjoy life, and yet I felt incomplete, inadequate."

And, thus, was a seeker born.

September 15, 2001

Dearest Ramesh,

It was so enriching to see and hear you again in Schermau, Germany. For family reasons, I had to leave before the seminar was over but on my way back, the thought and memory came of a very recent event where I could see a big change in my life. The story is the following.

During the last six years, I have been acting as neutral Chairman at ordinary shareholder's meetings with 300/400 shareholders in a public company with many conflicts between 2/3 groups of shareholders. It used to be a burdensome task sensing a worry of what would come next and for reactions to my ways of leading the discussions and making the propositions for voting.

This year, however, having been with you for a little over a year, a dramatic change showed itself. No matter how stupid or ill-willed the suggestions were, they were handled neutrally without any judging and then taken to various votings which, in themselves, were just flowing in a series of raising hands for 'yes' or 'no'.

Afterwards a lot of appreciation and admiration was received. One comment was that I never lost control or did not even seem affected by the attacks in between the shareholders and sometimes towards the Chairman.

I simply acted or performed whatever came up in my mind in the moment, using my experience and sometimes quickly consulting the legal secretary of the meeting. I was leaving the scene completely relaxed, surrounded with thanks and congratulations from the President and the Board of Directors of the Company.

With highest regards,
Göran Ekdahl

P.S.

Thank you for your latest book *The Ultimate Understanding*. It is the best thing I have ever held in my hands. To sense your wording slowly sink in is an adventure. THIS is how it is.

CONTENTS

What does Self-realization really mean in day-to-day living?; what brings about peace and harmony in day-to-day living?; consciousness, in which everything happens like a dream, is the dreamer in this living dream of life; true perceiving; the Buddha's statement – *samsara* is *dukkha*; the thinking mind in daily living; advice from an avatar, Ramakrishna Paramahamsa.

The sense of personal doership; convincing the ego-doer-seeker; the peace in life that is sought is not something to be 'achieved'; the basic cause of fear; a distinction between the experience and the experiencer; any form of escape can only lead to isolation and greater resistance; the importance of silence; what is meditation?

The essence of life and living would seem to be problems; making a decision; in the quiescence of the mind comes not the answer to the problem but action; the mind creates the problem; the inability to accept What-Is; hell is other people; a personal experience in my career.

FOREWORD

The famous psychoanalyst and social reformer, Erich Fromm, said that "Man is the only animal for whom his own existence is a problem which he has to solve." Most of us view life from this perspective, getting caught up in the web of daily living – its ups and downs, highs and lows and the emotional turmoils that usually go with it. As *Advaita* sage Ramesh Balsekar says, "What is not realized is that life is like a wide and deep river flowing incessantly, continuously, always in movement – whereas the day-to-day living for most people, seemingly out of choice, is a preference for the security and stagnancy of the little pools beside the river."

Ramesh avers that what usually disturbs our peace and tranquility – is a thought. A thought about something that we should or shouldn't have done, or that which someone else should or shouldn't have done to us. Such thoughts result in feelings of ill will, hatred, jealousy, guilt, shame, fear, arrogance and self-righteous anger. Paul Valery, the French poet, could not have put it better when he said, "Man's greatest misfortune is that he has no organ, no kind of eyelid or brake to mask or block a thought, or all thoughts, when he wants to."

The Indian philosophy of *Advaita* is based upon the concept of 'non-duality' which affirms that there is only 'One Source'. Ramesh uses an apt metaphor to describe this: just as electricity passes through different gadgets and each of them, in turn, produces that which it is designed to; the impersonal energy operates, in a similar manner, through different body-mind organisms and each body-mind organism produces an output based on its programming and conditioning. No one is a 'doer' but, rather, all actions are happenings which could not have happened unless they were ordained by this 'One Source' which some identify as God.

We all seek the courage to face whatever life brings, while being anchored in peace. Through this book Ramesh shows us how, by accepting the words of the Buddha, that "Events happen, deeds are done, but there is no individual doer thereof," we can find the way to this state of 'being'. And, when are we at peace? Ramesh could not have put it more simply when he says: "We are at peace when we are comfortable with ourselves and comfortable with others. Or, inversely, when we are not uncomfortable with ourselves and not uncomfortable with others."

Ramesh is, perhaps, the most lucid and compelling spiritual teacher on the subject of *Advaita*. He is indeed *Advaita's* priceless treasure and this brilliant book is the jewel in its crown. Why do I say this? I say it because, of what use is *Advaita* and all spiritual talk unless you can apply it in day-to-day living? This is precisely what the book is about. So go ahead and start reading this offering from one of India's foremost contemporary sages. And, you may just find the way to peace and harmony in your daily living. As Ramesh would say, "It will happen if it's supposed to happen." I would think, however, that the chances are good since this book has already found its way into your hands. And, finally, to use the words of Jonathan Swift, "May you *live* all the days of your life."

In happiness and in peace.

– Gautam Sachdeva
December, 2002

*E*DITOR'S
NOTE

For a number of months during 2001-2002, Ramesh's morning talks conveyed a common theme: peace and harmony in daily living. The apparent inspiration for this book on daily living was the story of a seeker from Sweden, a man named Göran Ekdahl, reputedly one of the topmost lawyers in his country. In his introductory talk with Ramesh, Göran explained that he had everything that a man could want in life – success, money, good friends and family, fame and good health. Yet, at the same time there remained a sense of incompleteness, inadequacy, of something yet missing. After he learned from his accountant that he had even more money than he thought, he decided to retire immediately and set out to discover what the missing element might be. The active spiritual search had been launched. Within a short time, having come across a couple of books by Ramesh, he was compelled to visit him in Bombay. From the outset, with a little gentle guidance from the Master, it was readily understood that what Göran was really seeking was peace and harmony in his daily living.

The teachings of *Advaita* (*a+dvaita* = non-duality) are for here and now, for life as it happens on a daily basis, not for some other life in some unknown future, and surely not for some unknown somebody in another lifetime. When the sudden realization happens (the happening called 'enlightenment') that there is truly no doer in life, and that all action is not something done by someone but a divine happening, Ramesh emphasizes that one continues living as the same individual but without the sense of doership, without the load of sin and guilt, hatred and malice, which is the familiar human 'bondage'. Accordingly, the Ultimate Understanding is not removed from daily living; the apperception brings the deepest possible acceptance and peace while living life in the world as we know it. According to Ramesh, it is just that simple. It is important at the outset that the seeker be clear about the seeking: that the seeking happens – there is seeking and no seeker; and that the goal of the ego-seeker, really, is to be comfortable with oneself and with others, which in essence means peace and harmony in daily living.

Ramana Maharshi said that a concept is like a thorn – an instrument used to remove another thorn, and then both are discarded. The concepts are not the Truth, but are pointers to the Truth. Much confusion arises from the rhetoric of putative spiritual masters, *gurus*, enlightened teachers, and new-age therapies. Only a man of Understanding, one totally steeped in the Understanding, can convey the Truth and project the force of the Truth. The prevalence of teachings that offer consumable comfort reflects the financial reward that often goes hand-in-hand with popular teachings. Hence the perpetuation of a variety of practices, beliefs and thought patterns. The inherent contradictions and conflicts in such doctrines may be felt by the practitioner, but are so disguised that they either escape the scrutiny of the confused seeker, or may cause such suffering as to force the seeker to seek a new approach seeking to look deeper into the problem.

Concomitant with the refusal or oversight of many teachers to elaborate upon the nature of the seeking is the propagation of the various myths about enlightenment. Numerous practices, holding the promise of enlightenment, may be given in an enticing variety: one individual may be told to be a *sadhu* or a wandering mendicant for a number of years; and another may be told to chant and meditate for hours and hours in a glamorous ashram; and, of course, there is the option of self-inquiry and contemplation, whether in three, seven or eleven prescribed steps. Rare is the teacher who bothers to clearly mention that the understanding is necessarily that there is no one doing the practice – that the valid inquiry is to find out 'who is the doer?' How many times is the seeker told to 'kill the ego' without ever being told precisely what the ego is? If the seeker can successfully 'let God function through him', he is told that enlightenment is close at hand in this lifetime, or surely the next one or two.

The seeking is in phenomenality, in duration; daily living is in phenomenality, in duration. The point of both is to be comfortable – peaceful – comfortable with oneself, with others and with the Creator. Beyond that, what more can one possibly want? Never has there been a time without suffering (*dukkha*), never has there been a time without peace (*shanti*). What every human being experiences as *dukkha* or *shanti* is one's destiny, God's Will. Never does one exist without the other. All one can do is to do what one wants and then accept What-Is.

Oft-times the fuel for the fire of seeking is the notion of *karma*, in a variety of interpretations. 'As you sow, so you reap': yet is this actually the experience in everyone's daily living? *Karma* means 'action' – nothing more. And there is no implicit assumption of *punya* or merit being gained on the basis of quantities of good deeds done. Life can go on, without foregoing the pleasures and benefits of this life to experience more of the same in the next life. The magnanimous assertion of a human being to want to bring a halt to the suffering of all humanity for all time can only arise from sheer neglect of the potency and the supremacy of God's Will. This in itself brings about the frustration, the bondage of the seeker in his sense of doership. Ramesh himself gives credence to the notion of 'original sin' in a most precise and practical way: the usurping of the pure Subjectivity by an individual object in relation to another object. When engaged in such an inevitably futile battle – the battle itself being the obstruction to the peace and harmony being sought – it would be rendered impossible to even catch a glimpse of the goal of the seeking.

Whatever happens cannot happen unless it is according to the Will of God. If war is to happen, it cannot be other than it is God's Will, and so a reign of terror, and so a reign of peace. Once there is the complete and total acceptance of God's Will – in every possible circumstance – then the life of this 'seeking seeker' is necessarily put to rest and all that continues is a functioning in Totality. The understanding is the peace and harmony in day-to-day living. However, if the question still arises 'what should I do?' whether in the context of making a decision, doing spiritual practice, or giving guidance to a child, the answer is, of course, 'do what you think you should do, and leave the rest to God'.

While having benefited from the guidance and practices of one particular 'spiritual path' for 10 years, my unexpected meeting with Ramesh and his concepts brought immediate relief and resolution to the confusion and conflicts which had been gnawing away for over a year while still living in an ashram. What was apparent was a certain inconsistency between the practices which were very much 'done', purportedly usually to improve oneself, and often under supervision and guidance as 'trainings' and 'contemplations', and the corresponding plea to 'let the presence of God function through you', which had its own certain appeal: yet, somehow the practices and the plea did not match, nor did the plea itself survive the scrutiny of reason. Not only did Ramesh's uncompromised concepts of non-duality bring a relief from relentless irking attempts to control by incessant doing, but more important, relief from the blame of oneself and others for what were identified and perceived as various actions of wrong-doing and mutual disapproval.

I was stunned, completely taken, by Ramesh's ability – and willingness – with so few words to explain so very clearly, precisely how life happens: that nothing at all happens unless it is God's Will, and moreover that this is in essence ensured in the manifestation, in Totality, by the singular functioning of one Primal Energy. He made it clear that it is not even a question of 'letting' this happen, it is simply what happens. The confusion just vanished, along with the suffering of guilt and blame, making way for peace and harmony in daily living – even while living in the challenging city of Bombay! A second major impact was the confirmation by Ramesh that *dukkha* and *shanti* do go hand-in-hand; and once the acceptance of What-Is settles in, life and living become more like a game, with whatever share of ups and downs, but with less and less involvement and more and more amusement and enjoyment. With the peace and harmony, the wonder of life is seen with a fresh glow, and full participation in one's role in the totality of manifestation happens naturally with ease and comfort.

Ramesh is clearly not unduly concerned about 'selling' his concept, whether it is accepted or not. His primary concern is that the seeker should understand the concept thoroughly, without any confusion, in all its aspects. And for that reason, he invites the seeker to ask any question – personal, pertinent or impertinent – and even suggests possible questions and provides the answers. One morning, one seeker came and challenged Ramesh with great enthusiasm, asking if he could have a "confrontation" with him. Ramesh was obviously delighted. By the end of a most entertaining talk, the seeker had been deeply impacted by the confrontation, and Ramesh had totally enjoyed it.

As an intellectual understanding goes deeper into total under-standing, the concept of non-doership becomes so appealing, bringing with it relief from the bondage of the load of shame and guilt. Indeed, the seeker may confess that it is an intellectual understanding and that he is eager for it to 'take hold'; the ego then asks what he can do to help bring this about. Ramesh stresses again and again that the concept can become the truth only when it is tested in the fire of one's personal experience. The only *sadhana* (spiritual practice) Ramesh recommends is to investigate one-by-one any number of actions that happen during a day and find out whether those actions are 'your' actions, or if they could have happened without some preceding action having happened. One will surely come to the convincing conclusion that 'no action is my action'. Of course, it is to be understood that whether the seeker must investigate 5, 50 or 500 actions is his destiny and the Will of God, and moreover, whether the investigation actually happens is also the Will of God!

Day-to-day living and spiritual seeking are neither mutually exclusive nor isolated happenings. The beauty of Ramesh's concept is that the apparent 'benefit' of the seeking is the impact in daily living.

Susan Waterman
Mumbai, India
July, 2002

*Events happen, deeds are done,
but there is no individual doer thereof.*

$\mathscr{I}$NTRODUCTION

There is so much confusion around what is sought by the spiritual seeker, and yet one cannot really imagine anything being sought without the seeker knowing what it is that is being sought. If an answer is ventured, it would be something like 'enlightenment' or 'Self-realization' would give me superhuman powers, or it would make me a perfect human being. Only a little thinking would make it clear that such an expectation is quite unrealistic, only a romanticism: no one can be perfect because the very basis of life as we know it is the existence always of the polaric opposites of every kind; also, the criterion of perfection itself would vary an awful lot. Another answer could be that Self-realization would prevent rebirth; but then rebirth itself is a concept not acceptable to everyone. In any case, no one has ever known of any previous birth, not even those who believe they remember their own previous birth, because what they do have is a memory of some previous life, not their own previous life. The fact of the matter is that there is great confusion about what the seeker expects to get out of enlightenment in this life, and it is for this reason that many seekers are forced to confess that at the end of 20 or 30 years of discipline of various kinds, there has been no change in their lives.

What the seeker does know, deep down, is that what he is seeking is not what is generally sought in this life: good health, good looks, money, fame, etc., but something vitally different. It is precisely because he is generally led away from this most necessary enquiry straight into the disciplinary practices of the particular system he has approached, that there exists such enormous confusion, frustration, misery and distress among seekers. It is precisely for this reason too that the spiritual seekers are generally regarded by the rest of the society as 'drop-outs'.

The Buddha has given a simple definition of enlightenment as 'the end of suffering'. Indeed, this definition is complete in itself because the end of all seeking is to end suffering. To ask what is left when there is no more suffering is to miss the point altogether. What is left is that there is no more of what was considered 'suffering', which had completely negated all the other advantages that life might have bestowed on the seeker: good health, good looks, money, fame, etc. The real point to consider, therefore, is what could the Buddha have meant by the word 'suffering'? Obviously it excluded the pain that could result by the absence of good health, good looks, money, fame, etc., because many seekers had all the goodies in life like these, and had yet been compelled to seek because they had felt incomplete, unfulfilled.

In other words, the Buddha had realized that it was ridiculous to expect that anything could possibly remove the very basis of life and living, that is to say, the polaric opposites of pain and pleasure of the moment. The Buddha had obviously known that it was the basis of life that the moment would bring sometimes pleasure of various kinds or sometimes pain of various kinds. This simply had to be expected as the very basis of life and, therefore, accepted. Is there some kind of suffering which exists even after this basis of life has been accepted – and which the spiritual seeker wants to remove? That would seem to be the relevant seeking of the spiritual seeker.

This specific goal of the seeker itself has to be examined: is it a feasible goal or is it an imaginary one? The Buddha certainly knew the answer: it is not an imaginary goal because He had actually experienced this absence of 'suffering' at odd moments, but the experience had not lasted beyond a certain time. Therefore, He knew that 'the end of suffering' that He was seeking was very real; only it had not lasted! So the real search was: how to get rid of that obstacle which prevented the 'absence of suffering' from being founded or anchored! What is this obstacle, and how to get rid of it – this is what the real spiritual seeking is all about: how to achieve the *shanti* (peace) of *nirvana*, the absence of *dukkha* (suffering). Now, the seeker knows that the goal of his search is not something imaginary, not something that cannot exist in daily living. In other words, the goal of spiritual seeking is very much a part of daily living, not something imaginary or romantic or out of this world, like being able to walk on water, or being able to know whatever is happening all over the world, or being able to effect a cure of all illnesses, or being able to be in more than one place at any time.

Now that we know what it is that is being sought – the end of suffering – and what the suffering referred to is not, we have to find out what it is that obstructs the happening of that experience which most of us have experienced at some time or the other – some more than others – and does not allow the experience to remain anchored whenever it does happen. Any personal investigation would quickly reveal that what disturbs this wonderful experience is usually a thought. And, of course, it is generally well accepted that the arising of any thought in anyone is absolutely not in anyone's control. The physicist explains that any thought happening anywhere is the actualizing of a particular probability among thousands of probabilities, and, therefore, not in the control of the individual concerned. Now the question really is: what kind of thought merely stirs the 'absence of suffering' that is being experienced, and the kind of thought that absolutely shatters the very foundation of the experience? Any thought that concerns life as it is happening will be countered by another thought suggesting the solution for the problem created by the earlier thought: the experience is only stirred but not shaken or shattered.

What then is the kind of thought that cannot be controlled and could shatter the very foundation of that rare, wonderful experience? I think everyone's experience would confirm that this is the kind of thought that arises from memory – again beyond anyone's control – that refers to something harmful one did to some friend, or something one could have done for a friend, which the friend expected from him, but which one did not do, for some reason or the other with the result that the friend suffered a great deal of damage. It is this thought of something one did to someone or something one did not do for someone – and this could have happened 20 years ago! – that truly shatters the very foundation of that great experience. There is, of course, the other aspect of the same thought: the enormous load of hatred and malice towards 'the other' who did some harm or did not do the substantial favor he could have done. Therefore, what really totally shatters the experience is either the load of guilt or shame for something one did or did not do or the load of hatred and malice for what the 'other' did or did not do. In other words, what shatters the very foundation of the experience is volition or the sense of personal doership – whether it is 'me' or the 'other'.

What we have arrived at, from almost everyone's experience, is the fact that one has had the actual experience of 'the end of suffering' in daily living, but that it does not last because it is shattered by the volition or sense of personal doership in the life of the human being. So now the question is: is it at all possible to give up the sense of personal doership so that one can be anchored in the experience of 'the end of suffering' while facing life from moment to moment? The answer, of course, is yes it can be done because there have been people who have been accepted by the world as 'sages' who have indeed been actual examples of individuals for whom 'the end of suffering' has happened. What this 'end of suffering' means positively can be clearly seen in the way these sages have fared in their own daily living. What we see is that these sages seem to live from moment to moment, enjoying the same pleasures and suffering the same kind of pains that the ordinary person is subjected to, but anchored in peace and harmony.

The question arises at this stage then, what precisely is meant by 'the end of suffering' in the Buddha's terms? What it obviously means is clearly to be seen in the daily living of the sage: the sage lives his life, doing the daily chores, doing his regular daily work in order to earn a living, and enjoys the usual pleasures and suffers the usual pains from moment to moment. Yet it can be clearly seen that his face is usually without anxiety, his body usually relaxed, and he generally seems to be 'in good humor'. People seem to seek his company not just for 'time pass' but are often seen seeking his advice in situations in their daily living; they see him offering his advice, only when it is sought, and with an astonishing sense of humility combined with compassion, sometimes even with affection. They see him as someone transparently open, without any guile at all and, yet, he is obviously no one's fool! This is perhaps what is meant by the high-sounding words: he is anchored in peace and harmony. But what one actually sees is that while he is not particularly keen to offer any advice, he does so when asked, with a great deal of simplicity, confidence, and utter humility.

One is so impressed by the personality of the sage, the utter naturalness of the sage, that one finds oneself in his company more frequently than one would imagine, even when there is no particular situation to be discussed with him. On such an occasion, one might find oneself asking the sage what made him what he is – so likeable. The sage would perhaps smile and say, again with utterly simple humility, "nothing but God's Grace" and you would know that he really meant it. If you were to gently pursue the matter, the response you would get is quite likely to be that he has a deep conviction in God's Will being present all the time, at all places. Indeed, he has accepted with total conviction that, whatever one may think one is doing, whatever is actually happening, could not be happening unless it was God's Will, according to a Cosmic Law. At this point, you find yourself asking whether the sage truly believes that all action is not anyone's doing but a happening that simply had to happen. The sage may seem to hesitate a little, but the answer will come with great confidence, "without any exception". You are, frankly, not quite ready to accept this unequivocal assertion. So you persist: does not that mean abrogating your responsibility for your actions?

The sage would probably look at you a little piercingly but when he finds total sincerity in your probing, he would open up completely. He is likely to explain to you:

"There is really no question of any responsibility. When I do believe totally, without any reservation, that nothing can happen unless it is God's Will, it certainly does not mean that, in a fatalistic manner, I shall stop doing anything. I know I cannot do nothing; and, therefore, if there is something for me to do in my daily living, I shall, of course, make a decision on what to do and how to do it. Having made the decision, I shall put in my best effort to make that decision fructify. However, having done that, I know with total certainty that whatever happens, thereafter, will be out of my control and will depend entirely on the Will of God. I shall be waiting comfortably without any stress and strain for the result of 'my action'. The result could be successful or not successful and, therefore, the consequences of that result would again depend entirely upon God's Will. A happening is God's Will and the consequences – good, bad or indifferent – would also be God's Will and my destiny. There's truly no problem, no avoiding responsibility."

By this time you are ready to accept the concept that there is truly no individual doer as such. But you know that this readiness to accept has not brought you the quiet confidence of the sage; you also know that the reason for this is that you are by no means ready to take a 'truth test' about your conviction. Therefore, the conviction is not total – indeed, you are not really even totally willing to want the conviction because of the conditioning of thousands of years: "If I am truly convinced that I am not the doer and, more important, no one else is a doer either, how can I live my life henceforth in a society which simply will not accept this fatalistic attitude of everything happening because of God's Will?" You put this difficulty before the sage, and you are surprised that the sage agrees that this is a valid difficulty. He strengthens your argument by adding that you also have the most inconvenient feeling of being a hypocrite: how can I truly accept that no one is a doer, and yet proceed to do actions and to live my life as if nothing has changed?

Then he proceeds to give you the answer:
"I assure you that all you have to do is to live your life as if you are the doer." And, anticipating your problem, he says: "No, you will not feel like a hypocrite because that is what you have been doing all your life. You know that the sun does not move and that all the planets revolve around the sun; yet, you have had no hesitation in using the words, 'sunrise' and 'sunset' as if it is the sun that is moving. Similarly, go ahead and do your actions as if you are the doer and so is everyone else. In other words, in any given situation, go ahead and consider all the facts and the data very carefully and then decide between the various alternatives available; having made the decision, go ahead and put in your best effort to fructify your decision. So far, nothing has changed; you have set a goal based on what you want to achieve, there has been proper 'motivation' – you have made an effective plan and put in your best effort; no one, not even you, can accuse yourself of being a hypocrite. So far, what has happened is precisely what has always happened in your life and nothing has changed. What happens after this will also be precisely what has been happening before: you have no control over what happens after this. You know from experience that any one of three things can result: your action will be successful, or it will not be successful, or there will be no result. The point is that nothing has changed. All you can do is

to set a goal, make a plan and put in your best effort; what happens thereafter has never been in your control. Life continues to be what it was."

"Then", you ask, "where is the big change?" Then comes the answer: "There is a very big change – it is not what happens in life, which is precisely as before – the big change is not in what happens in life but in your own personal attitude to life, which truly decides whether you are comfortable with yourself and comfortable with others, whatever happens in life."

You confess you are puzzled. The sage continues:
"Even previously having done what you felt you had to do, it was your life's experience – and everyone else's too – that thereafter the doer had no more control over it. Now, with your new understanding, there is really no change in what happens. But there is henceforth, a big change in what happens to you. Previously, accepting that it was your doing, success meant pride and arrogance, failure meant guilt, shame, resentment. Now, with the understanding that your doing was not really your doing but only a happening, success means only pleasure but not pride and arrogance; failure may mean a sense of regret but not frustration, guilt or shame – it was never your doing, but a happening over which you truly had no control. This is the big difference: instead of fighting with the flow of life, now you go with the flow without any stress."

You remain for a while with your eyes closed, enjoying the sense of living your life without stress. It is an unusually fulfilling feeling, brought about by the absence of volition, the sense of personal doership.

You have, however, not reached the end of your search. You have one more question for the sage. By this time, somehow, the deeper personality of the sage, together with the outpouring compassion from him, has subtly changed the relationship between you and the sage since the moment the sage has accepted you as a sincere seeker and not just a curious or impertinent questioner; the stranger has disappeared and a personal relationship has taken over. There is more and more feeling in the sage for you; your friendly affection for the sage has gradually but noticeably changed into a respectful love for the *Guru* with an enormous amount of gratitude for what is happening to you that is beyond your imagination. So, in this apparently new relationship, you now ask your question with great love, respect and devotion: "I have one more question, *Guruji*. What I now have is an intellectual acceptance of the concept that no human being is an actual doer and even the intellectual acceptance has brought about an awesome feeling of great freedom. I can only imagine what the final effect could be if I am able totally to accept this concept not as a mere concept, but as absolute truth. I know this can finally happen only if it is God's Will, and my destiny. But, since the sense of doership is still very much there, I ask: is there not something I can do to hasten this process?"

The sage-*Guru* looks at his new disciple with great affection and compassion and says:

"I can understand exactly why you are asking this question. You can feel that you are nearing the end of your quest. I shall suggest to you what precisely you should try to do because you have accepted that the final happening can only depend on the Will of God. What I am suggesting is really quite simple. All you need do is to test the concept in the fire of your own experience and at the end of it you will either reject it or accept it totally, not as a concept anymore but as truth itself, because it is you who have done the testing and it is in your own experience that the test has been conducted.

All that you have to do is take a single action and investigate it thoroughly and honestly – not with a view to seeking confirmation that it is indeed your action but with an open mind. At the end of the day, take 20 minutes off, relax totally by yourself and investigate a particular, single action which you are convinced is your action. How did that action happen? Did I at any moment decide, from out of the blue, that I would do that action? Your investigation would immediately disclose that what started that action was actually a thought and, of course, you could not have had any control over that particular thought happening at that particular moment. And, really important, if that thought over which you had absolutely no control had not happened, then your action would not have happened. In these circumstances, can you really call that happening your action? The answer is obviously 'No' – it is not your action.

In this way, you can investigate any number of actions, and every single time you will arrive at the same conclusion: if the thought that happened had not happened, my action would not have happened. If I had not happened to see something when I did, my action would not have happened; if I did not happen to overhear the conversation, I would not have done what I did; if I had not happened to read something when I did, I would not have done what I did... In other words, when one investigation after another brings you to the same conclusion that you cannot really call that action your action, at some point in the series of investigations, a flash of total acceptance happens. At what point it happens is obviously God's Will and your destiny. And when you accept that you are not the doer, you have to accept that no one is a doer either."

One has to clearly understand that the investigation refers to one specific action and not a whole incident over a period of time. Somehow or the other, this is not clearly understood, and when a visitor reviews his process of investigation with me, it becomes amply clear that the investigation process has not been properly understood or practiced. The investigation certainly has to be done by the ego himself from his own experience – no one can effectively do it for you. The only point is that it is the working mind working in the present moment that must do the honest investigation, and not the thinking mind always functioning in the past or the present, trying to prove something for the apparent benefit of the ego.

Once the flash of total acceptance happens that there simply cannot be any individual doer – oneself or the other – but that every single apparent action is not done by any individual doer but that it is a happening produced by the Primal Energy, functioning through the body-mind instrument, precisely as electricity produces through each electrical gadget precisely that which the particular gadget has been designed to produce, there is a corresponding result. There is the personal experience of the Buddha's statement, "Events happen, deeds are done, but there is no individual doer thereof", which, in turn, produces an intense, deep feeling of total freedom from personal pride or arrogance, guilt and shame for what was earlier considered to be one's own actions, and also total freedom from any hatred or ill will or malice towards anyone. The deep understanding, is clearly, that if I am not supposed to get hurt according to my destiny or God's Will, no power on earth can hurt me; on the other hand, if it is my destiny to be hurt, through which individual body-mind instrument the relevant action happens is for me totally irrelevant.

The Ultimate Understanding works very simply in daily living; daily living becomes the going with the flow, witnessing impersonally whatever happens not as anyone's doing but a series of happenings according to a Cosmic Law – total freedom from personal doership, total freedom from pride and arrogance, from guilt and shame, total freedom from hatred and malice towards anyone. That is living one's life as a sage.

One point needs to be very clearly understood. The Ultimate Understanding of non-doership – Self-realization – does not mean the total annihilation of the ego. This cannot happen for the simple reason that the ego is necessary for the sage to live the rest of his allotted span of life. The sage responds to his name being called and functions as an individual entity in his allotted role in life. But the ego of the sage is without any sting because the sense of personal doership has been annihilated. In the words of Ramana Maharshi, the ego of the sage is like the "remnants of a burnt rope" – absolutely helpless and harmless.

We do not have
to seek a solution to the
problem of happiness or suffering
but merely to understand that in reality
there never was a problem.

CHAPTER 1

PEACE
AND
HARMONY
IN
DAILY LIVING

There have been moments in almost everyone's day-to-day living when one has experienced the true joy of living, which translated in phenomenal terms, would be calm, peace, tranquility in day-to-day living. What has disturbed such moments? What has usually disturbed these moments are memories of something one has done that one should not have done or something that one did not do that one should have done: a load of guilt and shame, that has been carried by the ego for quite some time, that comes up in one's memory every now and then and makes one extremely uncomfortable. Or, if it is not what one has done or not done oneself, it could be something that someone else did that affected one adversely one way or another: a load of hatred or jealousy for someone!

It is, therefore, almost everyone's experience that those rare moments of the sheer Joy of Being are suddenly disturbed by thoughts of blaming oneself or someone else for something done. What would the position be if one could have been absolutely and totally convinced that no action is anyone's doing, that all action was merely a happening that simply had to happen?!

This is what the spiritual seeking is all about. The Masters may talk about enlightenment or Self-realization, but what does it really mean in ordinary day-to-day living? It can have no meaning unless the Self-realization brings with it the peace and tranquility that the sage enjoys in his day-to-day living.

A sage is considered a sage because he seems to be anchored in peace and tranquility while facing the usual pains and pleasures of day-to-day living in his chosen field of activity, like any other ordinary person. The ordinary person is attracted to the sage for this very reason: the sage obviously suffers the same pains, and enjoys the same pleasures that he does, but continues to remain comfortable with himself and with others, while he himself yearns for the peace and tranquility of the sage.

What does 'Self-realization' mean to the sage? 'Self-realization', to the sage, simply means the realization – the absolute, total conviction – that in the words of the Buddha: "Events happen, deeds are done, but there is no individual doer thereof." In day-to-day living, both the sage and the ordinary person respond to their respective names being called. Therefore, in both cases, there is identification with the body and the name as an individual entity separate from all others. Where then is the difference between a sage and an ordinary person? The answer lies in the fact that the sage knows that, "events happen, deeds are done, but there is no individual doer thereof", whereas the ordinary person has the conviction that each individual performs his or her action and is responsible for it.

What brings about the peace and harmony in the day-to-day living of the human being is the understanding that the Buddha has stated so precisely and so succinctly: "Events happen, deeds are done, but there is no individual doer thereof." In other words, every action is a happening according to a Cosmic Law (which no individual human being could ever possibly understand) and not something 'done' by an individual human being. If this is accepted, it also has to be accepted that the human being cannot blame anyone for whatever happens through any body-mind organism. Therefore, he need not blame himself for any action, need not feel guilt or shame for any action; nor can he hate anyone for whatever might hurt him in life. The result is that anyone who is able to have this acceptance in his day-to-day living would carry no burden of guilt or shame, nor any burden of hatred and malice, jealousy and envy. In other words, the result is that he is anchored in peace and harmony: he is continuously comfortable with himself and also comfortable with others.

The total acceptance that no one is a doer of any actions is based essentially on the understanding that perceiving in phenomenality as such is an impersonal, noumenal function of the manifestation of the phenomenal universe. Such perceiving is pure perceiving because there is nothing seen and there is nothing (object assuming pseudo-subjectivity) that perceives. In other words, there is no object who can perceive anything. Although our long and persistent conditioning will not easily let us accept it, the fact does remain that as sentient beings we are objectively nothing but illusory dream-figures. All phenomenal existence itself is merely an appearance in Consciousness, and all the characteristics of sentient beings – the form, the perceiving, the knowing, the feeling, etc. – are also nothing but movements in Consciousness as in the dream. All actions are movements and events are extensions in the conceived structure of space and time in order that they may be sensorially perceived and measured in duration, but they all happen in Consciousness, precisely as in the dream.

The significant point to be understood is that Consciousness, in which everything happens like a dream, is the dreamer: this is the *subjective* and dynamic perceiving aspect of the static Consciousness, while the *objective* aspect is the perceived, dreamed and discriminated element. In other words, the dream that is the phenomenal manifestation occurs in Consciousness. It is perceived and cognized in Consciousness and is interpreted by Consciousness through the duality that is the basis for all phenomenal manifestation: the subject-object relationship. This duality of subject-object relationship, it must be constantly remembered, is merely the mechanism or the instrumentation (like space-time itself) through which the manifestation occurs – and is, of course, a concept – with the result that the perceived can be nothing other than the perceiver. Consciousness is all there is: the subject and the object, inseparably united when unconceived and unmanifested, only appear as dual and separate when conceived in the phenomenal manifestation.

This would be clearer and, perhaps, more convincing if we analyzed the dream state. What appear to us in the dream as living factual characters with feelings and reactions – *including ourselves* – are seen on awakening to be mere illusory figures wholly devoid of any choice or volition. This day-to-day living, in which we think we are the subjects in relation to other human beings as our objects is really a living-dream which, in essence, is not different in any way from the personal dream. We are totally mistaken when we think we are autonomous and independent entities who can think and choose and make decisions. If we would but calmly review any period in our lives we would surely find that, while we thought we were making the decisions, actual events have happened according to a master plan on a vastly magnificent scale in which we were mere pawns.

The point is that in this living-dream that life is, all characters are merely objects in the dreaming mind (which is the content of Consciousness) through a process of duality that is given the name of 'causation'. There cannot be any subject other than the Consciousness, with the inevitable result that the object is the subject, that the perceived is the perceiver! There is an interesting anecdote about the Chinese sage Chuang-Tzu. One morning he told his disciples that he had dreamt that he had become a butterfly flitting about in the garden from flower to flower, and now he was worried. The disciples laughed and said: "It was only a dream, Master". Said Chuang-Tzu: "Wait. If you think there is no reason to worry, you are mistaken. Now, when I am awake, I am puzzled. I have a very serious doubt: If Chuang-Tzu can dream that he has become a butterfly, why cannot the butterfly dream that she has become a Chuang-Tzu? Now, who is really who? Am I a butterfly dreaming that she has become a Chuang-Tzu or am I Chuang-Tzu dreaming that he has become a butterfly?"

The living-dream, viewed phenomenally, is merely an appearance in Consciousness, perceived and cognized by Consciousness, and to that extent is indeed an appearance as illusory as the appearance of a mirage. But viewed noumenally, the phenomenal manifestation is not only not thinking, but is everything inasmuch as the *essential elements in the dream cannot be anything other than the dreamer himself*. This-that-dreams, the subjective aspect of Consciousness, is indeed the dream and everything in the dream. In other words, the sentient beings that are phenomenally mere objects in the manifestation are truly the pure Subject, the Potential Plenum. Phenomenally it may appear as the void of nothingness that results when the interrelated opposites of duality are superimposed, into total negation. In this living-dream what awakens is not the object. The awakening happens in the disidentification of the dreamer from his object, in the disappearance of the illusion, in the dissolution of the entity in the discovery that what seemed like an object is indeed the pure Subject.

When true perceiving is recognized as the objective functioning of the Subject, the pseudo-subject disappears and the ego-entity gets annihilated. *True perceiving is thus not seeing phenomena as our objects:*

as soon as we perceive phenomena as our objects, we establish an objective relationship with things and create a dichotomy between subject and object, between 'self' and 'other'. It is this apparent separation that is the cause of human misery and what is known as 'bondage'. Perceiving noumenally is perceiving not objectively but subjectively, seeing phenomena as ourselves, with the understanding that neither the object nor its subject exists otherwise than as an appearance. True perceiving is thus ceasing to conceptualize, *seeing the phenomenal universe without comparing, without choosing, without judging, without getting into a subject-object relationship.*

What is the significance of this true perceiving? What happens? The answer is 'nothing happens' and 'everything happens'. 'Nothing' because whatever happens is nothing but conceptualizing and when this stops, nothing happens except that we (as the subjective 'I') remain what we were 'before we were born'. And 'everything' because the nothingness of the phenomenal void is really the fullness of the phenomenal Potential Plenum. In other words, when conceptualizing stops, the false-seeing, the out-seeing stops, and what remains is the in-seeing, the source of all seeing – not the seeing by the entity but the seeing from within, seeing from the Source, which is noumenal seeing without any entity.

True perceiving establishes a direct relationship between the noumenal unmanifest and the phenomenal manifestation: the manifestation may adopt any number of forms, but the substratum of all of them is the Consciousness that is immanent in each and every phenomenon – like gold is immanent in all gold ornaments whatever their shapes and names. Whatever is perceived is then seen to have no existence independently of the noumenal Consciousness. In other words, true perceiving means the understanding – the deepest acceptance – that the universe is not different from us, that there is no difference between the manifest and the unmanifest, the temporal and the intemporal. The difference is only in appearance, and while this difference seems irreconcilable like all opposites phenomenally, it disappears altogether in the absence of conceptualizing because 'difference' itself is only a concept! In deep sleep, when there is no conceptualizing, there is no question of difference or differentiation: there is neither the conceived, perceived object nor the conceiving, perceiving subject – all there is, is noumenal functioning in the whole-mind without the dualism of the split-mind.

In its static state, when Consciousness is in repose, there is nothing for Consciousness to perceive or cognize because there is no manifestation; when movement gives rise to the manifestation and the conceptual perceiver therein, there is nothing other than Consciousness. In brief, whether there is any phenomenal manifestation (and the conceptual individual perceiver) or no manifestation, what is constant and changeless is the substratum of Consciousness.

Man intuitively knows the peace and harmony of the permanence of his basic, changeless, Beingness. He experiences it in deep sleep and in those rare moments in the waking state when the mind is still and vacant; but it is in his movement that he seeks for that immobility in vain, because he has mistakenly identified himself with his dynamic body-mind organism as an individual achiever.

The Buddha's statement, "*samsara* is *dukkha*" – life is all suffering – is quite often not clearly understood. It surely cannot signify that the human being does not experience joy and the hope of happiness. The Buddha's statement merely signifies that man cannot actually enjoy happiness *as he conceives it*. What constitutes the suffering is the wanting to tear oneself away from the present moment and pursue an ever-fleeing conceptual happiness in the future.

The Buddha found himself forced to identify life with suffering because of the perfectly normal state of our development in which we have to live our life: our relationship with the outside world. It is not the way of living that constitutes the problem but a lack of understanding in our interhuman relationships. The lack of understanding lies in the fact that we rely for our happiness on our interhuman relationships, what we do to others and what others do to us! In other words, our happiness lies not in our way of living but in the understanding of what 'living' as such is. We do not have to seek a solution to the problem of happiness or suffering, but merely to understand that in reality there never was a problem. We see something as suffering when there is truly no such thing as suffering.

The reality in the phenomenal living is that we do not live our lives; living happens through the billions of dynamic body-mind organisms. All that needs to happen is for us to be the spectator of the spectacle that life and living is. Identified experiencing makes one a part of the spectacle.

Omar Khayyam, the great Persian poet born at the end of the 11th century, known for his extensive pursuit of knowledge, said something similar about daily living in his famous *Rubaiyat:*

> *The Ball no Question makes of Ayes and Noes,*
> *But Right or Left as strikes the Player goes;*
> *And He that tossed you down into the Field,*
> *He knows about it all – HE knows – HE knows!*
>
> *The Moving Finger writes; and having writ,*
> *Moves on: nor all your Piety nor Wit*
> *Shall lure it back to cancel half a Line,*
> *Nor all your Tears wash out a Word of it.*

There is a page in the "Far Side" Calendar of cartoons that shows a picture of hell, with Satan standing with a spear and watching a line of people passing by. There is a notice on the wall that says: "Today is the first day of the rest of your life." It is as if Satan wants to make sure that none of the people would ever be able to live in the present moment!

It is our everyday experience that the mind can create problems that need never exist and are entirely the result of the mind wanting to escape from the present moment because the present moment is too dull! The mind wants the future because it can invest the future with its own desires and fears and thus make the future more interesting than the present moment. And it is this flight of the mind into the future – hope and pleasurable anticipation or anxious problems – which is what prevents one from being anchored in the peace and harmony of the present moment.

This does not mean that you do not deal with practical matters that must necessarily involve horizontal time of past and future. But it is the working mind that is concerned with working out the solution for the practical problem in the present moment. It is the thinking mind, dipping into the past and projecting itself into the future uncertainties, which interrupts the smooth and efficient working of the working mind in the present moment. The only way to prevent this from happening is not to let the thinking mind have any sustenance. The arising of a thought is not in one's control, but ignoring it and putting the concentration once again into the present moment deprives the thinking mind of the sustenance necessary for it to prevail in horizontal time.

What the thinking mind does in daily living is to deprive you of the very essence of life in the present moment, to prevent you from enjoying the magnificence and variety of life in the present moment. The next time you see a flower or an insect, give it your full attention and you will be astonished to realize that the difference between the two is purely a conditioned reaction, and not real at all.

Being anchored in peace and harmony means remaining relaxed and immersed in the cool light of Reality and, at the same time, enjoying the cool breezes of phenomenality, merely witnessing the arising and subsiding of thoughts and events in daily life. This is interpreted by others as never being uncomfortable – with one's self or with others.

When one talks of what one would want most in daily living – being anchored in peace and harmony – what precisely do we mean by daily living? A little reflection would show us clearly that the very basis of life is the concept of 'time': the concept and experience of a beginning, a middle and an end – a journey beginning with a wanting or desire, proceeding with effort towards the realization (or the failure) of the goal. This process happens to be applied by the individual to everything in his life: one has to do something, to achieve something, and to become something. In other words, the concept of 'time' and the flow of time, brought with it the concept of purpose, the investment of effort and the expectation of the result of the effort. And surely this is the very basis of one's 'daily living', beginning with going to school, then the university, and the end of education; then falling in love and marriage, to be followed by the happy family; in the meantime, one's career, again a beginning, middle and end, with the purpose of eventual 'success'.

Thus daily living gets based essentially on time – purpose – effort – expectation. Success means happiness; failure means frustration, unhappiness. The entire process itself is based on one's personal doing, whatever the purpose and the expectation. One has been conditioned, from day one, to believe totally in the adage, 'as you sow, so you reap'. One's very faith in the fairness of life, epitomized by the adage, gets severely shaken when this adage is proved again and again to be quite wrong. Even this, however, does not really affect one's faith in personal effort.

This total reliance on personal effort gets carried to almost all purposes and goals, including the spiritual goal whether the background and conditioning are Western or Eastern tradition. Both are based on personal effort: original sin, prayer, confession, repentance, forgiveness, communion and purification in Western tradition, or the repetition of a *stotra* or God's name (*japa*), worship in various temples and ashrams, sitting in meditation, fasting on certain days and several other disciplines in the Eastern tradition.

Purpose, effort, hope and belief become the inspiration but, when one pursues these values, one is usually unaware of the interconnected opposites to which they are inevitably attached: hopelessness, confusion, failure, frustration. It is, therefore, the usual result of one's personal effort: either success, ecstasy, pride, or failure, frustration, guilt. And the pity of the whole process is that in relying on one's personal effort, one has totally forgotten the basic principle in every religion: Thy Will Be Done; Inshah Allah; Thou art the Doer and Thou art the Experiencer.

There is the age-old story of God and the Devil – the basis of dualism, with the total ignoring of the One Source – both watching man discovering the Truth. "Aha", said God triumphantly to the Devil, "now that man has found Truth, you will have nothing to do." The Devil replied, "on the contrary, my friend, it will give me great joy to help him organize it."

In this entire process of daily living – time – desire – purpose – effort – goal – there are usually several ups and downs, all of which lead only to the strengthening and reinforcement of a self-identity, personal volition, a self-image, with the ultimate aim of being an effective, well-balanced, efficient individual. The volition itself becomes the very basis of the final frustration, because it is in the personal experience of almost every individual that the final result, in any enterprise, ultimately does not depend only on one's own effort but on several other factors totally out of anyone's control. Call this whatever you will: luck or destiny!

However, it cannot be denied that for someone who realizes that at least to some extent, apart from personal effort, a great deal depends upon one's personal attitude to life in general and to personal and other relationships, the contemporary therapeutic world offers some very beneficial alternatives – which basically affect one's existing conditioning – in order to have a better-balanced personal attitude. Such therapies could certainly help to produce the groundwork necessary to generate the kind of energy that would lead to a deeper and more realistic perception of the Awareness, the Presence, the Impersonal Energy that is the very basis of the functioning of the phenomenal manifestation, which we know and understand as 'daily living'.

In what we know as daily living, the individual arrives at some point of time (depending on his destiny, which is a reflection of God's Will, according to a conceptual Cosmic Law), at the conclusion that there is a distinct possibility, if not the total conviction, that perhaps what happens in life does not depend on one's own effort: that several other factors could and do affect what happens in daily living. And then, the individual arrives at the threshold of keeping himself open to that happening generally known as 'enlightenment' or 'Self-realization'.

In everyone's daily life, there are many occasions when one very deeply wishes one could get from a really reliable person – not a thinker or philosopher but one who has actually practiced his concepts with obvious success – how to act in life. Therefore, when one comes across a specific piece of advice from a recognized *avatar* – a direct, fully conscious manifestation of Divine Reality in human form – one should pay deep attention to it. One such personality was Ramakrishna Paramahamsa, the 19th century saint and sage of Bengal, also known as the 'Great Swan'. Les Hixon in his book *Great Swan* recounted several conversations Ramakrishna had with his devotees. One of these conversations was retold as follows:

Ramakrishna: *"The mature spiritual person, one who is truly awakened, need not remain involved in social responsibilities or religious observances. The sense that one must, or even can, initiate any action begins to disappear as one realizes that it is only God who acts. This realization is the final fruition of all aspirations and disciplines. When the fruit appears, the flower petals fall from the tree. Passages from holy scriptures will flutter away from the mind like petals in a strong wind.*

The mantra, the condensed inward invocation of Divine Presence, may remain active for a while, but eventually even those sacred words will blow away, leaving only the primordial resonance – Om; Om; Om – which is not just a word passed down by tradition but a humming tone at the center of awareness, audible at the core of every sound in the universe. Om is the open portal to Supreme Reality.

How long will it be necessary to practice various levels of religious disciplines? As long as you do not shed tears and feel tingling sensations coursing through your body while repeating one of the precious Divine names, you are still subject to the structures of moral and religious training. How does a small child learn to wake from a sound sleep in order to go to the bathroom? Until this ability develops, the child must continue to wear diapers.

This outrageous analogy, often used by the Master, brings forth gales of laughter. Sometimes the playful Master suggests that *Gurus* are like soft toys for children to chew on while cutting teeth. He cherishes no sanctimonious attachment to any religious form... Often he will say: '*Follow conventions of purity and piety only as much as absolutely necessary. Persons who are obsessed with religion cannot attain profound wisdom.*'

The Master was then asked how one should regard money and the efforts to obtain it.

Ramakrishna: *To worship God in order to generate material success or to be victorious in some litigation is not the sign of a true practitioner, who simply remains open to whatever gifts of abundance flow spontaneously and mysteriously from Divine Reality. This attitude does not preclude working hard at some honest occupation. Yet when engaged in personal effort, the lover of Truth experiences the miraculous flow of Divine Sustenance, and then can never be obsessive about earning or saving money. Such a person becomes constitutionally incapable of being obsequious, servile, slavish or deceptive in order to receive material or emotional compensation of any kind.*

Nevertheless, surprising abundance often comes to such a person... The lover of God is like the child of a powerful king. This royal prince or princess is always relaxed and confident in every circumstance. The Bhagavad Gita describes this person succinctly as 'one who remains spontaneously content with whatever comes'.

The person who loves Truth alone, free from any self-centered motivation whatsoever, can gratefully receive the gifts of basic sustenance or immense wealth from any direction whatsoever. By not desiring it – and not pursuing it – this person purifies it and uses it generously for the common good.

The Master was then asked how the spiritual seeker should live in the practical, mundane world.

Ramakrishna: *Live in the ordinary structure of family, religion and society as the mudfish lives in the soft mud at the bottom of a lake. The fish does not consider this mud distasteful, but is also never confined there, being capable at any time of swimming into the spacious crystal-clear water, without even a particle of mud adhering to its body...*

Certainly you can live at home, surrounded by your extended family, attending your place of business daily. Simply maintain the sense of perfect freedom, clarity and expansiveness, moment to moment, under any condition. Who cares if the world is strewn with thorns? Simply put on sandals and walk over them: the sandals are the knowledge that God alone exists [God created the world; let Him look after it].

The visitor then asks the Master: 'Venerable Sir, I was under the impression that the householder's life is an obstacle to spiritual progress and that full realization is impossible in the context of worldly enjoyments and responsibilities'.

Ramakrishna: *One can awaken fully into Divine Presence only if one feels a fundamental freedom from all limited, egocentric motivation, whether connected with family affairs or religious pursuits. The person who cultivates commitment to liberation from self-involvement experiences his own personal selfishness and various collective forms of selfishness as forest fires dangerously out of control, threatening the lives of all people.*

The person of dispassion clearly perceives that the obsessive attachment to spouse and children which seeks to own and control their lives is like a deep well with no way of escape... The person whose heart belongs to the radical path of total freedom, total renunciation of selfish effort, simply refuses to exist within any conventional categories, even for a moment; no family, no monastery, no wandering life, no self-doer – nothing but God [Thy Will Be Done].

The delusive power that makes the selfish habitual environment so dangerous is simply the instinctive urge to perpetuate the limited self and its limited existence. This becomes the atavistic drive to possess, to dominate, to control, to consume. Sexuality, when it is not spiritually consecrated and elevated, becomes an obvious instrument for this delusive power. So is the possession with wealth and hierarchical position. But this delusive power, this maya, begins to dissipate by itself, the more it is recognized, confronted, refuted, unmasked... Just recognize the power of maya for what it is – mere empty pretense – and it withdraws spontaneously, although the ego-doer tries to return again and again [the 'flip-flop'], under an astonishing array of disguises.

No one can cultivate radical freedom simply by wishing to do so, or even by desperately trying to do so! One must deal skillfully with various subtle tendencies – those inherited physically, those imposed socially and those deposited in the mind-stream by previous experience. This complex tapestry of mental and physical tendencies is difficult to unravel.

Listen to a story. Once a forest yogi, advanced in concentration but lacking in wisdom, invited a powerful king to retreat with him into the wilderness in order to be liberated from the heavy cares of the kingdom. The sovereign, a sage in wisdom and action, replied: 'Dear sir, I am afraid you would be disappointed. I could easily divest myself of palace, courtiers and refined comforts to live in your forest retreat. But the subtle tendencies within me to create and rule a kingdom would still remain active, attracting various persons and events to fulfill themselves. Your peaceful solitary retreat would gradually become a busy ashram and eventually the bourgeoning center of a new empire.'"

*The basis of
tranquility is the absence
of the sense of personal doership,
the absence of personal greed
and guilt, hatred and malice.*

CHAPTER 2

*E*GO:
THE
'ME'-DOER

For let Philosopher and Doctor preach
Of what they will, and what they will not – each
Is but one Link in an eternal Chain
That none can slip, nor break nor over-reach.

And that inverted Bowl we call The Sky,
Whereunder crawling cooped we live and die,
Lift not your hands to IT for help – for It
As impotently rolls as you or I.

– Omar Khayyam, *Rubaiyat*

In day-to-day living, it is the mind, the 'me' that is making the necessary effort to attain whatever it wants to attain. This 'me' that is making the effort – the identification with a particular body-mind organism and a name, with volition, *the sense of personal doership* – is truly merely an accumulation of memories and experiences, and what it seeks is based only on this accumulation. And, at some point in life, whatever the cause, this very 'me' seeks escape from its own activities and seeks peace and harmony in life. And, therefore, this very 'me', seeking peace and harmony, makes an effort that may take the form of some kind of discipline, yoga or meditation or whatever. Whatever this effort, the whole tragic joke is that this 'me', the mind seeking peace and harmony, forgets that what it is seeking is freedom from itself!

Only when this 'me'-mind realizes this fact most deeply will the mind cease to make any effort. Only then will the mind be induced – not forced by some discipline – to be still, completely still, free from seeking anything. Only then will arise the possibility of being receptive to the unknown, which is truly the experience of peace and harmony.

The method itself becomes the distraction because method means duration and duration means the absence of tranquility in the moment! Method – the 'how' – means duration and duration means not seeing the immediate necessity of the 'moment' of tranquility. A completely still mind – the happening of it – is the tranquility that cannot be pursued and hunted through a method of discipline.

The deep seeing of this very fact is the only 'method'. And it can only happen in the moment, not in duration. In other words, the mind, the 'me' cannot achieve it. It can only happen when the 'me'-mind, the 'me'-doer itself understands this very basic fact that it is itself the culprit. It can only happen when it is very clearly understood that there is in fact no division between the thinker and the thinking, between the doing and the doer. When this foundation gets laid, that all doing is truly only a happening, then the disappearing of the 'me'-doer means indeed the disappearance of the entire psychological structure of volition: freedom from fear, effort, greed, envy and sorrow. This is indeed the real Self-realization or salvation.

The basic structure of the ego is the identification with a body-mind organism as the individual entity, separate from all other entities in the phenomenal universe. The essence of the ego, however, that which gives it the lateral characteristic, is the sense of personal doership. The ego himself does not really understand this important distinction, and is naturally confused and afraid when, as the spiritual seeker, he is told that there can be no Self-realization unless the ego is killed. The ego would naturally wonder what kind of Self-realization would be acceptable when he himself would not be there to enjoy it.

The ego-seeker, therefore, needs to be convinced that what is to be annihilated is not the basic structure of the ego – the identification as a separate entity – but the sense of personal doership. Indeed, the ego-seeker has to convince himself, through investigation into his own personal experience, that not only will he not die when the sense of personal doership is removed, but that he will continue to live with an enormous sense of freedom and peace.

When the sense of personal doership gets annihilated with the final total acceptance that 'I cannot be the doer', perhaps the most important change that happens is that the overpowering sense of responsibility for the personal doership disappears. The immediate result is that the sense of 'get it over with' disappears, the sense of impatience with 'something I have to do' disappears, and 'something that is happening' takes its place, something always fresh, always new and interesting that can be enjoyed as part of the total magnificence and variety of God's continuous creation. You become one with the happening after the demolition of the sense of personal doership.

The sense of doership invariably means tension: I am doing this; as soon as I finish this, I must not forget to do that; any interruption could make me forget it... and this kind of tension happens not only in the case of important executive work, but even in the case of the most ordinary work. I remember when I visited my daughter in Bangalore, I noticed a servant doing the most menial work, mumbling to herself while she worked. I mentioned this to my daughter, and she laughed and said, "she vocalizes the work she has to do: 'I am doing this now, as soon as I finish this, I must do such and such a thing before I do the other work'" (i.e. I must not forget the chain of actions...). Needless to say, absence of tension means better efficiency.

In the daily cycle of living, there is a period when the ego, the 'me'-doer is not present. We are not unaware of the basic fact that our mind is never at rest except during the relatively short period of deep sleep. From the moment we wake up until we go to sleep, the activity of the mind hardly ever ceases. Indeed, the activity does not really cease even when we fall asleep: we dream. The problems of the day have been carried over into our sleep, and we dream. When we wake up, the moment we do wake up, the mental activity has already started: 'I have to go to the office earlier than usual today; I can't help it if my wife would be upset if I go without my breakfast; I have to tell the boss about the loss of the contract that I have withheld from him.' How earnestly we wish we could break this vicious circle!

At the moment we wake up, what is present is not the ego, the 'me'-doer, but the impersonal Awareness of Being: I AM. What usually happens is that the ego-doer quickly takes over from the impersonal Awareness of Being, and the vicious circle is not broken. Perhaps there is a simple way to prolong the impersonal Awareness of Being that arises at the moment of waking up. Let the moment drag itself into several moments; let looking out of the window happen smoothly, merely looking out, without mentally reacting to what is seen – not suppressing any thought that might arise – but being passively aware of the response of the body-mind organism to what is seen out of the window. Then, let the mind drown itself into the impersonal Awareness of Being – I AM. Finally, when the ego takes over, it will hopefully do so without its usual hectic activity and you can observe this take-over of the ego, merely observing the happening. We shall know only when we try the experiment!

The source of problems that disturb what we want most in life is the 'me', the 'thinking mind' which is always concerned with the experiences in the past and the fulfillment of desires in the future. The 'thinking mind' is distinguished from the 'working mind', which is only concerned with doing the job at hand irrespective of the possible results and consequences. The thinking mind is the 'me' – the thinker, the doer, the experiencer – which is the very cause of the disturbances that prevent the happening of the peace. The solution would seem to be that the mind – the thinking mind – must be made still. But that cannot be the answer because a mind that is 'made' still by a 'me' through force and discipline and control cannot be a 'still' mind. It is an imprisoned mind.

A man who is lustful, and hangs on to his passion but has suppressed it for a while, and driven and willed the mind to be still, cannot possibly have the peace that can only happen. It is only when full, alert but passive, awareness is centered on the lust or ambition or whatever, without a sense of personal doership, that the mind can become still and peace can prevail.

The disturbance that drives away the peace that every one of us has experienced spontaneously at odd moments is the constant urge to do something, to improve oneself, to achieve a noble goal. Just the deep awareness that this ambitious, competitive doing is itself the cause of the disturbance, is all that is really needed to preserve the peace which is the very essence of our being. Peace is not something to be achieved.

Hence, the essential malevolence of the ego does not lie in the identification with a particular body-mind organism (and the relevant name) as a separate entity, but in the sense of the achieving doership of the separate entity. This distinction, so very necessary in the understanding of the concept of the ego, was made clear by the sage of Arunachala, Ramana Maharshi, by stating clearly that the sage also does have an ego but that the ego of the sage is harmless, "like the remnants of the burnt rope".

When the Ultimate Understanding has happened, the proud resistance of the vanity of volition has given way to the softer, tractable, more pliant acceptance of non-doership. The restless anguish of the resistance has given way to tears of peace and joy of the acceptance of non-doership. This is the true humility of the sage.

It is necessary here to remind oneself of what Ramana Maharshi said of any concept: a concept is to be used as a thorn to remove another thorn imbedded in one's foot. Once that is done, both the thorns are to be thrown away. The concept is not to be pursued to its bitter end by comparing and analyzing each and every aspect of the concept.

In our day-to-day living, perhaps the most prevalent feeling is that of fear, not fear of some particular person or thing, but the prevalence of fear as such, fear of the unknown happening, a sort of underlying presence or tension. This is obviously because we have been brought up from our childhood to think in terms of guarding ourselves: all our defenses, both physical and psychological, are based on this underlying source of fear of the unknown.

So, the question before us is usually: can we free ourselves from this phenomenon of fear? This question is based on a total misconception: that we, the thinking mind operating horizontally in time, can do something to negate fear! How can a mind, conditioned so strongly, ever think of anything to negate fear? The thinking mind, based on the sense of personal doership or volition, is itself the very process of fear.

The only answer to the problem is not to seek an answer but to be aware of the problem itself: the fear based on a future that simply does not exist now. This psychological fear is simply not concerned with the actual precautions that can be taken for possible contingencies that can be anticipated. When the mind, instead of seeking a remedy for a problem that it has created itself, remains fundamentally quiescent, really empty and quiet, passively witnessing the various fears as they arise, without wanting to do something about them, it is only then in that passivity, in that true quietness lies the possibility of a spontaneous action if and when necessary.

In such passive quiescence there is a genuine possibility of an unconscious transformation, a fundamental change in perception in which the illusory future gets set aside. The important point is that the basic cause of fear is the existing conditioning in the mind, and that it is this conditioning that needs to be transformed through fresh conditioning that is not based on conscious personal effort. Reading this, itself, can be the fresh conditioning that is necessary for the required transformation. The conscious mind cannot free itself from the fear that it has created itself. What is basically required is for the mind to be quiet, merely to be deeply aware of the fear itself, without consciously trying to do anything about it.

The conclusion we have arrived at is truly very simple: we have to be able to live in the now, in the present moment, and this can only happen when we have understood that the whole mechanism of conscious thought is the basis of the fear that we want to get rid of. The very basis of the fear is the future, and the future only exists in the mind. And the mind can only project, for the future, its own needs and desires: its own fears. When the mind is able to remain in the now, in the present moment, there is no projection of fear in the future that does not exist now. There is silence, peace, absence of fear, in the very understanding of this process of horizontal thinking.

The natural arising of fear is a thought in the moment, usually leading to an immediate action based on the instinct of self-preservation. It has nothing to do with time. Thought is in the moment; thinking is in horizontal time. Thinking causes fragmentation in our lives. One of the prominent factors concerning the fragmentation in our lives is fear based on horizontal thinking, and not fear arising in the moment. Fear based on horizontal thinking means 'being frightened': 'I am afraid'. Such fear has existed from time immemorial, and the human being has never solved the problem – and he never will. This is because fear, as being frightened, is based on time, and the solution can never be found in time. It is only the understanding of the problem that can dissolve the problem.

One seems always to be afraid: afraid of losing one's job, afraid of falling ill, afraid of public opinion, afraid of the boss, afraid of the dark. In fact, the very word 'fear' makes us afraid! In other words, thinking brings about fear. Taking out a life insurance policy is an act in the moment that pre-empts being afraid of the consequences of death. It is only being able to accept totally that the future does not depend upon our free will – whatever we may plan to do – but on the Will of God, which would halt our horizontal thinking and the fear in it.

The very words 'pain' and 'fear' cause powerful responses in the body-mind organism because of the strong conditioning attached to these words. The same applies to the word 'suffering'. The fact of the matter is that pain or suffering or fear arises in the body-mind organism. If one were able to look totally at what arises, silently and objectively – as if it were happening in some other body-mind organism – the result would be startlingly different. In other words, what prevents one from doing this is thought or, more accurately, thinking in horizontal time about something that is in the present moment. It is this thinking that brings about an identification with the pain or fear or suffering. The suffering, as such, turns into self-pity: I am suffering and I do not want to suffer. If one is able to avoid this identification and look at What-Is in the moment absolutely silently and objectively, then the picture becomes totally different. This does not really refer to physical pain in its intensity except to the extent that the pain and even the crying out in pain will be both witnessed as if the crying out were happening through any other body-mind organism. In other words, the lack of personal involvement is the big difference. And this has actually been proved by personal experience, and is not just a theory.

In day-to-day living, the basis of living and working is the desire to succeed, which itself is based on the fear of failure. We are afraid not to be a success in life and, therefore, we want to be disciplined. And yet, the mind that is disciplined wants at the same time tranquility, peace, harmony. This is impossible. The basis of tranquility is the absence of the sense of personal doership, the absence of personal greed and guilt, hatred and malice. Tranquility is not a fish to be caught in the net of discipline and wanting and competing. Tranquility in the unknown needs freedom from the thinking mind. This is what is to be deeply understood while living our life from day-to-day. In other words, it is to be deeply understood that while we seem to. be living our lives, what is truly happening is that the living of our lives is happening. And it is only in this freedom of non-doership (neither doing nor not doing) that tranquility, peace and harmony can happen.

In the happening of the silence, the tranquility, there simply cannot be present any knower, any experiencer of that silence. Whenever there is an experiencer present who wishes to experience the silence, true silence cannot happen. Whenever there is an experiencer who says, 'now I have experienced the silence that I have been longing to experience' – 'I have done it' – it is not stillness. It can only be a trick of the mind, a kind of self-hypnosis. It is important to understand that stillness can only happen in the moment and, therefore, there cannot be an experiencer, the doer who wanted to achieve that silence in that moment. Indeed, the moment of silence, of tranquility, is an impersonal happening, not an experience as such, at all. What this means in effect is to let the silence happen without any desire to have more of the same, without letting the greedy mind take over. You can remain submerged in that silence as long as it happens, and this can happen only until the ego-experiencer takes over.

It is purely because of making a distinction between the experience and the experiencer that the problem of suffering exists, basically and essentially, in day-to-day living. If there is pain, the problem arises essentially because the ego at once identifies himself with the pain, goes into panic, and immediately seeks relief. If there is no ego identifying with the pain as the experienced, the pain is merely witnessed consciously, and there is no sufferer of the pain. There is pain but no individual sufferer of the pain. I have had an experience of this phenomenon after my appendix operation. Lying in bed, waiting for the pain to arise, which the surgeon had warned me about, there was a thought that perhaps I could just witness it consciously, instead of rushing to the nurse for a pain-killing injection. And that is what I did. I could witness the pain rising gradually, until it settled down at a certain point. Then another thought occurred: if I had been born with this amount of pain, it would have been accepted as a normal part of the body! The result was that I could bear the pain the whole day, until the nurse insisted on giving me the injection in the evening so that I could have a good night's rest.

In our day-to-day living, why do we find ourselves struggling against What-Is? The house in which we live may be hideous and ugly and we struggle to improve ourselves and our situation. The result is frustration and unhappiness. The only answer is to be able to accept the What-Is, while doing whatever we feel like doing to improve the condition. In this acceptance, which is not a forced yielding, there is the understanding that if we could have done something about our condition, we would have done it. Such acceptance, not a forced yielding, is the result of – or leads to – a certain quietness and silence of the mind. And in that silence of the mind, all actions in our day-to-day living happen without the strain of a continuous series of reactions by way of horizontal thinking.

What does living mean to us? Do we accept What-Is in the moment without thinking about What-Is in terms of time and future? We are afraid of dying only because we have been afraid of living.

We are, say, at the moment enjoying a wonderful meal. Are we one with the enjoyment itself in the moment, or, as is more likely, are we thinking of the enjoyment in terms of such enjoyment that we had in the past and such enjoyment that we may or may not have in the future?! In other words, what we do is to considerably reduce the intensity of the enjoyment in the moment by thinking in horizontal time – an utter waste of enjoyment.

Living for most of us is hardly anything more than the usual deadly routine of work, accompanied by the continuous fear of existence: despair, conflict, anxiety, loneliness and depression, guilt, greed and hatred. This is what we call living, and it is this that we are afraid of losing when death comes! As a matter of fact, can death mean anything other than going back to what we were before we were born?

In other words, our day-to-day living is usually a process of continuous conflict and turmoil, constant agitation and anxiety about our relationships, personal or official, about security, about life in general, or finally about death. Most of our activity seems to be based on thinking about ourselves, based on a pattern of self-centered thinking. It is our experience that such activity, based on a series of reactions of the ego, leads to various forms of confusion and conflict.

In pursuit of the desired tranquility, what we seem to do instead of understanding the problem itself with a calm mind, is to seek escape from the conflict through any available means through some religious ritual or some kind of social service or through drugs. It is absolutely necessary to realize that any form of escape can only lead to isolation and greater resistance. The only way out of the problem is to look at the problem totally – objectively and silently – and accept the problem without seeking an escape. It is only out of this objective looking at the problem, without seeking an escape, that acceptance can happen; and such an acceptance is not a forced acceptance. And, it is only this spontaneous acceptance that can bring tranquility, a kind of tranquility that is not dissimilar to death. Suicide is an escape; such acceptance is salvation – acceptance of What-Is in the moment.

The real problem is whether it is possible not to function in our day-to-day living within that pattern of continued reactions, whether it is possible to live with a sense of freedom from our supposed action. We know that it is indeed possible because we can see a few people, very few people, actually doing so: they live their life, doing whatever needs to be done in the moment, enjoying and suffering whatever happens in the moment, and still anchored in a kind of peace and harmony, comfortable with themselves and comfortable with others. What is it that the sage has that the ordinary human being does not seem to have? The answer is extraordinarily simple: the sage is *totally* convinced that all activity is a happening, not the 'doing' by any individual entity, that nothing can happen unless it is the Will of God – God being the Source from which the entire manifestation has emerged.

More specifically, what happens in the case of the ordinary person? For example, being a 'good conversationalist' is an enormous social advantage and also effective in one's working life. The more vocal you are at social gatherings, private meetings or even public functions, the greater your perceived value as an individual. The disadvantage, of course, is that as a vocal person you are almost always forced to take a position. If the talk is about exploitation of women, you have to take a position either as a 'feminist' or 'anti-feminist'. The trouble in such a situation is that this either-or situation prevents one from seeing the larger picture from a wider perspective.

Similarly, it is also the experience in our day-to-day living that, at some time or the other, one feels intrigued by the world we live in. It has been called a play, a divine *lila*, a dream. But basically, the problem seems to be: is there anyone controlling it? Whatever the answer, it can only be a concept, and a concept always has two sides: it is accepted or not accepted. 'God' is a concept. So is the other alternative: 'Ultimate Reality' or whatever. What is the nature of the Source or Ultimate Reality or Primal Energy? *Katha Upanishad* puts it thus: "The Ultimate Reality cannot be known through speech or through eyes. Who but the one who says 'It is' can know It."

Any discussion about the Ultimate Reality is ultimately fruitless because discussion means words, and all discussion has ultimately only led to the one real conclusion: the need to be silent! This was undoubtedly the reason why the Buddha refused to answer questions on the existence or non-existence of God. He would ask the questioner to sit near him for a couple of years in silence, and then ask his question. Those sincere seekers who did so found that when total silence prevailed, all the questions they had also vanished. This is clearly because what we are has always been before there was any thought, vocalized or otherwise. Silence is our very existence, the Ultimate Reality.

The sage Ashtavakra explained to his disciple, King Janaka, that we can attain true freedom only when we transcend duality, only when we rise above all doubts and questions. The sage asked:
"Where is the world and where is the aspirant for liberation? Where is the contemplative man and where is the man of knowledge? Where is the soul in bondage and where is the liberated soul for me who am non-dual by my very nature? Where are creation and dissolution? Where are seeker and success for me abiding in my non-dual nature? Where is the knower, the means to knowledge, the object of knowledge or the knowledge itself that is sought? Where is anything, and where is nothing for me who am ever pure?"

Even in our day-to-day living we find that silence can be a very useful tool that can sharpen the mind and that can help us to reflect in solitude and take stock of the larger picture in perspective. And it has often been seen in practice that quite often silence has been more profound in its eloquence than any speech could have been. Of a distinguished general, it was said, "he could hold his tongue in ten languages!" The whole point is that words cannot possibly express that which can only be known in silence. The map is not the territory. Words can only describe the known, and the Ultimate Reality is prior to words, prior to thought.

It is truly an unfortunate fact that the day-to-day living of the modern human being is essentially based on the psychological structure of society: wanting, competing, fear of failure, envy, greed, frustration, guilt, hatred and malice. And yet in such day-to-day living, man wants and hopes to get peace and tranquility. He believes that he will be able to achieve this peace through personal discipline, meditation, good deeds, and he gets frustrated when after a time he finds out that he is not nearer to the tranquility he yearns for.

The reason for this frustration from failure is really simple: the mistaken notion that tranquility can be achieved by self-centered activities – selflessness, being virtuous and noble. Tranquility is not a reward for personal good deeds and self-discipline. You may ‘meditate’ but you will not know that state of the ‘Real’, that state of the ‘unknown’, that state of silence and quietude. Meditation is not a disciplined, directed activity. Meditation can only be the activity of the silent, vacant, empty mind in which thinking is totally absent.

Zazen, or ‘sitting’ in meditation, is supposed to be an indispensable preparation for *satori*, the Zen experience; the intention is a ‘concentrated pondering’ on a koan, concept or a word. But this system of meditation does not seem to suit all people. Sitting still for a long time in the lotus position is not possible for many people.

Meditation is often misunderstood as ‘concentration’ on some word or image, but concentration means excluding everything, rejecting everything. It is a self-centered activity. Meditation really means absolute clarity, which can only come about in the total silence of the mind, not the self-centered concentration. Clarity can only happen when you are not concentrating on something, not when you are excluding everything, but you are merely silently being aware and attentive to every thought, every movement, without trying to correct anything. Meditation truly means clarity: being attentive to every thought, every word, every feeling, every desire, without in the least trying to correct anything according to a pre-conceived pattern.

The real intention of meditation would seem to be to extricate oneself from the mechanical, habitual, acquisitive automatism of our society, which leads to an over-stimulated nervous system, what Wei Wu Wei called "an overloaded switchboard". One system could be a discipline of 'pointed mindfulness', of focusing attention to the point where the insight breaks through. On the other hand, there could be a system that lets the mind be fully open and free, and merely witness, without comparing and judging and getting involved in any way, whatever appears in the mind.

Hui-Neng, the 7th century Zen patriarch, pointed out that the true relationship between the self and the other is "immanent in our minds" as part of man's spiritual equipment: "The truth is understood by the mind (*hsin*, heart), not by sitting still in meditation." There is the story of the Buddha holding up a flower and asking his disciples to comment upon it, something 'relevant'. The disciples tried to outdo one another in the profundity of their remarks. Only Mahakasyapa truly 'saw' the flower. He smiled and remained silent. In other words, Mahakasyapa saw the flower not as a flower but something without any label. The seeing was total, intense, not watered down by any predigested conditioning. The eye that sees is the I AM, the impersonal Awareness that experiences Itself in what it sees, becomes Self-aware, as "an integral part of the great continuum of all that is in the moment". Every thing or object is separate and yet not separate. In such seeing, curiosity gets dissolved in wonder.

Meditation simply cannot be a trained, directed, controlled activity. Out of that clear awareness of every thought and feeling, without altering it in any way, without either justifying it or rejecting it, merely witnessing and moving with it, arises that silence, that tranquility which is vibrant and not simulated or controlled. Such silence and tranquility is not the self-hypnosis that arises out of meditation as it is generally understood (or misunderstood!). Meditation cannot be based on discipline and control over the body. The body has its own intelligence that must be allowed freedom without any interference from the thinking mind of personal doership.

Meditation is truly seeing into one's own nature, far from self-analysis, the experience of Nature as it manifests itself both within me and outside me. It is the leap from out of the isolation of the 'me' into the totality of Being in the present moment, the Absolute Presence. And, this need not happen only when practicing some form of discipline. It can happen while crossing a busy thoroughfare or at a railway platform, if the mind happens to be in an appropriate state of receptivity.

When one admires a spiritual talk by a Master, one is inclined to forget that a true Master is very deeply convinced that he is not doing the talking but the talking is just happening through him. It is this forgetting of the very principle that makes a listener bristle with anger or impatience if what is said at any point of time seems to offend his sensibility. This was seen very clearly a number of times when people found talking happening through the famous Bengali Spiritual Master, Ramakrishna Paramahamsa.

"Today the Great Swan is visiting the residence of his beloved friend Adhar, a place of warm hospitality that Ramakrishna calls 'my ultimate Calcutta living room.' Adhar meets often with the Paramahamsa at the Temple Garden after an exhausting day of legal and administrative work. The tender sage always requests a mat to be spread on the floor of his room and Adhar sleeps peacefully at the holy feet of his guide, missing the oral teachings but receiving a strong infusion of Divine Presence.

The dignified well-dressed Adhar now welcomes the ecstatic, disheveled God-man with great devotion and enthusiasm, openly adoring this perfect union of Divinity and humanity, even before the critical gaze of other deputy magistrates and colleagues whom he has invited to his home for this festive occasion.

Adhar: 'Revered Sir, you have not graced our residence with the dust of your holy feet for much too long... But now the fragrance of your love for God pervades the entire house. Everyone is cheerful. This morning, I even wept during prayer and meditation, contemplating your arrival.'

The Master smiles like a delighted child, gazes intently into the eyes of his companion for a single moment, and steps into the reception hall, stammering with rapturous joy: *'Is that so? Tears of love. How wonderful!'*

Several important Calcutta intellectuals have also been invited today to meet the Paramahamsa, who is, for most of them, a quaint survival from the ancient Indian past. Certain of these guests regard Adhar as eccentric for retaining such deep contact with primitive forms of knowledge, rather than fully embracing the British cultural and educational model, as they have had the foresight to do. Others among the sophisticated visitors are open-minded enough to observe the Master objectively and test the authenticity of his teaching in the crucible of their Eastern sensibility and Western predilection.

Ramakrishna passes among these impressive gentlemen and ladies without even a sidelong glance, and unites with a small circle of ecstatic lovers gathered on one side of the elegant dining room which is filled with flowers and sumptuous refreshments. We begin to play and laugh, as if we were sitting together at the Temple Garden.

Attempting to integrate the gathering, Adhar brings forward the most prominent guest and introduces him to Ramakrishna. 'Revered Sir, may I present the renowned Bankim Chandra Chatterji. He is a great scholar and the author of books that develop new interpretations of ancient scriptures. He eloquently advocates social reform.'

Manifesting precisely the same delightful smile with which he greeted his beloved Adhar, the blissful sage turns to welcome this great Bengali literary figure of the day, bowing respectfully and inquiring: *'What has caused you to become so bent, so bankim?'*

Some conservative guests are disconcerted by this strange display on the meaning of Bankim's name, but Bankim Chandra himself obviously enjoys the wry humor and unconventional air [of an innocent child]. Seating himself on the Persian carpet with the sage, he answers back immediately, with humorous irony: 'Good Sir, your perception is completely accurate, I have been bent by kicks from the boots of our British colonial masters.' The nervousness in the room subsides as everyone senses that a most interesting conversation is about to ensue.

Ramakrishna: *No, no, my dear sir. You must not underestimate yourself this way. The sublime Lord Krishna was also bent in three places – knees, waist and neck – bent by ecstatic love for his exquisitely beautiful consort, the passionate Radha. This is how the ancient commentators interpret the traditional icons of Krishna, the incarnation of Divine Love. Do you know how they explain his dark blue complexion?.. Does it not strike you as strange that the Lord of the Universe appears as only three and a half cubits tall, measured by the span of his own delicate Divine Hand?*

Like the deep waters of the deep ocean, so Divine Reality appears dark blue when seen from a distance. If we draw near to the ocean and take the water directly into our own hands, we discover it to be brilliantly clear, perfectly transparent. The same holds true if one is courageous enough to come close to that ocean of Being-Consciousness-Bliss that appears from a certain distance as the dark blue Krishna... We must cultivate this direct acquaintance with the true nature of God. The Divine Reality will no longer be experienced as bent in three places, dark blue, small in stature. But, my noble friend, what an extraordinary attainment it is to make this direct acquaintance. This intimacy with Supreme Reality is not possible through ordinary modes of perception, knowledge or belief. Only the total concentration of our conscious being, called samadhi, can actually take us to the shore of the ocean. Beyond that no words apply.

As long as 'I-ness' and 'my-ness' remain habitual, we will continue to experience each other as names and forms, and will, therefore, most appropriately relate to God through Divine Names and Divine Forms. But this situation need not be experienced as a depressing separation from God. The dynamic universe of name and form is not a dim, miserable, musty place. It is the magnificent lila, the Divine Play – filled to the brim with the delight of tasting God, serving God, and wondering ceaselessly at the awesome Divine Mystery.

The heart-melting Krishna is actually Pure Consciousness. His captivating consort, Radha, is the primordial power of Pure Consciousness that projects complex worlds of name and form. What is the meaning of their ecstatic union depicted by the traditional icon of Radha and Krishna dancing side by side, merged into a single current of Divine Delight? The interpretation is simply this. Pure Consciousness and its own Primordial Power are one Reality and not two. You cannot realize the Absolute without participating in the dance of the relative. You cannot understand the play of relativity without being immersed in the radiant stillness of the Absolute.

A profound silence comes over the drawing room, decorated and furnished both in British and traditional Indian fashion. Our instinctive attachment to duality evaporates for just a moment. Bankim Chandra and his admirers, who have been educated in European and Indian modes of thought, are experiencing the profound impact of the perennial tantric teaching just unveiled with such power by the Paramahamsa. Their composite modern world view is being non-violently challenged at its very foundation."

*The essential cause of
almost any problem is the fact
that the individual entity concerned
is not able to accept the fact of
What-Is in the moment,
but wants something different.*

CHAPTER 3

*T*HE 'ME'
AND THE
'OTHER'
THE BASIC CAUSE OF PROBLEMS

The essence of life and living would seem to be 'problems': all kinds of problems, personal problems, problems about interhuman relationships, problems that we can anticipate and those we cannot. The Greek derivation of the word 'problem' originally denoted 'something thrown at you'. When something is thrown at you, whether you anticipate it or not, the only thing you can do is to catch it or dodge it. The point is that the decision and action are spontaneous and simultaneous.

We do get distressed by problems, but they also provide fresh experience, fresh conditioning, which amends our existing conditioning and makes us see problems in another perspective. We cannot but see, if we are alert and open to the moment, that problems do enlarge our compassion towards others, educate and humanize us. In facing daily life, there is no greater mistake than not finding contentment with one's own sufficiency; there is no greater calamity than to be covetous. When one is content within one's own nature, one will always have enough; the fictitious, illusory problem will dissolve into its own illusoriness.

There are certain problems that the individual cannot deal with. Such problems are those that people have to face at the poverty level. An extreme case of such problems is the one that is so often reported in the Indian press: a woman, without any source of income, threw her four children in the well and then threw herself in. But this is not the kind of problem that an average man at the middle level of society is usually concerned with. His problems are usually psychological problems – problems connected with the mind. We are so eager to find a solution that we do not care to study the problem, to observe the problem itself in silent contemplation.

What this means is that in seeking an answer, we are in fact seeking an escape from the problem because quite often the apparent solution turns out to be only a superficial remedy. What is necessary is to seek the source of the problem, and it is only full awareness of the problem in total spontaneity that can reveal the source of the problem. Passive but alert and spontaneous awareness would reveal that the source of most such problems is the 'myself', and then the problem collapses. For instance, suppose the problem is: how can I get even with someone who has insulted me? Silent observation of the problem itself is necessary to see the real source of the problem. And when this is seen, the anger that arose together with the supposed problem would give way to amusement and the problem itself would collapse in the amusement. The real problem lies in condemnation and justification, and it is only seeing the problem itself in its intensity with unbiased awareness that can produce a solution that is not superficial; this could actually result in the problem itself being unnecessary and, therefore, any solution unnecessary.

How do I deal with what happens in life? When it happens I welcome the happening, experience it while it lasts and let it go when it leaves. Happenings that at one time would have seemed serious now seem trivial, sometimes even amusing. At one time, I noticed that even the possibility of a war with the neighboring country, which caused quite a scare worldwide, seemed amusing. Not that one had become 'insensitive': whatever were to happen would happen in due course by Divine Will.

Daily living for most people means 'problems' and how to deal with them. It is for this reason – the acceptance that life and living mean problems – that our hearts at once go out to those who suffer from life's problems of one sort or another. But the fact of the matter is that the only real 'problem' in life is for those who are hovering around the poverty line, numbed by the fact that they are faced with the dire problem of starvation. Any other 'problem' is not really a problem as such, but a 'conflict' based on the non-acceptance of What-Is. Non-acceptance of What-Is is an outcome of the concept of what should be!

One day my friend was giving me a lift in his car, and we had to stop at a traffic light. A lame young boy hopped along in the busy street and put his hand out to me with a happy smile. While he was waiting for me to give him something his friends from the sidewalk called out to him, "hey Langda (Lame One), come here". He replied with a cheerful smile, "in a minute". No bitterness, no anger at being called a 'lame one' – he had accepted he is lame. My friend, who had been wailing all along about the medical expenses for his handicapped son, simply drove on.

In most cases, life's problems focus themselves on one point: making a decision. In making a decision the ordinary person faces the 'problem' of deciding between the different criteria laid down by one's conditioning: personal, social, religious. This is the real problem. The only answer is to realize that what is to happen has already happened, and then it really does not matter what decision you make. Whether what you have decided happens or not has never been in your control: neither the happening of the action behind the decision, nor the results or consequences of the decision. This is what Lord Krishna told Arjuna in the *Bhagavad Gita*: "You think you have to kill your relatives, friends and even your preceptors, but the fact of the matter is that as 'Time' I have already killed them, and you would only be the destined instrument through which their deaths will occur at the appropriate time. Therefore, even if you decide not to fight, your decision will be futile."

The most difficult situation in day-to-day living is one in which one does not know what to do in a set of given circumstances: what do I do? Where do I turn? The situation really is not much different than being lost in the woods: one is confused, there is no one to turn to and ask for directions. Indeed, they are the ones – the society, the family, friends, enemies, the church or the temple – who have brought one to this condition of utter confusion and discomfort. In such a situation there is only one thing to do – only one thing that can happen. Just stop. Wait and see what happens. In that state of confusion one simply cannot understand anything; one simply cannot know what is right and what is wrong. Therefore, stop doing anything. Let the mind be quiet, really and truly quiet, quiescent, empty, vacant; if thoughts come let them come and go. In that quiet, quiescence of the mind, comes what? Not the answer, but the very action that is necessary.

The way the understanding works when facing problems in day-to-day living is little short of miraculous. Occasionally in the morning talk a visitor will share how the understanding, at whatever level, has impacted the daily living. Göran Ekdahl, recognized as one of the top lawyers in Sweden, shared that the moment he decided to retire, although all conceivable worldly benefits were there, what he recognized was that there was still a feeling of discomfort, of dissatisfaction. As his active spiritual search began, what he came to understand was that the missing piece was true peace and harmony in his daily living. Below is a letter I received from Göran Ekdahl:

September 15, 2001

Dearest Ramesh,

It was so enriching to see and hear you again in Schermau, Germany. For family reasons, I had to leave before the seminar was over but on my way back, the thought and memory came of a very recent event where I could see a big change in my life. The story is the following.

During the last six years, I have been acting as neutral Chairman at ordinary shareholder's meetings with 300/400 shareholders in a public company with many conflicts between 2/3 groups of shareholders. It used to be a burdensome task sensing a worry of what would come next and for reactions to my ways of leading the discussions and making the propositions for voting.

This year, however, having been with you for a little over a year, a dramatic change showed itself. No matter how stupid or ill-willed the suggestions were, they were handled neutrally without any judging and then taken to various votings which, in themselves, were just flowing in a series of raising hands for 'yes' or 'no'.

Afterwards a lot of appreciation and admiration was received. One comment was that I never lost control or did not even seem affected by the attacks in between the shareholders and sometimes towards the Chairman.

I simply acted or performed whatever came up in my mind in the moment, using my experience and sometimes quickly consulting the legal secretary of the meeting. I was leaving the scene completely relaxed, surrounded with thanks and congratulations from the President and the Board of Directors of the Company.

With highest regards,
Göran Ekdahl

In one's daily living, one often comes across a problem like: should we or should we not plan everything we are supposed to do? Most such problems would disappear because they are basically only conceptual problems and all we have to do is to rely on our own experience in life. In regard to planning, everyone's experience is that: *a)* one does the planning and it works out; *b)* one does the planning and it does not work out; *c)* one does not plan anything and yet it works out; *d)* one does not plan and it does not work out. Therefore, the answer is simple. If it is your 'nature' to plan everything (if that is your 'programming'), you will be happier if you follow your nature. If you feel planning an awful drag – and your experience shows that planning does not always succeed – don't bother yourself to do any planning: act spontaneously. In other words, your 'nature' or your 'programming' happened without your choice; your success or failure in every venture is your destiny.

Where is the problem? If you are able to accept this analysis completely, can you not imagine the awful amount of strain and stress you will be able to avoid in your daily living? Whatever happens is your destiny; whatever was done or not done as preparation for it is also your destiny. The two saddest words in any language are "if only...".

For many, the very basis of life is dealing with problems: if there is no immediate problem in the moment, it is so easy for the mind to create a problem in the future. Again, it is our experience that in actual practice, the problem is finally not 'solved' but 'dissolved' when the problem is directly faced, directly understood, without the mind worrying about it seeking a solution. This is because seeking a solution is necessarily done by the mind which itself created the problem. This is especially so in the case of problems based on relationships.

In other words, looking for a solution or answer to the problem is really avoiding the problem: the problem belongs to the self, the individual entity. The answer, the decision, the action, can only come from within, in the absence of the individual entity. The self, the entity is indeed the real problem.

I want money, I don't have it. I do not want illness but I do have it: migraine. I can steal money, but if I am caught, I shall be punished; besides, I do not have the courage to do it. I can take medication for my migraine, but it comes back again. Is there any time when I do not have this problem?

Yes – when I am in deep sleep. But I cannot remain in deep sleep all the time; I have to earn a living.

Why did I not have this problem when I was in deep sleep? Because there was no 'me' to worry about it. But I was not dead; so I was there, but not there to worry about the problem. What does this mean? It can only mean that I was there, but there was no problem without the 'me' to worry about it.

How can this be? – no 'me' and no problem! Is there really a problem for the 'me' in this moment? It is not that I have no money at all. Therefore, in this moment I truly have no problem even when I am awake! There is no problem and no 'me', in this moment, if I do not assume that there is a problem.

Therefore, it is obvious that the problem has been created by the 'me' by thinking in horizontal time: not being in the present moment. In the present moment, there is no problem and, therefore, no need of a 'me' either.

But wait! Now, in this moment, there could be a problem about money: I have to pay to the bank an installment on my housing loan today. Is it not a problem? Yes – but is this 'money problem' that I have as severe as the problem which someone else could be facing, who has lost his job, or, someone who has no money, in the moment, to feed himself and his family?

Are there not always others who could be in a much worse situation than I am in?

Do I then really have a problem? Even assuming I do have an imaginary problem, is there something I can do in this moment? If not, I had better shut up my thinking shop, and enjoy my blessings in the moment with a deep feeling of gratitude.

Our conditioning – our education, our very culture – has trained the mind to be occupied and it is the very occupation of the mind that creates most problems. A mind that worries about spiritual progress is as fully occupied as another mind that is consumed with the world's problems.

When we are faced with a real problem that needs action, such action would usually come forth with a certain amount of spontaneity. It is the involvement of the self – the 'me' and the 'mine' – that creates fear and hesitation in the mind and seeks a solution that is in reality an escape and not the real solution. Silent, impersonal observation, without comparing and judging, is the only answer. This clearly and obviously does not apply when it is the working mind in operation. For example, when you are supposed to select one man for promotion from several candidates, the necessary comparing and judging does not present any problem, unless one's partiality comes into focus, and the problem then again focuses on the 'me' and the 'mine'.

In other words, the source of the problem almost always centers around the self. In fact, the problem is the self. If we understand this process of the occupation of the mind by the self, the problem itself in most cases would find an easy answer; it happens when we are not afraid of the source of the problem.

In day-to-day living, we are troubled by problems for which we cannot find solutions. The tragedy of life is that many of these problems are created purely because of horizontal thinking in time, and do not really exist in the moment. The problems exist in the flow of thinking, and the answer really lies in what is called the 'vacant mind' or the 'silent mind', a state of mind when it is emptied of its flow of thinking. This comes about when the vacant mind does not identify itself with the flow of thinking but merely witnesses it without discriminating between the various items in terms of right or wrong, important or unimportant, of value or no worth. Such witnessing of the passing show of thoughts, without any judgment at all, is of immense value in reducing tension and creating a real sense of peace and calm. Such impersonal witnessing, experience has clearly shown, not only dissolves most of the psychological problems but, importantly, yields sudden solutions to even practical problems. This is because the impersonal witnessing or passive awareness gives full flow to the creative or intuitive faculties of the silent mind, as the unconscious or passive awareness.

In his day-to-day living, the ordinary person may momentarily experience the quiescence of mind. Yet, the word 'meditation' frightens the ordinary person. The word has an ominous background of sitting on a particular kind of mat, with a straight back and a convoluted routine, at a particular time of the day. In actual fact, meditation can be practiced by any ordinary individual during any period when he happens to be alone. Meditation means, simply, to be aware of any thought, of any feeling, that is there at the moment, to merely watch it and go with it, without considering it as right or wrong, without trying to justify it or condemn it. Out of this kind of awareness, arises silence. This silence that arises of its own, that is not simulated or brought about or controlled, is itself true meditation, in which the observer, the meditator, is absent.

Indeed, such meditation can and does take place anywhere, any time: walking in a park, traveling in a bus, or even in the drawing room while sitting amidst your loved ones, preferably when there is no participation in a conversation! In other words, meditation, as is often misunderstood, is not an activity that needs isolation. You can be alone even in the midst of company. In short, meditation only means a constant state of total attention to whatever is happening, a constant state of total awareness, in which there is no individual observer doing any observing and judging. In this meditation that is really silence, the dividing line between you and me disappears.

The essential cause of almost any problem is the fact that the individual entity concerned is not able to accept the fact of What-Is in the moment but wants something different. It has been my experience that many a visitor, otherwise in quite happy circumstances, seems disgruntled, not at all comfortable with himself because, deep down, he has the feeling that he is not sufficiently interested in the welfare of others, not sufficiently concerned with the woes of the world. As one of them, an intellectual, expressed it: "Why is there no genuine love in my heart? Why is there this gap between the self and the others, between the intellect and the heart? This makes me extremely uncomfortable with myself."

In other words, in the case of this individual there was no acceptance of the programming – the 'nature' – as it was, of the body-mind organism with which the ego had identified himself. He wanted to know that he should be nobler than he is, and wanted to do something about it. The usual problem, therefore, is: what do I do in order to change the What-Is into what I want it to be?! The obvious understanding should be that one is what God intended one to be. Therefore, just BE. The problem is a self-created one, and just seeing this, the problem dissolves.

It is really astonishing how easily we forget the basic cause of a problem when dealing with one in day-to-day living. There is a joke about this. A young lady went to her doctor and asked him if there was any remedy to prevent pregnancy that was absolutely harmless and one hundred percent safe. She was delighted when the doctor assured her that he certainly had the answer for her question. When she eagerly asked for the prescription, he stood up and said: "Very simple – do not have sex."

The basic reason behind any problem in day-to-day living is that the 'me' concept, born in dualism (not 'duality', which is the necessary prerequisite for phenomenal manifestation), splits irreparably the unicity of Reality and makes a Sartre say: "Hell is other people." Whatever the 'me' concept may believe, the fact of the matter is that the 'me'-doer, the pseudo-subject *viv-a-vis* the 'other', is only a phenomenal object, and identification with it as a separate entity with choice of decision and action must necessarily bring about conflict, the basis of which is fear and hope, which brings in its wake various affective manifestations. Even after a victory over the 'enemy' has been achieved, the fear of the future with 'other' enemies is never overcome, although it may be masked as anger, frustration or revolt. Man is constantly afraid that the happiness achieved at one moment may not last for long and hopes for constant, changeless joy. He does not realize that constant change is the very basic essence of life in the phenomenal manifestation.

There was one particular incident during my career as a banker that had great significance for me as the empathy of life. I was not an active spiritual seeker at that time but there was an inherent appreciation of the fact that it is truly never a question of one against the other; it is really a matter of one complementing the other in the harmony and empathy of life.

It was when I was the manager of one of the larger branches of the bank, I must add, at a comparatively younger age. A particular customer, a borrower, was in difficulties, and at my request he was to meet me in my office at a designated time. I had completely cleared my desk, and there were no papers on my desk except those concerning the customer. My room was on the ground floor, and as I looked out of the window I was startled to see this gentleman sitting morosely in the car, obviously working up the necessary courage to enter the bank for what was certainly going to be a very difficult interview. My heart immediately went out to him as I could easily understand his state of mind.

Suddenly, he got out of the car when he looked at his watch and found that it was time for the appointment. I was myself quite worried about the bank's loan but, having seen the other, I deliberately greeted him, as he entered my room, with more warmth than I would perhaps otherwise have done. He was rather startled to see me greeting him so warmly, particularly because I had been recently transferred to the branch and his experience with my predecessor was notoriously bad. I showed him to a chair opposite my desk and I was about to go back to my own chair on the other side of the desk, when, somehow or other, something intuitive made me stop and take the chair beside the one in which he was sitting. There we were in that moment, our first meeting, sitting side by side, and I asked him whether he would like a cup of tea or coffee before we started our conversation. I have never forgotten the expression on his face at that time. He had tears in his eyes as he realized the attitude I had taken – we were not on the opposite sides of the desk.

I slipped out of the room for a few moments in order to give him time to compose himself. The meeting went off extremely well, the borrower came out of his mood of helpless panic, and between the two of us, we managed to nurse the account back to good health. This incident remained in my memory because it taught me a number of lessons. First and foremost, I could see the actual and immediate effect of demolishing the separation between the lending banker and the borrowing customer, between 'me' and the 'other', and establishing a closer relationship towards achieving a common goal. Secondly, the incident gave me the ineluctable insight into the way sincere sympathy and a genuine desire to help intuitively communicate themselves to the other. Thirdly, an open and frank discussion with the borrower brought out several factors about how and why the account got into trouble in the first place. And these clarifications undoubtedly helped both of us in our respective roles.

But the most important of all was the fact that the expressed goodwill thus created turned my 'enemy' into the best Public Relations Officer for the bank and for me personally.

In day-to-day living, a beautiful guidance is given by the famous Rudyard Kipling:

If you can keep your head
        when all about you are losing theirs and blaming it on you;
If you can trust yourself
        when all men doubt you, but make allowance for their doubting
        too;
If you can wait and not be tired by waiting,
        Or being lied about, don't deal in lies,
        Or, being hated, don't give way to hating,
        And yet don't look too good, nor talk too wise;

If you can dream – and not make dreams your master;
If you can think – and not make thoughts your aim;
If you can meet with triumph and disaster
        And treat those two imposters just the same;
If you can bear to hear the truth you've spoken
        Twisted by knaves to make a trap for fools,
        Or watch the things you gave your life to broken,
        And stoop and build 'em up with worn out tools;

If you can make one heap of all your winnings
        And risk it on one turn of pitch-and-toss,
        And lose and start again at your beginnings
        And never breathe a word about your loss;

If you can force your heart and nerve and sinew
        to serve your turn long after they're gone,
        And so hold on when there is nothing in you
        Except the Will which says to them 'hold on';

If you can talk with crowds and keep your virtue, or walk with kings –
        nor lose the common touch;
If neither foes nor loving friends can hurt you;
If all men count with you, but none too much;

If you can fill the unforgiving minute with sixty second's worth
> of distance run –
Yours is the Earth and everything that's in it,
And, which is more –
> You'll be a Man, my son.

*Total awareness plus
total relaxation in the
moment leads to spontaneity
and efficiency in action, and to
peace and harmony in non-action.*

$\mathcal{T}$HOUGHT
AND
THINKING

It is the experience of most people that contradiction, conflict and tension, which disturb the peace and harmony of daily living, are the result of constant thinking and objectivizing the future in terms of the past. The only answer is to realize that the conscious thinking process, the ego, is a creation of the split-mind of subject-object relationship.

It is only when the mind is let alone to function in its natural way, which is the integrated spontaneous way of the whole-mind, that one can witness its working resulting in a special indefinable effectiveness and power. The Chinese philosophy of Tao calls this power 'Te', which can only be loosely defined as natural and spontaneous virtuosity. Such a state of mind, in which its functioning is 'non-active', is called 'no-mind' or 'fasting mind'. It is by no means a state of idiotic vacuity. On the contrary, it is precisely the opposite: the mind, undisturbed by any horizontal thinking or objectivizing, is at its most alert.

This state of the alertness of the mind comes about when the split-mind of 'me' and the 'other' gives up the impossible task of controlling itself beyond a certain limit. It then surrenders itself in the sense that it realizes the futility of the perpetual operation of the dualism of thought and action, and lets the whole-mind take over. In other words, split-mind ceases to think, and act, and think on the action all at the same time continuously. This kind of blockage also occurs in the dualism of action and feeling, for example, not just feeling happy while enjoying in the moment music or food or whatever, but also wanting to feel oneself feeling the relevant feeling. It is precisely for this reason that it is said in *Yogavasishta* that the *jnani*, the sage, not only enjoys whatever comes his way – he does not pursue the pleasure – but that he is a *mahabhogi*, a 'super-enjoyer'. The *jnani* gives full attention with the whole-mind to whatever he is doing at the moment (more accurately, to whatever is happening at the moment) without any distractive thinking based on comparison and contrast with a previous experience or future expectation.

In the usual day-to-day living of most people, this non-action in the no-mind state is not generally apprehended in its true significance. On the contrary, it is misconstrued as idleness or waste of time in a society where what is traditionally approved and accepted and expected is a furious competitive spirit in order to strive and achieve a particular goal. What is forgotten is that all such thinking and doing is in dualism, that even the apparent success achieved in this manner is so loaded with an inherent depth of guilt – and even shame – that very soon the achievement and the success seem empty and ephemeral. The result is that the split-mind of 'me' and the 'other' goes ahunting for more and better success, leading to ultimate frustration and a sense of having wasted one's life. Over 800 years ago, the very same condition was described beautifully by Omar Khayyam:

> *Some for the Glories of This World; and some*
> *Sigh for the Prophet's Paradise to come;*
> *Ah, take the Cash and let the Promise go,*
> *Nor heed the rumble of a distant Drum!*

> *Were it not Folly, Spider-like to spin*
> *The Thread of present Life away to win –*
> *What? For ourselves, who know not if we shall*
> *Breathe out the very Breath we now breathe in!*

This truly is the basis of the concept of *samsara* (life and day-to-day living) being *dukkha* (misery), and more importantly, the concept of the world being *anitya* (not merely 'impermanent', but 'insubstantial' in the sense that worldly success cannot really be grasped into a deep feeling of *shanti* or harmony and quietude, peace and calm). Indeed, it is only when the real significance of these doctrines of *dukkha* and *anitya* is clearly apprehended that the mind ceases to grasp itself into a split-mind, that the mind achieves its pristine purity and becomes what is known as 'unborn' mind or 'whole-mind', and what results is action that is in reality 'non-action', spontaneous, intuitive action.

What actually happens in day-to-day living is that the human being attaches undue importance to past conventions, to conscious thinking, to communication by linear signs and mathematical symbols, and not nearly enough to the intuitive 'feel'. In other words, far more importance is given to the central spotlight vision and not enough to the peripheral vision, far more to the analytical data and not enough to the 'gut feeling'. It is absolutely essential to understand that it is not at all a question of one against the other, but really the *very important matter of one complementing the other*. What happens most of the time is that the conditioning of conventionality is so powerful and overwhelming that it completely smothers all spontaneity.

This can be clearly seen in the education of a child, where the stress on abstract, linear thinking combined with social conventions sometimes reaches such a degree of repression of the child's inherent spontaneity of expression that it could do positive damage to the thinking of the child. What is necessary is certainly not a surrender to a mad urge of caprice, but a rational recognition of an intelligence that does not base itself on the too orderly a working of reason and intellect: an intelligence, the actual working of which can be clearly seen in the way we are able to move our limbs and take our breaths. In other words, we seem to be afraid to forget our minds, fearing to fall through the void with nothing to cling on to. Man is afraid to rely to any extent on the spontaneous functioning with which he is naturally endowed but which gets blocked, when restrained, in its natural working by the efforts to understand it in terms of conventional techniques:

> The centipede was happy, quite
> > Until a toad in fun
> Said, 'Pray, which leg goes after which?'
> This worked his mind to such a pitch,
> > He lay distracted in a ditch,
> > Considering how to run.

According to Jesus Christ, 'Unless you become like little children, you cannot know the meaning of life'. The clear interpretation of this statement is that in day-to-day living you cannot find peace and happiness unless your attitude to life is like that of little children. The infant is regarded in many religions as an example of the way in which man should view the world and what happens in it.

The basis of this view is that the child is not loaded with a lot of concepts and, therefore, is not hampered in its action by a lot of horizontal thinking based on the past and projected into the future. The child lives in the present moment. The sage, in his deep Ultimate Understanding, also lives in the present moment. The query is sometimes made whether, since the child and the sage both live in the present moment, can the child be considered Self-realized?

The fact of the matter is that the child, not knowing what Self-realization is, does not need it! The child is not capable of any realization at all, let alone Self-realization, because to realize anything, there has to be intellect, and the child in its earliest stages does not have intellect except in its most elementary state. Almost every spiritual teacher has condemned conceptualization as the barrier to Self-realization. When Ramana Maharshi said, "kill the mind", he certainly was not unaware that the mind-intellect is the very instrument that has to be used for Self-realization.

Development of intellect is a gradual process. If this were not so, and if intellect had appeared at birth with all its possibilities and potential, the child, without the subsequent conditioning, would certainly have realized the immanence of the Absolute in all phenomenal objects, the one abiding principle in all phenomena, and could then be considered as being Self-realized. But then, if every child were to be Self-realized, the play of *maya* could never have started. The fact of the matter is that there is gradual mental transformation in human beings from the state of being a baby without any intellect as such, to that of an infant or child and then on to the level of the adult with verbal thinking.

Intellect appears in a child at the age of about 2 years or so, but until then the baby has only the animal level of thinking, which is neither verbal nor logical. At this level, the baby, like the animal, superficially resembles the sage inasmuch as the thinking of the baby at the pre-verbal level is totally fluid without any intellectual conditioning. The big difference between the baby and the sage is that in the case of the baby the two dual states of convergence and divergence, harmony and disharmony, exist together in the primordial state of apparent confusion and chaos, whereas in the case of the sage, the two states exist in perfect balance and conciliation because of the Self-realization which has happened through the intellect. It is thus the intellect that makes the difference between the infant and the sage.

The development of the intellect is gradual and progressive, from associating particular words with particular objects to forming verbal concepts about abstract matters, and then on to metaphysical questions like 'what exactly am I?' During this evolution the child, when it is 3 or 4 years old, comes across the phenomenon of death and the concept of 'disintegration', which until then was unknown. Then the child discovers the idea of 'life' through the interdependent concept of 'death'. From then on the idea is firmly established in the mind that 'integration' means 'being' or 'existence' and 'non-integration' means 'disintegration', 'death', the annihilation of beingness.

Thereafter, man does not realize that non-integration truly means not disintegration into nothingness but being merged into the unmanifest fullness of the Plenum, the totality of the potential unmanifest from which has emerged the totality of the manifest. The identification with a phenomenal object as a separate entity with volition and separate doership becomes so consummate that, though man may be prepared to accept death as denoting the destruction of only the body, he simply cannot give up his separate identity with volition. He conceptualizes that the separate entity (called by various names like the 'spirit' or the 'soul' or whatever) moves into another world in another form at some other time, *still retaining the separate identity*. He does not realize that by his refusal to accept death as a finality, man prevents himself from being the Reality. It is the power of the *maya* – divine hypnosis – that man accepts the illusory phenomenal world as real and rejects Reality as illusory nothingness!

From the time this partiality for integration (life, existence, happiness) gets firmly established in the psyche of the child along with its interconnected opposite, the aversion for disintegration, he starts pursuing happiness as an object, which in fact is a pure subjective state.

The 'me-entity' thereafter pursues this concept of happiness with determination and it is inextricably involved with the 'other' that is seen as the enemy. Each conflict with each 'other' makes the illusory problem that much stronger. This illusory chase after the illusory happiness cannot cease until there is a clear apprehension that the duration in which the chase happens is a concept (the physicist firmly tells us that 'time' does not exist), that what truly exists can only be in the moment, and that anything based on duration is illusory.

Volition and desire leading to the pursuit of the illusory happiness inevitably means the fear of not succeeding in the pursuit. And this fear of failure is, again, inevitably allied to the hope of one day being freed of this fear. So it is a sort of double-bind, chasing the illusory happiness and at the same time seeking freedom from this compulsive chase after happiness. And this is the ever-present problem in day-to-day living. While chasing the mythical happiness, man simply has no time to enjoy the present moment, and what actually happens is that he wants both happiness and the freedom from the pursuit of happiness as an object at the same time.

In other words, man seeks Intemporality within the framework of temporality, and the permanence of Unicity in the duality of the impermanent phenomenality. It is this awful problem that makes the human being suffer the horrors of hell in his day-to-day living. And this situation cannot but continue until there is the realization – the Self-realization – that the Supreme Subjectivity cannot be grasped as an object by another phenomenal object, which the human being basically happens to be.

Many people have had the experience of the happening of events in their day-to-day living when there has been an unusual balance of intellect and intuition, so that they were surprised how unusually effective their work had materialized. It was not, it is realized, that this principle of balanced thought and intuition excluded the concentrated attention that must necessarily be given to the routine or technique. Indeed, one cannot get away from the fact that concentrated attention, to the exclusion of distractive thinking, is the very essence of a successful piece of work.

The Zen term 'mindfulness' could perhaps be explained by the following incident: My daughter's mother-in-law was incapacitated by an illness into being confined to bed. She was a very remarkable woman. Instead of being bitter about her illness, she was extremely well-adjusted about her condition. One morning, the 'coconut man' came to do his job: climbing the two coconut trees in the garden and removing the coconuts. The man climbed the trees, removed each coconut and dropped it to the ground from above. He finished the job, came to the house and reported to the lady-of-the-house that there were 46 coconuts. The lady promptly told him that there should be 48 coconuts and that two of them could have rolled away and escaped his attention. The man was astonished; he went out, replaced the two coconuts that he had kept aside to take away for himself, and after a few minutes reported again that the two vagrant coconuts had been found and that the total was now, indeed, 48. While remaining helpless in bed, the not-so-old lady had been counting the 'thuds' as each coconut fell to the ground.

The essence of the Zen philosophy – perhaps the equivalent in a sense of the Hindu *Advaita* – is indeed what they call the 'no-mind' state, which is the most alert mind. At a certain juncture in one's daily work, one has found occasions when the thought-language has been given free rein by avoiding the natural partiality towards too much rational, convergent thinking. The Japanese master-swordsman knows that the unknown has no ego-consciousness (which conscious thought has) because it does not move at the level of dualism. Therefore, when conscious thought is left behind, and there is no thought of winning the contest, the sword moves almost *by itself* wherever it should move.

As Sun-Tzu, a great Japanese warrior, is said to have put it: "To win every battle is not the best aim; the perfect victory is to win without planning to win." The no-mind state means great alertness, and in this state the mind is free of all conflicting thoughts of life and death, victory and defeat and, therefore, functions at its most natural and effective level. In other words, in the no-mind state, the personal 'me' with its thinking mind functioning in the future, is absent. Like the master-archer in the Hindu mythology, the Zen master-swordsman is beyond all dualism.

In my own day-to-day living, I can recollect two instances of a similar nature. In the first instance, after passing my B.A. examination in

Bombay, I went to London to join the London School of Economics. There was an entrance examination in which I had to appear for an exam in economics, for which there was no specific curriculum. So there was nothing to cram up except to go cursorily through the basics of the subject. When the question paper was distributed, I found that there was a fair amount of choice and I selected general topics where the principles of economics could be applied and discussed, and not much relevant information was required. So I happened to write the answer in a relaxed frame of mind, perhaps, because I had gathered that the test was more to weed out the sub-marginal applicants rather than to test the caliber of each applicant. I had also come to know that for those who had done their B.A. and had applied for entrance to the B.Com. course (Commerce), the usual standard marking was 'partial exemption', which meant that I would have to appear for an examination next year in the accountancy subject, which I had not done for my B.A.

When the results were ready, I was supposed to see one Professor Plant about my score. When I met the Professor and gave my name, he went through the list, gave me a bright smile and said, "full exemption". When I explained that in India I had done B.A. and not B.Com., he again referred to the list and repeated, "full exemption". He held out his hand, we shook hands, and I came out of his room rather dazed. When I told my friends that I had been given full exemption, they would not believe it and told me to check again when the list was put out on the board. There was no correction, and I gathered later that the examiners were so impressed by my answer paper that they had recommended "full exemption" which made me the only B.Com. from the London University who had never passed a paper in accountancy! Of course, I did study accountancy later.

The one thing I could later recollect about the examination was that when writing the answers, I must have found myself in complete tune with the universal pulse, the body and mind working in total relaxation, without any thought, let alone anxiety, about what might happen. I do remember that when I came out of the examination hall, there was only sheer joy of the performance itself.

In the second instance, a similar thing happened once when I played a round of golf with the club professional. It was the first day of my vacation, and when I stood at the first tee, I had the most fantastic feeling of being at the peak of my physical condition, relaxed and looking forward to the round of golf. There was, of course, no question of really winning or losing – either face or money! When we returned to the clubhouse, I had played the best round of golf ever, with the lowest score of my life, and the club professional with whom I had played did not have to tell me that, at a certain stage of the game, he had to take the game really seriously so as not to lose face.

I found that I had learned a lot that day. First, that the best results 'happen' – are not 'achieved' – if there is concentration on the work itself, that is to say, on what is being done in the moment, whether it is a ball being hit or a report being prepared or whatever; that concentration does not mean tension but relaxation, which happens when there are no disturbing thoughts about the result of the effort being made; that in fact, if there is true concentration with relaxation, the actual effort turns out to be effortless like the winning effort of an expert in any field. Such effortless effort denotes the Joy of Being experienced in the effort itself, irrespective of the success that such an effort might or might not produce.

What is an occasional experience in day-to-day living for the ordinary person has become the common, usual experience for the sage. After the apperception of the true nature of Reality, the sage has realized that the interconnectedness of duality is the very warp and woof of the phenomenal manifestation. He has realized that the volitional acceptance of one aspect of life to the exclusion of the other is precisely what causes conflict in day-to-day living, and this realization has brought the sage to the inherent natural balance in life.

The sage continues his phenomenal existence until the end of his allotted span in perfect adaptation to whatever might happen, without losing his inherent sense of equanimity and harmony. His living then is non-volitional living, though the life of the sage may appear to others as being purposeless. However, in the words of a Zenrin poem: "The wild geese do not intend to cast their reflection; the water has no mind to receive their image."

What are you doing at this moment? – watching the TV; reading a book; taking a walk; resting in an easy chair or in bed; doing a job to earn a living; discussing business with a colleague or customer; talking to a personal friend or two; driving a car; giving a talk, writing a letter; doing a painting; taking physical exercise; attending a party; eating a meal; brushing your teeth; relieving yourself in the bathroom; enjoying a shower? Whatever you are doing, if you were asked at any moment, 'are you quite comfortable with yourself now?', your honest answer is most likely to be, 'I don't know'. If the question were, 'are you having fun?', again the likely answer would be, 'I don't know'. (Of course, it is assumed that you are not asked this question when you are pleasantly drunk!).

This means clearly that what happens very often is that, at any moment, one is not totally aware of the situation. In other words, the fact that there does not exist a clear, total awareness in the moment surely means that there exists an undercurrent of discomfort, uncertainty, perhaps even a fear of being wrong or being cheated. In any case, it means a continuous undercurrent of stress and tension.

This means that whatever you are doing – having fun or doing serious work – what is always needed is the *existence of total awareness in the moment*. Then there would be spontaneity and efficiency in the action that is going on – with the working mind focused on the job at hand, without the thinking mind creating doubts and problems by projecting itself into the uncertainties of an imaginary future. The working mind will have already taken into account the various available alternatives together with the projected results, based on the existing data, before starting the job. When there is no action being undertaken in the moment, total awareness together with total relaxation would produce peace and harmony, and absence of stress and tension, because whatever is happening in the moment would be witnessed impersonally, i.e. without comparing and judging.

In other words, total awareness plus total relaxation in the moment leads to spontaneity and efficiency in action, and to peace and harmony in non-action. This can happen only in the absence of the 'me', the ego-doer, creating imaginary problems in the imaginary future. And again, this can happen only if there is the total understanding that there is, in actual life, no individual doer – neither oneself nor the 'other', that whatever has happened could not have happened unless it was the Will of

God, according to a Cosmic Law. In other words, the total understanding has to be that an action happens because it is the Will of God; and whatever the result of any action, happening through whichever body-mind organism, would obviously also be the Will of God.

An area in which the spiritual seeker often finds himself in confusion is: how does the understanding – or the lack of it – work in actual living? This is a valid point that needs to be addressed squarely, without causing the confusion to be more confounded. In daily life, our experience is that almost anything that we do or experience begins with a thought or feeling; and the arising of a thought or feeling in consciousness is not in one's control. One sees something or hears something (or some other sense reacts to its respective object), and the reaction is a thought or feeling. This thought arises in consciousness, strictly in accordance with one's destiny, according to the programming in the body-mind organism.

A reaction in the moment could be anger or fear or pleasure or regret or disgust or compassion or whatever. This is the same whichever it is, according to the programming in the body-mind organism, and has nothing to do with whether or not any understanding has happened or not, whether the person concerned is a sage or an ordinary person. What happens subsequently depends to a certain extent upon the intensity or absence of the understanding.

What happens subsequently could be: *a)* the thought or feeling spontaneously turns into an action; or, *b)* the working mind comes into the picture and takes possession of the thought or feeling, depending upon the degree and depth of the understanding. Or, in the absence of the understanding, it is the thinking mind that comes into the picture and gets the ego thoroughly involved in horizontal time; the moment there is the clear apperception that the involvement has taken place, the involvement gets cut off. Or, if the thought or feeling does not result in any specific action, the sage or the man of understanding merely witnesses the thought or feeling as it disappears from the consciousness; more accurately, the understanding itself brings about the impersonal witnessing of the disappearance of the thought, without any involvement. This process shows the arising of the thought or feeling and the course it takes until it reaches the end of it.

I remember an event, an experience when I was a student in school. I was perhaps 12 or 13 years of age, when the subject Algebra was first introduced in the class. I was so enamored of the subject that I could not wait for the quarterly examination. I was seriously worried that I might die before the examination. In fact, it is everyone's experience in daily living that 'experiencing' is a judgment of partiality and is qualitatively absolute; and yet, it is a dynamic process – I experience because I *wish to experience*. The wish to experience is so constraining that it becomes a *need*. The source of this constraint can be traced to the will by which the Absolute Source brings about its manifestation. In other words, each creature wills its 'being' absolutely because the Absolute Source Itself wills Itself absolutely in each being. From the moment the human being identifies himself with the individual body-mind organism, his claim to his individual beingness is absolute: the individual's search for the consciousness of his Absolute Being becomes necessary – and constraining.

In actual fact, the 'will to experience' (and its activity) is absurd inasmuch as it can never achieve its goal. This very fact, to understand with the deepest conviction this very absurdity – that the individual being cannot realize its Absolute nature – is the ultimate goal of all spiritual seeking!

In the 'will to experience' there is basically no dualism between the outer world and the individual consciousness. When one goes to the outer world for experience, what interests the individual 'me' is not the world but the consciousness of the Absolute Being that the 'me' wishes to find in the contact with the outer world. And, deep down, it is not the individual body-mind organism that interests the 'me' but the consciousness of Being in the contact with the outer world.

When one has an ecstatic experience of being fulfilled, what has actually happened is that one has really lost all interest in the outer world as well as the individual body-mind organism. This actually can be interpreted as the 'me' being prepared to die with that ecstatic experience. Before the ecstatic experience happened, the expectation was, 'I must not die before I have completed the undertaking'. In other words, in regard to one's 'will to experience', the individual body-mind organism and the outer world had no difference between them: both are useful together for the experience and, after the experience, both cease to be effective.

This intimate connection between the outer world and the individual body-mind organism can be clearly seen in the psychological notion of the state of one's mind. When you are in a 'positive' state – life could not be better – the outer world and 'myself' are both equally positive. My 'state' seems to set up a kind of vortex which tends to fixate what I experience: I am sad because I see the world as overcast, and I see the world overcast because I am sad. The way in which I experience myself and I experience the world seems like the reflections of an object when there are two mirrors facing each other.

In other words, theoretically, I live in the present moment, continually moving in duration, but in practice, what actually happens is that I find myself immobilized in duration which seems to flow in spite of me: I live in a dream of the future continually repeated. I find myself, in other words, just not able to live in the present moment with my will to experience the ever-new experience; I find myself immobilized.

The inherent dualism in any will to experience seems to be reflected in my avidity for sheer existence combined with the fear of existence. This makes me a slave of my present existence, my present experiencing. This immobility in my will to experience is the root cause of my unhappiness: expectation of the future based on my present experience instead of calmly waiting for the future experience whenever it appears. We should see this absurdity not as a condemnation, but to affirm and realize the necessity for a change, a change that cannot be 'achieved' but can only happen with the deepest understanding. We cannot find a solution for the problem; the problem itself must dissolve when it is squarely faced.

Concomitant with the will to experience, what is generally pursued in day-to-day living is knowledge, information. A certain amount of technical knowledge about one's trade or occupation is certainly necessary. But what the mind gets used to and demands continuously is a process of accumulation of knowledge and experience, almost as a means of competing with all 'others'. And the unfortunate part of the situation is that this accumulation is mistaken for wisdom. A man of experience is usually mistaken for a wise man but, actually, wisdom can never be separated from spontaneity, whereas accumulation of knowledge and information is based on memory. This does not, of course, mean that an ignorant man is a wise man.

The truly wise man is he who is not continuously involved in the process of accumulation, but is usually free of such a process, so that he is relaxed and spontaneously open to whatever the moment brings. Whatever comes from that silence is spontaneous and not based on accumulated information and reaction. This silence is not achieved but is a natural result of being fully aware of every thought, every feeling, every reaction. It is in this awareness, pure awareness, that all thinking and reacting dissolve and leave the mind vacant and open to the moment. When the mind is quiet, whatever happens becomes the action of spontaneity and not based on accumulated information. Such action contains something sacred and mysterious for the very reason that it is not based on accumulated information and conditioning.

Our natural state – as an intrinsic part of the Totality – is one of relaxation. This state of relaxation, peace, tranquility, is what quickly distinguishes a sage from an ordinary person. A sage is one who has been able, by the Grace of God, to bridge this separation from Totality, which is the basic cause of aggressiveness, tension and fear. It is only the surrender to the Totality that can eliminate from our systems the totally unnatural tension and fear: a surrender not forced by a sense of frustration and bitterness but a softly induced friendly surrender, brought about by a clear understanding of our true nature. The understanding of the sage is simple enough: what we are in phenomenality are not independent entities with volition and free will but merely uniquely programmed body-mind organisms or instruments through which the Source – what 'we' truly are as 'I' and not the identified 'me' – functions. And, the sage understands that this functioning brings about actions or happenings as are supposed to happen according to a Cosmic Law, which is totally beyond human intellect to comprehend.

The basis of all fear, what brings the ordinary man out of the natural state of relaxation, is the individual entity, the identification with a particular body and name as a separate individual with autonomy and independence, with volition and choice. In one's day-to-day living, fear, desire, and all other forms of affectivity are mere manifestations of the pseudo-entity, and what needs to be eliminated is this pseudo-entity rather than the manifestations of that pseudo-entity. In day-to-day living, 'fear', as a phenomenon, needs to be clearly analyzed and understood. What-We-Are is the subjective noumenality, but the identification with one separate entity, as opposed to others, gives rise to the unhappy concept of fear. As an *Upanishad* says: "Fear exists wherever an 'other' exists." In other words, fear is a manifestation of the relationship between 'me' and the 'other', and its basis is aggression. In fact, fear and aggression are interrelated; one is the cause of the other. The basis of both is the need for satisfaction or gratification.

It is understandable when the need for satisfaction is a basic need like food for the gratification of hunger, but we move on to an entirely different level when the gratification sought is based on the need for power or status in society. Again, if the fear is based on the possibility of imminent physical danger, such fear will disappear as soon as the danger disappears. The primitive man's fear is based on an instinctive feeling of danger and disappears along with the danger, leaving the slate clean. Whereas, in day-to-day living, man is today almost constantly under tension as a matter of habit, because he is basically aggressive in opposition to the 'other' who is regarded as a threat to whatever he is expecting and trying to achieve for himself.

Today, man has become so habituated to the state of constant anxiety and fear that he is indeed an addict to psychological fear. What is in fact basically a mere physical, natural biological reaction to an imminent danger – almost every animal displays this reaction – has been turned into a chronic, psychological state that man today would think it is strange if in some unguarded moments he finds himself relaxed and without the stifling sense of fear that has become his second nature, as well as his bondage.

The human being is not physically in chains, so the 'bondage' generally referred to must obviously be bondage created by the mind; and anything created by the mind must obviously be an illusion. I have a friend in the USA, Gary, who told me of an incident in his life. Some years ago, his wife suddenly left him for no apparent reason with a 3-year old daughter to look after. One evening, after giving the child her bath and supper, he put her to bed and was sitting beside her, smoking quietly. The child, keenly sensitive to the mood of her parent, asked him if he were sad. When he said "yes", the child told the father, very simply, "daddy, if you don't think of mommy, you won't feel sad"!

As one writer has put it, man's greatest misfortune is that he does not seem to have any kind of organ, any kind of eyelid or brake to mask or block a particular thought – or all thinking – when he needs to! Reason and intellect are obviously important tools not only for survival, but for creating flying machines on the one hand and beautiful figures of speech on the other. However, even the greatest of scientists would admit that it is not the rational mind that comes up with the greatest discoveries, but something else, "something somewhere doing we know not what!" Albert Einstein confessed with the greatest humility that the equation ($E = MC^2$) came to him "from outside".

The fact of the matter is that we humans do not know how to think; in any case we think too much the wrong way. Our so-called rational mind is deeply conditioned – psychologically and culturally – and what is generally labeled as reasoning is often just the mind making excuses for its reactive behavior and emotional needs. As a proverb puts it: "Many complain of their looks, but not about their brains." Reason may be humanity's greatest boon but it is also our bitterest curse, perhaps even our fatal flaw: "What reason has gained for us by giving us some degree of mastery over the world, it has taken away by separating us from the world – a separation that is the prime cause of the bondage and misery of the human being."

Having separated ourselves from the world, we simply cannot accept that the meaning of life is simply that it stops. Our much-glorified intellect tells us that to accept that life is nothing more than the moments between birth and death would clearly be absurd! It would reduce us humans to the level of the animal! Our whole existence – our suffering – must surely have greater significance! And if the universe will not tell us what it is, well then, we must create something: thus enter the multitude of gods and religions, 'isms', or nation-states, or even life-styles. If we cannot discover one supreme reason for existing, for living, we create relatively satisfying earth-bound purposes: a 'utopian future' or 'freedom' or 'progress'.

Perhaps Joseph Campbell had the answer when he said: "I don't believe life has a purpose. Life is a lot of protoplasm with an urge to reproduce and continue in being." Maybe, that is all we are here to do: "Go forth and multiply." Maybe, all our questions will be answered, maybe they will not. This is what Gertrude Stein commented:

There ain't an answer,
There ain't going to be an answer,
There never has been an answer,
That's the answer!

There is a saying that God made man because he loves stories –
shades of *maya* and *lila*. Anyway, here would seem to be a good one:

> Once upon a time, in fact only a few hundred years ago, most
> Westerners believed that humans lived on a planet that was located at
> the very center of the universe. Then a great scientist named Galileo
> figured out that the earth circles the sun and, therefore, it must be the
> sun that is the center. The Catholic Church, believing that humans had
> been specially created and that, therefore, the earth simply has to be the
> center of the universe, forced Galileo to recant. This took place back in
> 1630, but the Church did not forgive Galileo until 1979! By then, of
> course, astronomers and physicists had discovered that the sun itself is
> a relatively small star located on the edge of a relatively small galaxy in
> a cosmos that includes billions of galaxies filled with uncountable
> billions of stars. The Vatican absolved Galileo, but made no further
> announcements concerning the center of the universe.

This crazy story has yet another twist: astronomers have recently
found that the Big Bang sent everything in the universe moving away
from everything else, every single point in the universe can be considered
the center. So, just as you believed – and hoped – you are still the center
of the universe! To add to this melodrama, comes the final twist in this
story: since Albert Einstein's discovery of space-time, it is impossible to
locate ourselves in space unless we simultaneously locate ourselves in time.
Perhaps the only way to locate ourselves is – HERE and NOW.

One basic problem created by the mind in daily living happens to
be simple; man doesn't really know what he wants out of life, and what is
worse, he simply does not take the time during his busy day to sit quietly
and give this problem some serious thought. He thinks he knows exactly
what he wants in life: fun! From this perspective, there is no problem.
The problem lies in the fact that he does not know what constitutes 'fun',
and how and where he is going to find it.

Most people pursue physical, material pleasures because they believe those things will bring them happiness, or they may seek various forms of psychological gratification in the hope that they will bring them 'fun' or happiness. But they soon realize that every time such fun or happiness is so short-lived, and the search for fresh avenues continues unabated. In other words, the fact of the matter is that what is sought is always in the imaginary future, never in the present moment. That is indeed the real problem.

Only a few fortunate people come to the understanding that what they are looking for is not something to satisfy their physical or psychological wants, but something that already exists in the present moment – HERE and NOW – when the mind is still in silence, and not actively confused in a distant non-existing future. True 'fun' in life consists of the freedom from fear, freedom from a feeling of insufficiency, freedom from passing experiences that can only lead to frustration and 'future chasing' in the imaginary future.

They will have found what they were looking for only in the realization that what they need is not some fun-giving momentary experience but fulfillment, peace and harmony in the present moment. True happiness, it will be found from personal, lasting experience, consists not in the positive 'fun' but from being never uncomfortable with themselves and never uncomfortable with others. Peace and harmony is in fact freedom from compulsive conceptualizing in the past and the future, freedom from the ghosts of the past and the illusory goals of the future. Only actual experience of this peace and harmony will bring conviction that this peace is not the boredom that they were once afraid of.

There is a passive cause for the deep feeling of 'bondage' that the human being has. Man has the continuous feeling of being trapped because we humans obviously seem to have some control over our daily lives – we do really lead 'our' lives from day-to-day – and yet cannot get rid of the deep, persistent feeling that we are helpless victims of another will, another incredibly superior order – what Schopenhauer called "a metaphysical entity, a kind of Universal Consciousness, compared to which individual consciousness is a dream compared to reality". Freedom from this feeling of bondage can arise only if we are able truly to realize the unbreakable wholeness of the universe, and unconditionally accept the fact that there is a mysterious, miraculous order being brought about, out of what appears to us as disorder.

One of the best kept secrets of the universe, which confounds the human mind, relates to the question of the *paradoxical nature of probability*, which has puzzled philosophers ever since Pascal initiated that branch of mathematics, which von Neumann (perhaps the greatest mathematician of the last century) called 'Black Magic'. The paradox consists of the fact that the Theory of Probability is able to predict with uncanny precision the overall outcome of a large number of individual events, each of which is in itself unpredictable. We are faced with a large number of uncertainties producing a certainty – a large number of random events creating a lawful outcome!

Let us take some bizarre examples cited by Arthur Koestler. The statistics of the New York Department of Health showed that the *average* number of dogs biting people, reported per day was: 75.3 in 1955; 73.6 in 1956; 73.5 in 1957; 74.5 in 1958; and 72.4 in 1959. A similar statistical reliability was shown by cavalry horses administering fatal kicks to soldiers in the German army in the 19th century. Then again, murders in England and Wales, however different in character and motive, displayed the same respect for the law of statistics. Since the end of World War I, the average number of murders was: in the 1920s, 3.84 per million of population; 1930s, 3.27 per million; 1940s, 3.92 per million; 1950s, 3.30 per million; and 1960s, 3.50 per million of population. How did the dogs know when to stop biting and when to resume? And the horses to kick and the murderers to commit murder?!

The modern scientists' answer is that this miracle can only be seen in the light of the Theory of Probability (or the Law of Large Numbers) – a 'law' that cannot be explained by physical forces. But paradoxically or not, the law works. It has indeed become an indispensable tool of physics and genetics, of economic planners, insurance companies, gambling casinos and opinion polls – so much so that the 'Black Magic' of von Neumann has been taken for granted! The order from disorder principle seems to be an irreducible, inexplicably 'just there'. To ask 'why' is to ask 'why is the universe there?'

The essential feature of modern physics is its increasingly holistic trend, based on the insight that the whole is as necessary for the understanding of the parts, as parts are necessary for the understanding of the whole. As Prof. David Bohm has put it: "Thus one is led to a new notion of unbroken wholeness, which denies the classical idea of the analyzability of the world into separately and independently existing parts."

The description of what we envisage as God's order in day-to-day living appears to us as the Principle of Uncertainty. There appears to be paradox and yet there is explicit order – utter confusion for the petty human intellect. We feel inadequate and helpless only because we attempt to discern a pattern. What the human mind demands is security and certainty in what is essentially an uncertain world. It is not realized that uncertainty is the very basis of the existence of this world: the world cannot exist in the absence of uncertainty. In a certain, definite world, the physicist tells us, with great authority, particles would follow well-determined patterns with exact locations at each and every point. But the alternative of a 'certain' world is scientifically known to be quite unworkable. The tiny electron inside of every atom would have to radiate continuously each and every instant, and it would, in consequence, lose all of its energy and quickly fall into the nucleus; all atoms would disappear, all electromagnetic energy would vanish, all nervous systems would cease to function. All 'life', in fact, would cease because life, as we know it, can only exist through the blessing of uncertainty. Security – personal or collective – is a myth.

A friend of mine came across a system of breathing which was supposed to cure his tendency to catch a cold easily. He practiced the system and the results were quick, and he was delighted. He could not wait to tell everybody about the new system. The other day when I met him, he was sneezing continuously, obviously about to catch a cold. And I knew this had been happening to him for quite some time. So we had the following talk:

> *'I thought you had conquered your cold. What has happened? Have you stopped doing your wonder breathing system?'*
> *'Yes, I have stopped doing it.'*
> *No question from me. So my friend said:*
> *'Are you not going to ask me why I stopped?'*
> *I said: 'No. I am not going go ask you why you stopped doing your breathing exercise.'*
> *He said: 'My wife says I am my own worst enemy.'*
> *I said: 'Did you ask her why you would choose to be your own worst enemy?'*
> *He said: 'No, she would not understand.'*

When a sophisticated, modern young man meets a Master, the impact is bound to be a most interesting one. It is bound to be even a startling one when it is the modern, well-known Bengali author, Bankim Chandra Chatterji, meeting a Master like Ramakrishna Paramahamsa.

When they met at a mutual friend's home, Bankim Chandra suggested: "Revered Paramahamsa, with your evident gift for language and your brilliance, why not preach from the various pulpits and podiums of Calcutta. It would far surpass what we are hearing from contemporary pandits."

Ramakrishna replied:

"The very word 'preach' is utterly distasteful. It suggests that someone can dispense Truth as if it were a commodity rather than the supreme and only Reality. It is chronic human vanity alone that assumes anyone can preach, that anyone can stand in front of an audience or a congregation and present Truth. Human egos are flimsy, insignificant structures. They cannot withstand the slightest impact of a genuine Truth-force. Divine Reality alone is capable of transmitting Truth, and the timeless essence of the soul alone can receive this powerful transmission.

Through the mysterious activity of its Primordial Power, Consciousness crystallizes the structures with which the human form exists – broad earth, life-giving sun, infinitude of stars. Divine light alone illuminates and eventually enlightens all manifest Being. To be a spiritual teacher, one must become transparent to boundless radiance. Is this an easy attainment? Can this transparency be brought about by study, by will-power, by public acclaim? No one can transmit Truth unless the Divine Light consciously shines through this person, not just partially but entirely. The initiative must come from God, not from individual ambition of any kind. Of course, no one can stop popular preachers from shouting slogans and creating an emotional response among their blind followers. People will listen to them for a few moments or a few years, and then forget all about it again, just like any novel sensation that eventually becomes tiresome.

Consider carefully, Bankim Babu. Even if intelligent readers and audiences congratulate you enthusiastically on your eloquent words, they will certainly forget your intended meaning. You will have to write more books and give more lectures to remind them. Afterward, your teaching once more slips away from their busy minds. Thus you become caught in a negative cycle. And when you die, all your work will disappear, instantly or gradually... You must gradually increase your capacity to bear and transmit Truth-force. How? Through intensive sadhana, through sincerely and selflessly practicing spiritual discipline. You Calcutta people try to teach without realization. As the wise proverb indicates, 'the one who has no room to sleep always invites a friend to sleep with him'... Unless you actually represent, in your very being, the awesome authority of the Divine Command, no one will heed your teaching.

Every guest is listening to the uneducated sage with respectful attention. An illiterate village man has become the acknowledged enlightener of the best legal and literary minds of modern Calcutta. The Paramahamsa now deepens his probing.

Ramakrishna: *Dear Bankim, since you have carefully considered the human condition after reading extensively, please tell us what you perceive our ultimate responsibility. What is the knowledge that remains valid and fruitful throughout all conditions of existence, even after the key moment of physical death? Do you accept the heavenly existence of the soul?*

Bankim: 'I do not cherish the slightest attachment to any notion of heavenly existence.'

Ramakrishna: *Excellent! When the physical body drops away, the person who has attained supreme knowledge does not need to enter any higher or more subtle plane of existence, but merges blissfully into the transparent Ground of Existence – not becoming unconscious but becoming Pure Consciousness. However, as long as the individual awareness has not fully awakened during this very life, into limitless awareness, even the most dedicated, purified person must visit heavenly realms for further transformation and refinement. This individual mind-stream must express itself again through living forms on the planetary plane, either upon this earth or somewhere else in the vast universe. Only the authentic knower of Truth, the jnani, is free from the need to be embodied or expressed through some finite mode – whether physical, subtle or formless plane of existence.*

The mysterious grace of God returns certain liberated souls into the various realms of finitude and embodiment in order to be true teachers and tender caretakers. But this return is a function of Divine Responsibility, not human desire. Pure Consciousness spontaneously manifests its *Primordial Power to teach and transmit Truth, and this miraculous process is what appears as the great guides of humanity, such as Sukhadeva and Shankara. This is true Divine Action, not human initiative.*

Well, Bankim, now please give us your answer. What is our ultimate responsibility?

The Master asks this question to probe and purify the mind-stream of Bankim Chandra, yet he presents it with a playful smile. Perhaps the literary man misunderstands the Master's spiritual mood, being accustomed to the crude joking of the conventional world. He responds with a misplaced attempt at humor.

Bankim: 'Sir, if you want my frank answer, I would say that our ultimate responsibility is to eat lavishly, to sleep soundly, and to enjoy reproducing the race.'

Ramakrishna: *Now I see your shallowness. What you are obsessed with, day and night, is involuntarily coming forth from your own mouth. The person who eats garlic with beans involuntarily emits the odor of garlic and beans from his body. The person who gorges on radishes belches the stench of radish.*

Once again the Master's directness has surprised and impressed Bankim and the sophisticated people around him. With downcast eyes, the literary giant humbly accepts this severe scolding from the unlettered sage.

Ramakrishna: *You are constantly surrounded, both physically and psychically, by the habitual ego-centric tendencies called lust and greed. This is a poisonous atmosphere. Women are regarded not as sacred vessels of the Goddess but as objects for momentary satisfaction. Wealth is regarded not as the Divine Mother's abundance, mercifully granted for the welfare of all Her created beings, but as a means to grasp power and to satisfy every obsession imaginable. Your mouth has become a machine that speaks about lust and greed automatically. Your surface mind may soar into impressive intellectual spaces, but your mind's eye is fixated, like the sharp gaze of the high-flying vulture, solely upon dead or dying flesh.*

This is not really you who speak in such obsessive patterns, Bankim, but a mind that has unconsciously permitted itself to become calculating, turbulent and deceitful. This very same mind can become serene, guileless and innocent by concentrating upon Divine Reality. A mind that has directly perceived Truth, even for an instant, would never jest as you have done, Bankim Babu. You have revealed the impoverished condition of your awareness. What purpose can broad scholarship, brilliance of expression and commitment to social reform really serve if there is no sound discrimination between what is exalted and what is merely conventional or habitual? And what kind of pundit or true elder of society, is he who has not utterly renounced the conventional and the habitual? This person may be able to quote long passages from scriptures. He may have produced highly technical treatises, composed in traditional or modern style. But if his mind does not spontaneously and effortlessly dwell on God and within God, can you call him a pundit, and man of wisdom?

Certain sophisticated modern people remark about the lovers of God: 'These poor, misguided souls are mad – conversing day and night about Divine Reality, cultivating no taste for any other subject, whereas we have the correct balance. We enjoy philosophy and religion as well as the pleasures that money, honor, and position provide. We pray to God, but we also thoroughly pursue the delights of the senses.' These self-willed people are like the magpie, which assumes that it is the most clever among the birds. But have you ever carefully observed the behavior of the magpie? The moment dawn awakens it, this bird begins to seek out and consume nothing but refuse. Then it struts about and chatters self-importantly.

There is shocked silence throughout the elegant residence of Adhar. We all experience the chastening touch of these fiery words at the center of our conscience, at the core of our personality, where one longs for integrity above all else. As the Master speaks – slowly, stammering slightly – the radiant smile of Divine delight never leaves his lips.

Ramakrishna: *By contrast, those whose thoughts instinctively move toward the One Reality – in every condition, at every moment – are like the adept swan of folklore that can drink from a mixture of water and milk, only pure milk, leaving the bowl half full of water. The great Swans, the paramahamsas, are simply true human beings. Like the swan flying North on its annual migration, the true human being moves powerfully forward in one direction, toward Truth alone, seeing nothing else, seeking nothing else.*

Ramakrishna adds, with great tenderness: *Please, dear Bankim, do not take personal offense at my words. I simply must speak Truth.*

Bankim Chandra is visibly moved. He replies strongly: 'Revered Paramahamsa, I really do appreciate your uncompromising attitude. I did not come to you to receive palliatives or flattery. I came here to encounter a Person of Truth.'

Bankim Chandra Chatterji is, at this moment speaking for everyone in the room. Each one of us, wherever we may be along the path, feels humbled and consecrated by this encounter between the ancient Paramahamsa and the modern pundit. Bankim has proved to be honest and resilient enough to receive the probing and the purification from a master spiritual physician, from a living manifestation of Truth.

Someone starts to sing. The Great Swan leaps to his feet and enters profound *samadhi.*"

*One does not make
any thought, a deciding
thought or otherwise.
Thoughts occur. It is quite a
common occurrence that our decisions
seem to be quite out of our control.*

CHAPTER 5

VOLITION
AND
FREE WILL

There is an ancient story:

A young farmer, Raju, worked hard on his land. One evening, as he rested under a banyan tree, the royal herald rode by announcing that the king had an unusual dream. Whoever could explain it to his satisfaction would receive 100 gold coins. In his dream, the king saw a sneering jackal trying to jump on to his lap. While trying to ward it off, he woke up with an uneasy feeling.

'If only I knew the answer', murmured Raju to himself. Then a sweet voice said to him, 'I'll give you the answer provided you promise to give me half of your award.' It was a beautiful little bird that had hopped down to a lower branch right above Raju's head. An enthusiastic Raju immediately accepted the offer. The answer was: 'The throne symbolizes the kingdom; the jackal symbolizes treachery and selfish cunning dominating the atmosphere. Ask the king to be cautious.'

Raju met the king the next day and interpreted the dream. The king was satisfied and Raju received the 100 gold coins. Walking back, Raju thought, 'what a pity I have to part with half the amount of the reward.' He took a detour and avoided the bird. He invested the money prudently and grew rich. 5 years passed. One evening the king's general galloped down to his house and called out: 'Hurry up. His Majesty has had another intriguing dream. He saw a bloody dagger circling his head.' Raju promised to meet the king the next day.

It was a moonlit night, and as soon as Raju approached the banyan tree, the bird appeared again and said, 'I know about the dream.'

Raju promised to give the bird half of the reward, and the bird explained that the dagger represented violence, that the atmosphere was steeped in it and the king should be on his guard. In the morning, Raju explained the dream and got a reward of 1000 gold coins.

Raju was afraid that the talking bird might report the matter to the king, and when he met the bird the next day he threw a stone at it, wanting to kill it. However, the bird escaped. Raju forgot all about it, until 5 years later, he was again brought before the king. This time the king had dreamt of a delicate dove resting on his lap. Once again he went to the bird, promised half the reward and was told that the dove symbolized peace and the king could now rest in peace. This time Raju received 10,000 gold coins.

This time Raju made a beeline for the banyan tree, and offered to the bird the entire amount in total surrender. The bird, however, had no use for it and advised Raju to spend it on the people's welfare. A tearful Raju pleaded to the bird to be pardoned for his conduct. 'Your conduct', said the bird, 'where was your conduct? On the first occasion, there was treachery in the atmosphere; the second time, there was violence in the atmosphere, and now there is peace and trust in the atmosphere. No one really acts according to his personal will.'

If one were to choose one single event in our daily living that is the most common happening, it would perhaps be the fact that in almost any group of people in almost any class of society, the subject of the conversation is a happening for which someone is being blamed: someone is responsible, someone should be punished! This has become the very basis of living and has been causing the 'suffering' which the Buddha considered the very essence of life: "*samsara* is *dukkha*" – life is suffering. He, therefore, concluded that the only way to end this suffering is to accept that "events happen, deeds are done, but there is no individual doer thereof."

This would promptly raise the question: 'Does this mean then, that if I find something wrong, I just keep silent and do nothing?' The answer is simple: 'Just don't complain. Do whatever you think you should do. Whatever is to happen will happen or not happen. Whining and complaining does not help you or anyone else.'

One's sense of volition or free will would seem to depend upon a certain balance between reliability and flexibility in relation to cause and effect, effort and result. Without the former, all outcomes would appear to be arbitrary and, without the latter, all outcomes would appear to be predetermined. In neither case would one's free will be concerned in an effective result. This would seem to be clear, but establishing a precarious balance has proved to be such a frustrating effort that Kant himself was forced to declare 'freedom of the will' to be one of only three metaphysical problems beyond the grasp of the human intellect (the other two intractable problems being 'God' and 'immortality').

Debate has been going on for several years regarding the belief that the human being is in control, not only of the environment but also of himself. Debate regarding this belief used to be primarily a religious matter known as the 'Free Will vs. Determinism' argument. Disagreement centered on the amount of freedom the Creator had given us to act – more specifically, to sin or not to sin. Back when most of the civilization believed that God was in control over our lives, it was often assumed that He could be bribed with a few good deeds or contrite supplications, which left us some degree of choice over our destiny. However, in the 20th century, science has investigated the issue by taking a close look at the biological and psychological makeup of the individual human being. And, as the ancient saying goes, self-knowledge is usually bad news.

What science is discovering – what mystics have known for centuries – comes down to this: we are not in charge of the cosmos or the planets, we are barely in charge of ourselves – we are chaff in the wind. As the poet Rumi has put it:

> *Do you think I know what I am doing?*
> *That for one breath or half-breath I belong to myself?*
> *As much as a pen knows what it is writing,*
> *Or the ball can guess where it is going next.*

It would seem that the old theological controversies still continue to have a lot more relevance today than what one might expect. There is the completely 'hands on' view of God's agency in the functioning of the manifestation: "Not a drop of rain falls without the express command of God." Such an extreme view of theological determinism posed problems such as the relevance of moral responsibility. This situation was not really different from the present situation in which problems are posed today by the 'physical determinism' of scientists like Colin Blakemore.

Kant's analysis of the situation was that while physical determinism held sway in the world of appearances, the world in which there is empirical knowledge, there might still be room in the hidden world of 'things-in-themselves' for free will. Kant's analysis has not prevented physical sciences from continuing to be unfriendly to the concept of free will – witness Albert Einstein:

"If the moon, in the act of completing its eternal way around the earth, were gifted with self-consciousness, it would feel thoroughly convinced that it was traveling its way of its own accord on the strength of a resolution taken once and for all. So would a Being, endowed with higher insight and more perfect intelligence, watching man and his doings, smile about man's illusion that he was acting according to his own free will...

Man defends himself from being regarded as an impotent object in the course of the Universe. But should the lawfulness of events, such as unveils itself more or less clearly in inorganic nature, cease to function in front of the activities in our brain?

Leaving aside the inconsistency of such a view, the influence of alcohol and other sharply controllable factors on our thoughts, feelings and activities should show very distinctly that determinism does not stop before the majesty of our human will."

So far as the physical sciences are concerned, it would clearly seem that the universe continues to go on its merry way as a thoroughly deterministic system, even if it is not totally predictable by man's limited intelligence.

Recent brain research has revealed that humans have actually three distinct brains: a reptilian brain, a mammalian brain and the new cerebral cortex or 'human' brain. Research has also revealed that we make maximum use of our reptilian and mammalian brains, and experiments show that we use our new human brain only at about 15% capacity and that even this 15% is used mainly in order to rationalize and justify the reactive behavior of the other two brains.

Most people feel that they act independently from moment to moment, but human freedom of action would seem to be severely circumscribed by our fundamental biochemical makeup. Science writer, Jon Franklin, in his Pulitzer Prize winning book, *Molecules of the Mind*, asserted that our belief in free will is itself determined: "And so, multi-leveled Mother Nature, wry and cruel but at times strangely benevolent, has inserted a mechanism, in the human mechanism, to prevent that mechanism from fully comprehending its mechanistic nature."

Also, biochemists are reporting that moods and emotions are closely associated with certain chemicals. Amazingly, what we call 'love', for example, may be understood as the presence of an 'excitantamine' known as phenylethylamine or PEA, in our system. Mice injected with PEA jump up and down and vocalize, while rhesus monkeys exhibit 'lip-smacking behaviour'.

Meanwhile, the latest evidence from biologists indicates that each of us is shackled from birth to a genetically determined future, bound by the chains of the DNA double-helix: we are imprisoned in our cells. Then again, molecular geneticists tell us that the DNA molecule is programmed with information that determines how tall we will grow and how strong our teeth will be, what illnesses we are likely to contract and, to some extent, how long we will live. It is as if we were born into a spy novel: as the past unveils, our identity is gradually revealed. As if this is not enough, our genes provide each of us with a face we must wear from birth, whether or not we like it (unless drastic measures are taken). Also given are a thick head of hair, or a near-sighted squint, or lop-sided ears – these features that affect how the world looks at us, and how we look at the world. Now, on top of all this, there is speculation that the DNA molecule programming may include our sexual proclivities and even 'perversions', and also the likelihood of our addiction to alcohol or drugs! Thus, at the physical level at least, we are not free to be ourselves; we are forced to be ourselves.

From another angle, psychologists tell us that individual freedom of choice and action is almost totally circumscribed by our early upbringing. "As infants we ingest our parents and then spend the rest of our lives trying to digest them: we eat them whole, from their genes to their judgments, we eat their values, their moods, their fears, their world-views. Even if we rebel against them, they shape that rebellion: their voices continually echo inside of us – we never really leave home."

So many strings tie us to the past, to people, to politics. Volumes have been written about how we are programmed to conform to the values and fashions of the society into which we are born. Even the strong identification some people have with 'individuality' and 'freedom' could well be a product of a particular set of cultural values. Adding another dimension, geological anthropologists talk about 'geographic determinism', the hypothesis being that our perception of Reality is shaped, at least partially, by the mountains or the flatlands or the forests or the deserts that surround us. As a Sufi suggested: "If you wish to know about Reality, go into the desert at night, and look at the stars."

Cosmic, geological, biological, psychological, cultural, political – so many forces shape us and our thinking, without even considering the possibility of past lives influencing the present one! 'Freedom' would thus seem to be just another word or notion without any real significance.

The perpetual blind spot that gives us the impression that we are separate from the rest of creation also may have fostered the belief that we are in control, not only of our environment but also of ourselves. We simply do not know who or what we are, why we are here, where we are, or what this life – or universe – is all about.

It would certainly appear that if the distinction between things we do through choice and necessity has no scientific validity, then the consequences would need to be addressed as a matter of urgency. In fact, the problem would seem to be moving beyond the parameters of armchair philosophers into a distinct concern for the welfare of society and civilization. It would appear that already scientists are beginning to draw some extremely radical conclusions regarding how the legal system needs to be recast on a more scientific basis. Of course, it goes without saying that any fundamental change in the legal system should only grow out of a major debate in which philosophy, sociology, religion, ethics, political considerations and various other viewpoints all had a voice. But we do see which way the wind is blowing.

Some scientists and philosophers seem to have taken a more robust approach to the problem and have indeed ended up with certain conclusions that have been branded as 'outrageous'. It is interesting to note that Erwin Schrödinger, one of the founders of quantum theory, pondered on this problem in the tantalizing epilogue of his classic, *What Is Life?* Schrödinger encapsulated the concept of consciousness in the form of two premises: "*1*) My body functions as a pure mechanism according to the laws of nature. *2*) And yet, I know, by incontrovertible direct experience, that I am directing its notions, of which I foresee the effects that may be fateful and all-important, in which case I feel and take full responsibility for them." He added, in view of the obvious contradiction: "The only possible inference from these two facts is, I think, that I – 'I' *in the widest meaning of the word, that is to say, every conscious mind that has ever said or felt 'I'* – am the person, *if any,* who controls the 'motion of the atoms' according to the laws of nature." In view of the fact that one could conclude that Schrödinger had provocatively suggested, 'Hence I am God Almighty' – a statement that would sound both 'blasphemous and lunatic' – the original Catholic publisher rejected *What Is Life?*

The fact remains that the idea – 'I' in the widest meaning of the word that would totally exclude the pitiful little 'me' – was hardly new! As Schrödinger himself noted, this "grandest of all thoughts" was recorded in the Hindu *Upanishads* more than 2500 years ago, and has long been considered the deepest insight in Indian philosophy. Said Schrödinger: "The singularity of consciousness, surely, is more intuitively convincing than the Western idea of a plurality of consciousness, which leads inevitably to the invention of souls – as many as there are bodies – and to unhelpful questions such as whether the soul survives death and whether animals (and bacteria) have souls?"

It may be pointed out that Schrödinger's remarkable viewpoint (from the Western perspective) has been remarkably consistent over a period of almost 40 years. Schrödinger referred to the ancient Vedantic vision, according to which: "Consciousness is only one, singular, identifiable with its universal Source (Brahman). The perceived spatial and temporal plurality of consciousness or minds is just an appearance or illusion." Schrödinger wrote in 1925: "...knowledge, feeling and choice (which you call *your own*) are essentially eternal and unchangeable and numerically one in all men, nay in all sensitive beings." Then 19 years later: "Consciousness is a singular of which the plural is unknown (perhaps, therefore, a more appropriate word could be 'Unicity'); that there is only one thing and that what seems to be plurality is merely a series of different aspects of this one thing, produced the deception." Then 30 years later:

"There is obviously only one alternative, namely the unification of minds or consciousnesses. Their multiplicity is only apparent, in truth there is only one Mind." And, 36 years later, shortly before his death, he wrote again, as a comment to a line in the *Upanishads*: "...the plurality of sensitive beings is mere appearance (*maya*); in reality they are all only aspects of the *One* being."

It is quite amazing that Schrödinger's view is echoed in the philosophy of Benedict de Spinoza, whose monist philosophy again echoes the *Upanishadic* view, even more closely than Schrödinger's, in spite of the amazing fact that Spinoza knew nothing of the *Upanishads* themselves. For Spinoza, like the *Upanishads*: "Ultimately there is only one thing in the universe, God or Substance, that which is in Itself and conceived through Itself." In other words, all individual consciousnesses are simply this One Ultimate Substance, "perceiving through the diverse orientations of individual body-minds".

Thus the monisms of Spinoza and the *Upanishads* clearly imply that free will is actually nothing more than an illusion. For, as Spinoza put it: "Once one's physiology has become integrated enough to see everything '*under the gaze of eternity*' – that is, once one has become 'enlightened' – one recognizes that the free will was only an illusion produced by one's prior inadequate perceptual and conceptual perspective: in *Upanishadic* terms, a product of *maya* (divine hypnosis). If there is in reality only One existent, all distinctions of beings, states and actions can only be appearances and not realities, and – from the enlightened state – all willing and, therefore, all freedom of the will is only 'as if'."

It must be mentioned that Michael Persinger has shown, using both electroencephalographic methods and questionnaires, that mystical experiences and paranormal beliefs are associated with "unstable temporal lobes or high temporal lobe liability". He has also been able to induce out-of-body and other experiences by applying rapidly fluctuating weak magnetic fields across the temporal lobes of subjects in the laboratory. Others argue that neurological changes can bring about not only tunnels, lights and out-of-body experiences, but the dissolution of the normal sense of self which lies at the heart of a mystical experience. In ordinary life, we hold the false notion of a persisting inner self that has consciousness and free will. In certain circumstances, such as mystical experiences and near death, this illusion breaks down, giving rise to a new sense of Self as one with the universe, or to a state of No-self.

When the sense of a personal self gets dissolved, there arises a sense of vivid realness, clarity of consciousness, and a loss of the normal sense of volition or free will. As the Buddha has put it: "Actions do exist, and also their consequences, but the person that acts does not." To those who have never experienced that state, it could certainly seem not only paradoxical but even a threat to morality, but when it does arise it seems to be the most natural and easy way to be: one ceases to carry the usual load of guilt and shame on the one hand, and another load of hatred and malice towards 'the other'. In other words, people who have had this experience are very demonstrably seen to have become 'nicer rather than nastier' when they live this way. They seem never to be uncomfortable with themselves, never to be uncomfortable with others. They seem to be anchored in peace and harmony.

The fact of the matter of free will is that there is no direct evidence about the claim for the illusory nature of free will; nor is there any evidence to the contrary – no evidence is available. The scientist, Benjamin Libet, whose research demonstrated that a thought occurs nearly half a second in a human brain before it is acknowledged, had this to say:

"The phenomenal fact is that most of us feel that we do have free will, at least for some of our actions and within certain limits that may be imposed by our brain's status and by our environment. The intuitive feelings about the phenomenon form a fundamental basis for views of our human nature, and great care should be taken not to believe allegedly scientific conclusions about them, which actually depend upon hidden *ad hoc* assumptions. A theory that simply interprets the phenomenon of free will as illusory, and denies the validity of this phenomenal fact, is less attractive than a theory that accepts or accommodates the phenomenal fact.

In an issue so fundamentally important to our view of who we are, a claim for illusory nature should be based on fairly direct evidence. Such evidence is not available.

My conclusion about free will, one genuinely free in the non-determined sense, is then that its existence is at least as good as, if not a better scientific option than is its denial by determinist theory. Given the speculative nature of both determinist and non-determinist theories, why not adopt the view that we do have free will (until some real contradictory evidence may appear, if it ever does). Such a view would at least allow us to proceed in a way that accepts and accommodates our own deep feeling that we do have free will. We would not need to view ourselves as machines that act in a manner completely controlled by the known physical laws."

Such a permissive option has also been advocated by the neurologist Roger Sperry. There is also a pertinent quotation from the great novelist, Isaac Bashevis Singer, that relates to the foregoing views. Singer stated his strong belief in our having free will. In an interview he volunteered: "The greatest gift which humanity has received is free choice. It is true that we are limited in our use of free choice. But the little free choice we have is such a great gift and is potentially worth so much that for this itself life is worthwhile living."

The practical aspect of this matter of whether or not we have free will is, fortunately, much simpler. It boils down to a simple practical question: in daily living, in a given situation, what do I do? And the answer is simple: do whatever you think you should do in the moment – as if you have free will! Let the theorists deal with the complicated matters of determinism vs. non-determinism!

Several years ago, there was a report in the American *Time* magazine:
Yoshiko Igarashi in Tokyo was at a loss to decide on a plan for her new kitchen. The more she looked at catalogues and store displays, the more confused she became. So, she looked into the future and it worked. She visited the sleek showroom of Matsushita Electric Works in Tokyo. There she put on an exotic looking headgear and simply walked into a kitchen of her own design. The headgear consists of a mask fitted with a small pair of liquid-crystal display TV screens that create three-dimensional images, along with a set of headphones that provide stereo sound. To interact with objects represented in the computer-generated kitchen, the client wears a glove equipped with optic-fiber sensors. When the system is turned on, a computer-drawn image of a hand appears among the images of the kitchen. By turning and pointing the index finger, one can move the hand in the direction indicated. With

other simple finger movements, one can explore the room, open a cabinet door, turn on a faucet, or put a cup in the cabinet. If one throws a dish, it will 'break' with a smashing sound.

A researcher at Matsushita's Information System Center commented: "In virtual reality, it is actually the mind that does the seeing and creates a sense of physical experience."

It is not only the external world that deceives us, but our internal world as well. For centuries, mystics have told us that we are not what we appear to be, that we have no separate 'self'. Now psychologists and biologists tell us the same thing: the 'self' that we think we are is not the real *Self*, that the so-called 'selves' are determined almost completely by genes, chemicals and our early conditioning. The conclusion scientists are approaching – but do not yet seem to have the courage to state – is that there does not exist any independent 'self' at all: we simply do not own one. That 'self', which each of us thinks of as an independent individual with free will, is as much of an illusion as the world of matter!

It is only a shift in levels towards a comprehensive Consciousness – the Universal or Cosmic Consciousness – as the fundamental of interconnectedness of life that might enable us to take those 'selfless' steps that could begin to solve our collective problems. The fundamental question really is whether there can ever possibly be two objects or factors in the world that are not in some sense related. In fact, the question of universal interconnectedness has been curiously anticipated by philosophers for millenniums. Anaximander of Milates in ancient Greece is said to have taught that "the primary substance of the world is infinite, eternal and all encompassing." Two thousand years later, Giordano Bruno went further in writing: "All reality is one in substance, one in cause, one in origin... and every particle of reality is composed inseparably of the physical and the psychic. The object of philosophy is, therefore, to preserve unity in diversity, mind in matter and matter in mind... to rise to that highest knowledge of the Universal Unity which is the intellectual equivalent of the love of God." As might be expected, the 16th century Italian philosopher got burnt at the stake for this and other similar heresies, but his thought lives on. Moreover, it has been reinforced by modern science, which finds that the earth's minerals, vegetables and animals have been found "to converse and interrelate in almost every conceivable way".

It is an established fact that the human body is microscopically nothing but emptiness, a dynamic pattern of concentrated energy, throbbing and vibrating at incredible speed: a veritable frenzied dance of Shiva in which creation and dissolution take place continuously and almost simultaneously. It would thus seem that a separate 'entity' should not exist, but the wonder of paradoxical nature is that it has so contrived that each emptiness, each body-mind organism, each personal identity (created by *maya* or divine hypnosis) has a set of personal characteristics that distinguishes it from all others. Personal identity with a sense of personal doership is, in fact the very basis of human relationships and, therefore, of life as we know it.

The botanist tells us that every leaf on a tree or a shrub is at least slightly different, in some way or other, from all others. The chance of two fingerprints being identical has been computed as being less than one in 60 billion. Brain wave patterns are observed as being distinctive. An effective voice print definitely identifies the speaker through the recorded voice frequencies, and a newborn baby's breathing pattern is supposed to be as distinctive as a fingerprint.

The All-in-Oneness of the Eastern mystic has now been clearly accepted by the modern scientist but he finds himself, along with the layman, facing seeming absurdities in the quantum theory conclusions that do not agree with what is generally considered as common sense. But accept them he must, because the theory works! A formulation made by the physicist J. S. Bell – Bell's Theorem – particularly emphasizes: "No theory of reality, compatible with quantum theory, can require spatially separated events to be separate." Simply, this means that distant events are interconnected. What is more startling is the implication that each electron must *know* what every electron *in the universe* is doing, in order to know what it itself has to do every moment. It further implies that each subatomic particle within is in touch with All-That-Is.

The mystic intuitively understands the situation that to the physicist is a problem: all there is, is the Primal Energy, an aspect of Universal or Cosmic Consciousness, which has produced on or within itself the mind-stuff of the universe (*chittamatra*) as an objective representation of Itself (*vijnaptimatra*). In other words, all there is, is Consciousness – Cosmic Consciousness – which has objectified Itself as the phenomenal universe and which, in its aspect as 'sentience', enables the senses in the sentient beings to function and cognize one another.

Unity and diversity – the one and the many – are dialectically embedded in each other. Experiencing this unity in existence happens only with the total realization that we are all separate entities only as separate, distinct instruments through which the same one Primal Energy functions and brings about such deeds – such happenings – as are supposed to happen according to a Natural or Cosmic Law. Experiencing the unity in existence can certainly alter one's relationships in day-to-day living, and profoundly change the way one accepts both living and dying. It increases compassion, eliminates judging and blaming either oneself or others, and brings about the capacity to see oneself as only one of the players in an eternal drama. The mystical experience that arises with the apperception of non-doership begins with Oneness and spontaneously gets integrated into day-to-day living.

The fact of the matter is that the universe is still and complete. Though, in perceiving it, we imagine that it is in motion, and unfinished, it is quite finished, and quite astonishingly beautiful. In the end, as things really are, any event, any happening, no matter how significant or insignificant, is intimately and sensibly tied to all others: "You pull out a blade of grass, and you shake the universe." And when all is perceived in such a way as to obviate time, justice becomes apparent, not as something that will be, but as something that IS.

It is interesting to know in this regard that the physicist's concept of time today is totally different from what it was in the 19th century. Sir Fred Hoyle has put this in his provocative way:
"You are stuck with a grotesque and absurd illusion... the idea of time as an ever-rolling stream. There is one thing quite certain in this business: the idea of time as a steady progression from past to future is wrong. I know very well we feel this way about it subjectively. But *we are the victims of a confidence trick.*"

Call it a 'confidence trick' or 'divine hypnosis' or whatever. We know what has happened.

And yet we must live our daily lives. Life is continually fired at us point-blank and we cannot say: "Wait a minute, I am not ready yet, let me sort things out." So what do we do? The fact remains that decisions have to be made and choices exercised. The answer is quite simple: in our day-to-day living we are free to choose. The fact that for many of us in modern-day living making a choice is itself a problem, is another matter! But we do have the freedom to believe that we can choose, but the whole point is – and our total experience has shown us – that we have no control over the consequences of our decisions.

As the German philosopher, Hans Vaihinger, has put it, man has no choice but to live by 'fictions' – *as if* the illusory world of the senses did represent Ultimate Reality, *as if* man had free will which made him responsible for his actions, *as if* there were a God to reward virtuous conduct, and so on. Similarly, the individual today must live as if he is not under sentence of death, and humanity must plan for its future as if its days were not numbered. Also, there is the undeniable fact that we are dealing in probabilities and not in certainties: there is always the possibility of the unexpected and unforeseen.

So, what should we do in daily life? Is this a thinking process you recognize?

I have a problem – I have a big problem: my health is indifferent; my financial circumstances are uncertain; there is a law and order problem in my city; there is a political mess in my state; there are serious communal riots in the adjoining state; the state government and the national government are at loggerheads; two of the largest states in the north of the country are financially bankrupt; corruption is at its worst all over the country; the army has been on alert on the borders for the last several months; AIDS is almost rampant; there is an explosion in population, and starvation deaths in several states have been reported; industrial growth is almost non-existent; there is total disorder in the functioning of the parliament; prices of all commodities are shooting up; my age is not creeping up, it is galloping; I must not forget to get an appointment with my dentist; my neighbors are becoming impossible; the traffic problem in the city is getting worse every day (it is a fortuitous fact that I don't have to get out of my house too often!); it is only the beginning of the summer, and it is already quite unbearably hot; I don't know what the forecast is about the next monsoon; the city will have an awful water problem if the monsoon fails; more and more, taller and taller buildings are under construction with total disregard to the fire hazard; there is the Israeli-Palestine conflict in the Middle-east, Maoist conflagration in a neighboring country...

Is anything in my control? No. Is there anything at all that I personally can do today, now, about anything at all? NO. Is my family desperate about money or health? No. Am I in a hospital? No. Am I in jail? No.

Do I have a problem, in this moment? No. Do I really have a problem at all?! NO. God created the universe – let Him look after it.

To repeat the question: what should we do in daily life, if we have no free will? The answer is that it is impossible to live life without an implicit belief in personal responsibility. So, act *as if* you are responsible for your actions: live in the present moment; forget the past; do not worry about the future, which is not in your control. And this, is it not precisely the burden of Lord Krishna's advice to Arjuna in the *Bhagavad Gita*: "You were born a warrior; you have been trained to fight. Whom you fight and whether you win or lose is a matter of destiny – it is not in your hands, so, fight!"

If you find that the concept of non-doership – as the Buddha put it, "events happen, deeds are done, but there is no individual doer thereof" – not only intriguing but really acceptable because it appeals to your sense of logic and reason, but you cannot truly accept it with total conviction, with 'gut-feeling', then you should pay attention to what a Nobel Laureate had to say about it. When English scientist Francis Crick and his associates won the Nobel Prize in Medicine for deciphering the DNA code that defines genes, he stunned the medical world by saying: "You, your joys, sorrows, memories, ambitions, your sense of identity, free will and love are no more than the behaviors of a vast assembly of nerve cells."

One can really wonder why it is that people believed for so long that the sun went around the earth. To this query, Wittgenstein is reported to have replied: "How would it have looked, if it had looked as if the earth went around the sun?" The answer, of course, is: 'pretty much the same'. The real question is: why is there such a resistance to the 'folk theories' being questioned, let alone revised? There are several reasons. The first, of course, is the necessity of specialized equipment or testing procedures before any alternative theory can be entertained. The second is that, depending as they do on 'common sense', they offer a comforting model of individuals and their place in the scheme of things – the idea that the sun goes around the earth places the human being at the center of creation, as 'God's chosen', than as the provisional outcome of a vast concatenation of historical accidents. And third, the contrary evidence to the consensual view may become virtually hidden when perception itself becomes selective and skewed, and persistent interpretations become self-reinforcing. For one culture, intrinsic to a particular belief system, it is a simple 'fact' that the crops failed because the gods were displeased; to a different culture, the floods and storms that ruined the crops are the effects of demonic activity in the remote corners of the planet. It takes sharp, disinterested, 'honest' observation to acknowledge that the way things seem may not be the way they are.

The way people think about their 'will' – the immediate causal relationship between our intention and action – is a good instance of the folk model. It certainly *seems* that each of us is a center of volition and that conscious deliberation plays a causal role in determining our plans and actions. This is the 'common sense' view: 'if one didn't have free will and self-control, we would all run amok!' It is only an honest disinterested inquiry into the phenomenology of free will that can reveal the actual position. As D. Dennet says:

> "If having free will matters, it must be because not having free will would be awful... But what exactly are we afraid of?.. Not having free will would be somewhat like being in prison, or being hypnotized, or being paralyzed or being a puppet... Any admission of the unconscious would be based on vague but powerful images: zombies, aliens, Machiavellian manipulators, or sinister 'brains' behind the delicate sensitive operation that we take ourselves to be."

It is an accepted fact that intentions are really neither necessary nor sufficient for intelligent actions to occur. There are any number of occasions when actions occur without any preceding intention. When asked subsequently how or why we did as we did, although we may produce a plausible rationale, we have to admit that this reasoning represents a *post hoc* inference rather than a prior intent. Even our getting out of bed does not furnish any real evidence of volition. What actually happens, very often, is that we are in the middle of a totally unrelated train of thought and suddenly 'come to' finding ourselves already in the process of getting up. The fact of the matter is that we frequently do not get up when we decided to do so. In other words, failures of will power are more the rule that the exception.

It is quite a common occurrence that our decisions seem to be quite out of our control. We have to wait for our own decisions! And when we do decide, the decision suddenly rushes into our consciousness. According to D. Dennet: "We do not witness it being made; we witness its arrival. This can then lead to the strange idea that Control Headquarters is not where we, as conscious introspectors, are; it is somewhere deeper within us, and inaccessible to us." E. M. Forster famously asked: "How can I tell what I think until I see what I say?" – the words of an outsider, it seems, waiting for a bulletin from the interior. In other words, we have the recurring experience of being the recipient, rather than the architect, of our decisions. But what we do is that we build a psychological theory of 'decision-making' by inserting the decisions not where we have the actual experience of them but where the theory demands!

The consequence of this fact is that the misconception of conscious monitoring and intention often leads to self-consciousness, and a concomitant shuddering or even a breakdown of performance. And it has been a very regular experience, in various performances, that the fluent execution of complex skill under demanding conditions, in the state known as a natural 'flow', is clearly characterized by a total absence of intention, deliberation or self-consciousness.

In other words, 'intention' would appear to be not a form of control, but internal prediction, and 'free will' itself a phenomenon of anticipation rather than conscious instigation. This world seems to provide the basis for the prescient definition of 'intention' by Ambrose Bierce: "The mind's sense of the prevalence of one set of influences over another set: an effect whose cause is the imminence, immediate or remote, of the performance of the act intended by the person incurring the intention." This approach obviously means that *a)* conscious intentions are more likely to arise when decisions are complicated and processing is protracted; and *b)* they are often wrong. The conclusion we seem to have reached is that, like the realization that the earth goes around the sun and not *vice versa*, his reframing of 'will' and 'intention' may appear less comforting but is, in fact, more veracious and, therefore, more functional.

On a daily basis, one might consider the question: 'Did I get out of the bed or did getting out of the bed happen? Did I brush my teeth this morning? I do not remember brushing my teeth.' Getting out of bed is usually the first deliberate act one makes in one's day, following an extended period of passivity, and then brushing one's teeth follows. Often, getting out of bed does not feel mediated by will. Rather, it feels like an automatic response: we are jolted upwards, whether this jolt was prompted by the sound of the alarm clock or the feeling of pressure in the bladder or the image of being late for work. In other words, we more often than not get up without any struggle or decision at all: we suddenly find that we have gotten up. At other times, however, our movement does indeed seem to involve a decision on whether or not to abandon the warm and comfortable bed, especially on a cold morning; we feel that we have made a choice between two alternatives.

As Hubert Benoit has put it: "When man studies himself with honest impartiality, he observes that he is not the conscious and voluntary artisan either of his feelings or of his thoughts, and that his feelings and his thoughts are only phenomena which happen to him." Thoughts arise. This becomes strikingly clear if one sits still and brings one's awareness to only the movement of the breathing, as in meditation. However hard one tries, one very soon finds oneself watching random thoughts, "arriving unescorted to consciousness", experienced more as a happening than as being made by one deliberately. This is so not only in meditation, but it is rather one's everyday experience in daily living, even if one does not at the time assess it as such. Mark Twain describes his thought process as, "racing along from subject to subject – a drifting panorama of ever-changing, ever-dissolving views manufactured by my mind without any help from me".

One does not make any thought, a deciding thought or otherwise. Thoughts occur. In other words, just as we say in normal conversation, 'it rains' or 'it blows', we could quite truthfully say, 'it thinks'. One does not make thoughts – choice, decision or otherwise; one can only say, 'thoughts go on'. The actual deciding moment occurs without any decision at all. As J. Krishnamurti put it: "If you watch very carefully, you will see that, though the response, the movement of thoughts seems so swift, there are gaps, there are intervals between thoughts. Between two thoughts there is a period of silence which is not related to the thought process." This gap, though, is part of the uninterrupted flow of the stream of Consciousness;

in fact, it is precisely because the stream of Consciousness is an uninterrupted continuity that the gap between thoughts can be perceived as such. In fact, thoughts appear and disappear against the background of Consciousness. When one hears the thunder happening, it is actually thunder breaking upon silence (Consciousness) and contrasting with it.

Indeed, it is precisely the existence of this underlying, abiding, 'unbroken' witnessing Consciousness, that the practice of meditation helps make manifest. According to the Hindu tradition, Witness-Consciousness, or 'Seer' (*drishta*) is the pure Awareness that abides eternally beyond the senses and the mind, uninterruptedly apperceiving all the numerous and changeable contents of Consciousness. All schools of Hinduism agree that the Ultimate Reality is not a condition of stone-like stupor, but Super-consciousness. This assertion is not mere speculation but is based on the actual realization of thousands of yogis, a discovery corroborated by the testimony of mystics in other parts of the world.

The arising of the ego – identification with a particular body-mind organism, as a separate entity, with the volition or a sense of personal doership – is an interesting phenomenon. The ego does not exist in early infancy; the first symptoms of any distinction between self and another relate only to the body. This process gradually extends from mere 'my arm' or 'my leg' to the identification with a host of complexity of memories, experiences, feelings, hopes and fears as 'mine', and thereby arises the ego.

The ego is thus originally a mere complex of perceptions, experiences and memories, but when the sense of doership deepens with time, the shadowy ego acquires more and more substance as a separate entity, with quite a degree of self-esteem and self-importance as an individual with responsibility for his actions. As this originally insubstantial entity gains more and more substance as the originator of his actions, it assumes more and more authority and a sense of responsibility that separates him from the world of 'others'.

It is this same ego who becomes the spiritual seeker, seeking his 'true nature' or 'self-transcendence'. And when his real non-existence is pointed out to him, he is not only confused, but full of rage and fury.

The fact of the matter is, that while in reality the ego does not exist, for all practical purposes it is the ego who is the seeker and it is the ego who needs to be convinced that his 'existence' is merely a matter of divine hypnosis. And, furthermore, he is told, his notion of free will or volition is based on the programming in the body-mind organism – genes plus environmental conditioning, over which he has had no control.

It is only when the ego himself comes to the conclusion, from personal investigation into his own personal experience, that 'his' every single action has been based on a prior happening over which he has had no control, that he finally is compelled to surrender his sense of personal doership. Simultaneously, he accepts that he is only the operating element in the body-mind organism in which the Source (or Primal Energy or Consciousness or God) is the only true functioning authority. Any other way for the ego to seek freedom from himself would seem to be an utter absurdity.

In day-to-day living, the ordinary person carries a monstrous load of sin and guilt, only because he is not able to accept the concept that nothing – 'good' or 'bad' – can happen unless it is the Will of God. As Shakespeare has put it: "There is nothing either good or bad, but thinking makes it so."

There is the incident of a young married man going to Ramana Maharshi and, with tears in his eyes, expressing his fear that he might be tempted to commit adultery because he was carried away by the sight of his young neighbor's breasts. He begged for help. Ramana Maharshi's answer would cause astonishment to the ordinary person: "*You* are always pure. It is your senses and body which tempt you and which you confuse with your real Self. So first know who is tempted and who is there to tempt. But even if adultery does happen, do not think about it afterwards, because You yourself are always pure. *You are not the sinner.*" It would be an event which had to happen according to God's Will, whatever the consequences.

There is an enormous complexity in our day-to-day living that gives rise to stress and strain almost continuously. Our present day living has lost all its simplicity and we are bewildered by the complexity and multiplicity of choices in almost whatever we do. And yet, deep down it is everyone's experience in day-to-day living that while we try to shape our day-to-day life, what really happens is that things seem to happen the way they are supposed to happen. And, in the odd moment, the thought occurs: 'Why do I bother? Why don't I just float through the flow of living instead of struggling? It is definitely my experience that all I can do is to make a choice and, thereafter, in spite of all my efforts, what actually happens (or does not happen) has never been in my control.' Indeed, the more one thinks seriously on these lines, one cannot help coming to the conclusion that the limit of one's free will is to make a decision and try one's best to transform that decision into action. Whether our efforts succeed or not has never really been in our control – that is definitely one's actual experience in life. It would clearly seem, therefore, that the strain and stress of life is the result of expecting our efforts to succeed. Therefore, why not make a decision on the problem of the moment, put in your best effort and leave it at that? Expectation of results leads to frustration.

Another constant underlying feeling – a result of modern hectic living – is a feeling of uncertainty which commonly haunts anyone who is not naturally a slob: have I left anything undone? It is my experience that one can rid oneself of a great deal of this discomfort if one is able to get into the habit of *a)* keeping a small notebook on one's person or close by, so that a note can be immediately made in it of something to be done at a later date (and, of course, the notebook must be referred to as often as possible); and *b)* more important, one must get into the habit of doing immediately whatever can be done at once. I remember a very dear friend of mine saying that his father was always at him, when he was young, yelling some bit of advice or the other all the time, and that he had managed to forget most of such advice which was, of course, meant to make the father's life easier. But he had never forgotten one piece of advice that he has been following scrupulously as long as he could remember: do it now! (And he said he still remembered the way his father said it, grinding his teeth!).

Which of us does not remember the many times we have uttered the words of anguish: 'If only I had done it when I thought of it', or 'why did I not do it earlier?' Would it not contribute a lot to peace and harmony in our daily living if such anguished words became an exception rather than the rule?

It is quite a usual experience that one makes a decision in a responsible way, but having made that decision there is a lingering doubt: have I made the right decision? In this situation the really vital point is that there cannot ever be a 'right' decision. One's supposed 'free will' extends only towards making a decision. It is everyone's actual experience that having made a decision and having made the necessary effort to put it into action, what happens subsequently has never been in one's control because other forces in the circumstances come into effect, over which one cannot possibly have any control. And, what is more, the action when it happens – or does not happen – produces results quite contrary to what was anticipated. And, what is even more extraordinary, the actual results affect not only the apparent doer of the action, but other people who were not directly concerned. And this is the fact that produces considerable confusion and uncertainty in life, which leads to a continuous sense of discomfort in living.

The only answer to this situation is to try and have an awareness of the present moment, a realization of the fact that one's place in the fabric of all that exists in the moment has never been in one's control. What this realization means in effect is that in the moment, every single moment, "all living things of the Earth open their eyes wide and look Me in the eye." It is the simple realization that whatever exists in the moment is precisely as it is supposed to be, according to a Cosmic Law that is forever beyond the conception of the human intellect.

This radically realistic and experiential approach to Reality, although more prevalent in the East – especially in India – was not unknown to the great mystics and authentic creative artists all over the world. The summit of Awareness cannot be different in the East and the West. The 9th century Irish mystic, John Scotus Erigena, knew: "Every visible and invisible creature is an appearance of God." And Meister Eckhart in 13th century Europe said: "The eye with which I see God is the same eye (seeing) with which God sees me." Eckhart's 'eye' is the very same that in the East is called the 'Buddha Eye', or what the *Upanishads* speak of: "Verily, oneself is the Eye, the endless Eye." It is the Eye not of the 'me', but of "God born in man's soul", of the true Self. In other words, it is not the eye with which one human being sees another, not the eye that operates in a subject-object relationship in relative phenomenality.

One evening I had a telephone call from Subbarao, a retired gentleman living in one of Bombay's suburbs. He has been deeply interested in the spiritual seeking over a long period and has an intense conditioning based on the sense of personal doership and personal morality extending over several lives through rebirth. When he came across my concept of non-doership, there was a violent psychological crash that he has not really been able to handle. He does not keep good health and is, therefore, unable to attend the morning talks as often as he would like to.

Subbarao is a really sincere person and repeatedly assures me that it is not his intention to challenge my concepts, that he has been compelled to accept my concepts, but somehow cannot altogether sever himself from the deeply-grounded feeling that the human being is himself responsible for his own actions. He, therefore, telephones me occasionally with a lot of apologies for disturbing me. Knowing his situation, I have enormous sympathy for him, and each time we go through the same routine and find that he has, every time, come to the core problem: what can I do to make my intellectual acceptance of non-doership total and unconditionally complete?!

And, each time, he puts the phone down reluctantly, but confessing that he has to accept the position that there can be no free will or doership for the human being, that the human being is, basically and essentially, a uniquely programmed body-mind apparatus through which the Primal Energy functions (like electricity functioning through the thousands of electrical gadgets) and brings about precisely that which the particular human organism is designed and programmed to produce. Subbarao also, each time, accepts that the final acceptance is not something he can achieve but that it is something that has to happen. I look forward to the time when Subbarao will call me one day and happily announce that there is no longer any problem.

In one of his *abhangas*, the saint Tukaram said:
> *Where God abides, let us hasten,*
> *There let us seek our restful haven,*
> *To Him our weak and woe we must surrender.*

These lines, said so confidently by the saint, raise wonderful expectation in the heart and mind of the ordinary human being, living his day-to-day life that is usually full of competition and conflict. At the same time, the word 'surrender' is not an acceptable word against the background of the usual conditioning of the modern man.

Therefore, the modern man wants to know what exactly all the saints and sages mean by the word 'surrender'. What is man to surrender? Is he supposed to surrender the identification with the body-mind organism as a separate entity? – the ego? This is unthinkable because without that identification as a separate entity even a sage would not be able to live the rest of his span of life, whatever role he is supposed to play in life. One can only imagine living one's life without any identification in a Himalayan cave in utter solitude. So long as one has to live in society, identification as a separate entity must necessarily be there. Without that, even a sage would not be able to respond to his name being called.

This is a valid objection that needs to be dealt with. Why is the identification to be surrendered? The identification is to be surrendered supposedly because it signifies the stifling source of separation that is the cause of the burden that the human being feels in his day-to-day living. But what one has to consider is the nature of this burden. Does it lie merely in the separation as an entity different from all other entities, or does it in fact lie not in the mere identification, but rather in the sense of personal doership or volition that usually goes with this identification?

One cannot deny that one enjoys bathing in salt water because it brings about a feeling of lightness; when an obese person loses a substantial amount of weight, the immediate, welcome reaction is certainly one of relief. In one's day-to-day living, what is the burden one would love to be relieved of? That is the real question. And the answer obviously is that the burden is in fact the burden of the responsibility for one's supposed individual actions.

Again, the real question to be considered, therefore, is: does an individual human being really have volition or free will? It is the experience of everyone that free will in fact simply means the free will to make a decision. How many of one's decisions have in fact been translated into actions? And among those that have in fact turned into actions, how many have had the precise results expected when the decisions were made? The answers to both these questions would clearly indicate that the free will that man values so much, and which is the cause of so much guilt and shame, and hatred and ill will, is really a myth. All it does is create the burden that would be instantly lifted if it were possible for the ego genuinely to surrender its volition or sense of doership and responsibility. Such surrender means the total and absolute acceptance that it is the Will of God – according to a conceptual Cosmic Law – that prevails all the time. In other words, the surrender of one's illusory free will means, in effect, the acceptance of the Buddha's words: "Events happen, deeds are done, but there is no individual doer thereof."

Immersed as man is in the cares and responsibilities of day-to-day living, one can sympathize with him if anger and confusion do arise when he is told by the saint to rest his cares and fears on God, for He is the ocean of bliss and cheer. The only way he can interpret the saintly advice is that he cannot but continue to retain his cares and fears, that he cannot but continue to think about what he wants – and keep worrying and fearing that he may not get what he wants – but that he should appeal to God to grant his wishes because He is the only One powerful enough to do so. This would in effect mean the same thing as waging a war and then appealing to God to take one side against the evil enemy!

What the saint meant by his words is quite basically different. What he suggested is that we should abandon conceptual thinking, which is the basis of our anxiety – "On Him we shall rest our cares and fears" – and surrender our volition to Him for the simple reason that our will would necessarily be short-sighted. What we want in the immediate future may not be in our real interest. In any case, what actually happens has never been in our control; why then carry the burden of our cares and fears unnecessarily?

Much as a parent would love to indulge a child, he would not give a bottle of poison to him to play with in spite of all the fuss that the child might make. An excellent illustration of the limited view of the individual's split-mind and the whole-mind of the sage with the Ultimate Understanding could perhaps be found in the fact that, at a certain level of magnification, the cells of an organism would appear to be engaged in a fierce and relentless battle for individual survival, but if the organism were to be observed as a whole through a different level of magnification, it would be clearly seen that what appeared as a conflict at the lower level was indeed harmony at the higher level of the entire organism.

The sculpted figure of the Dancing Shiva – with its four arms and their gestures, so dynamic and yet so superbly balanced – very beautifully expresses the rhythm and unity of life as such. It personifies the continuous and ceaseless flow of energy passing through infinitely different patterns, merging into the Totality of the phenomenal activity of the Brahman through the ceaselessly changing myriad manifestations in the phenomenal world. Even more impressive, in the same way, is the sculpted figure of Mother Kali in action – Primal Energy personified.

When the saint Tukaram sang, "On Him we shall rest our cares and fears", what he obviously meant was that at any given moment, What-Is is an indisputable fact that simply could not have happened unless it was precisely what was supposed to happen according to God's Will and a conceptual Cosmic Law, which the puny intellect of man could not in a million years be able to grasp. Accepting this means resting our cares and fears on Him who is the ocean of bliss and cheer. In other words, we do not like the short legs of the duck but they cannot be lengthened without considerable discomfort to the duck; the same thing applies to the long ugly legs of the crane that we do not like. Similarly we accept our own imperfections as right and proper in the larger perspective.

Such a wider vision at once restrains our tendency to conceptualize and to compare and judge What-Is in the present moment, and becomes conducive to a surrender to the Totality of the manifestation and its natural functioning. This surrender is not the abject surrender of defeat but the elevating surrender of the understanding that our volition is nothing but the usurpation of the subjectivity of the Source. When the subject-object relationship is seen in the correct perspective as the result of the surrender of our false sense of doership, we are capable of experiencing the present moment in which the whole manifestation is Brahman, in which we see ourselves as mere units for perceiving the universal functioning. We no longer see distinct and separate organisms with supposed responsibility – with the attendant fears and cares – for independent choice, decision and action.

To the followers of *bhakti*, 'surrender' is quite easily understood to mean, "Thy Will Be Done". To the seeker of knowledge, 'surrender' would mean the acceptance that the conceptual individual entity, being only an infinitesimal but nonetheless intrinsic part of the totality of manifestation, cannot possibly have, as a three-dimensional object, any independent existence with volition.

Such an acceptance does not come easily to the seeker of knowledge because of the conditioning over thousands of years that he is an independent entity responsible for 'his' actions. Yet he cannot but accept the fact that in the entire phenomenal manifestation, being the objective expression of that pure Subjectivity, there cannot be any individual independent entity with volition. The real problem for the seeker of knowledge, even after accepting the fact that he cannot possibly be an independent entity with volition and choice of action, is: 'If I am not an independent entity with choice of action and the relevant responsibility for it, how do I conduct my daily life in the world? How do I carry on my business in day-to-day living?'

The answer is given by the Chinese sage, Huang-Po:
"If you were to practice keeping your mind motionless at all times with the aim of not creating any thinking, the result would be an absence of dualism, no dependence on others and no attachment; if you would allow all matters to take their own course throughout the day as if you were too ill to bother, without the specific desire to be known or unknown to others, with your mind like a block of stone that mends no holes, then the Universal Law would deeply impregnate your understanding. And, very soon you will find yourself firmly unattached and your reactions to phenomena rapidly decreasing and your ceaseless flow of thought coming to an end."

In the state that follows the absence of conceptualizing and the fabrication of objects in the mind, all thought and all action assume a noumenal nature. In other words, wherever action is needed, the working mind provides the thought and action, without any interference from the thinking mind concerned only with the results and consequences in the future. With the understanding that all events are predetermined parts of the totality of functioning, actions take place without any anxiety about the success or failure of the actions. In other words, when the understanding that subject and object are one is clearly and deeply entrenched in the psyche, all actions become spontaneous and natural without the taint of the dualistic separation between the self and the other.

What is, perhaps, more important is the fact that the purity and naturalness of one's actions cannot but evoke a sympathetic response from the 'others' concerned even though these actions may not in fact be in their immediate interest. In short, a deep understanding working mysteriously, miraculously, would make life unbelievably more pleasant and considerably less complicated.

"What will you do if someone comes at you with a knife?" It is precisely such a question – or similar thinking – that makes life a hell. All that such thinking does is to create enormous disturbance, agony and turmoil in the external world; each one separates himself from the others, wanting security. And security in this world, all of us know from personal experience, is an illusion. There may be a belief that asking such hypothetical questions provides us with answers about what is to be done. Again, it is our experience that what actually happens is almost always something quite different from what one has planned.

"What will you do if someone comes at you with a knife?" The only answer is: "I really don't know. I do not know what I shall do." This is because, again, according to our experience, in any circumstances what actually happens in the moment is a happening, not one's doing. That is our personal experience, which we choose to ignore, and we continue to wallow in our fear of the future, ending in our being afraid of death.

It has also been the experience of most of us that we have enjoyed moments, even brief periods, when there was a sense of total lightness and freedom, in tune with the silent pulse of the entire universe, which betokens an innate synchrony and Oneness. There is no specific 'reason' for this feeling and, indeed, the feeling itself disappears when one seeks the reason for it. Thinking – thinking in horizontal time – encroaches upon the natural rhythm of the moment and breaks it and destroys it because the thinking is based on the hope and fear, based on the dualism of 'me' and the 'other'.

It must be clearly understood that there is a basic difference between pleasure or enjoyment as such and the desire or demand for enjoyment. It is not enjoyment as such that causes any conflict in the mind, but the thinking that the desire or demand for such enjoyment may not be fulfilled in the future. In other words, thinking pursues pleasure, sustains its memory, demands its continuance and produces the fear that it may not succeed. The only way to get rid of this fear is to enjoy the pleasure or the experience of the moment in that moment and finish it so that there is no image or scar left on the mind. This is what happens to the sage, and that is why the sage is sometimes described (to the surprise and confusion of many) as *mahabhogi*, i.e. the supreme enjoyer.

The great moments of ecstatic harmony arise when there is no conflict, when there is no division between the thinker and the thought, between the experience and the experiencer, when thinking in horizontal time does not bring about a dichotomy between the me and the other. A deep acceptance of this fact is all the 'action' that is necessary, because when the body relaxes and the mind expands beyond the dualism of the me and the other, the heart is free from the fear of failure.

Harmony prevails when thought ceases to demand and seek experience and merges in the experiencing. Detached from the rigid and immovable center of the 'me' and its demands and desires, the experiencing is a beautiful free movement without any limiting boundaries of the thinking in horizontal time. Harmony then prevails because, while thinking and reasoning regarding the job or work at hand continue unabated, the mind, freed of the incessant demands of the 'me', is free to move in boundless space.

Harmony means absence of conflict: it means stillness and silence, peace and tranquility in day-to-day living in our world of today, not in a Himalayan cave! Life goes on and What-Is in the moment is accepted so that the immeasurable vital energy of the universe continues, not hampered by the real limitations of the 'me' and its confinement and conflict. And such silence and stillness necessarily comports the understanding that all that exists is the totality of the manifested universe in its unbroken wholeness, that the individual is an intrinsic part of that Oneness, merely an appearance in Consciousness, endowed with the sentience which enables it to perceive and cognize the other appearances, and most importantly, that such a mere appearance cannot possibly have an independence or autonomy, nor any volition or choice of decision and action.

When the first principles of non-doership in the world of duality become intellectually acceptable – that all actions are happenings based on the Will of God, according to a Cosmic Law, impossible for the puny intellect of man to understand, and not the doings of any individual doer – there arises an apparent difficulty in the day-to-day living of the human being. It is the ego, with the sense of personal doership still very much present, who has this problem which seems very real indeed. The problem according to the ego is: 'I like the concept of non-doership very much, particularly because it takes away my personal responsibility for all actions which are supposed to be entirely according to God's Will. But my problem is that the society in which I have to live is not prepared to accept this principle and holds me responsible for my actions. I have to face this problem all the time. When I have a problem, *what do I do?*'

The answer is astonishingly simple. Let the ego, with the sense of personal doership, do whatever he likes, whatever he thinks he should do, after the most careful consideration of the various alternatives available to him. He is flabbergasted with the simplicity of the solution to the problem only because he has not understood in depth the principle of non-doership. The principle itself is, again astonishingly simple: nothing happens unless it is the Will of God. Therefore, the arising of the problem itself is the Will of God. The solution which the ego comes out with cannot, again, be anything other than the Will of God!

The real point in the arising of the problem, and its solution by the ego, is that whatever action happens apparently through the solution cannot be other than according to the Will of God. But the more important point is that the action – the problem and the solution – is the Will of God, and so also are the results or consequences of the action that has happened, *whomsoever they might affect.* The principle of responsibility is based on the ego considering the effects of 'his' actions on himself in the first place. The point, however, is that the results or consequences could be much more widespread! Many more persons could be involved. And whoever is affected would be affected because that is the Will of God.

Once the ego has done a thorough and honest investigation into his own personal experience, he will come to the unequivocal conclusion that every single action that he thought was 'his' action turns out on investigation to be merely the reaction to an earlier happening over which he had absolutely no control. Soon the simple action of scratching his nose turns out, on investigation, to be the reaction of the brain to an itch over which he had no control. In other words, if there had been no itch, 'his' action of scratching his nose would not have happened. The ego, who earlier had enormous anxiety that his very existence was in danger if his sense of personal doership were removed, is very soon convinced that the basis of his existence, the identification with the particular body-mind organism as a separate entity not only continues unhampered, but that his day-to-day living has now become enormously simpler, with the load of personal doership removed.

The ego now finds that his day-to-day living continues precisely as before, but now life in true faith is possible: the ceasing of self-centered striving, with all irresolutions and doubts having vanished, has freed him from the bondage of the responsibility of the sense of personal doership. Without the interference of the thinking mind, all is clear, transparent, almost self-illuminating.

The ego now finds that in order to be in direct harmony with this Oneness of Reality, all he has to remember – and even this has become natural and spontaneous – is that there is only the One Reality functioning through every single body-mind organism, without the slightest interference with the body-mind organism as a separate entity, which continues to function as an essential part of the One Whole. The provocative Persian philosopher, Omar Khayyam, depicted the human condition this way in the *Rubaiyat*:

> *We are no other than a moving row*
> *Of visionary Shapes that come and go*
> *Round with this Sun-illumined Lantern held*
> *In Midnight by the Master of the Show;*
>
> *Impotent pieces of the Game He plays*
> *Upon this Chequer-board of Nights and Days;*
> *Hither and thither moves, and checks and slays;*
> *And one by one back in the Closet lays.*

To live in this realization that all there is in phenomenality is the One infinite universe – all definitions and divisions have vanished – is to live being anchored in the peace and tranquility of Self-realization.

All there is,
is Reality, and any
illusion, any appearance,
any shadow, cannot but be
a reflection of that very Reality.

CHAPTER 6

DVAITA:
THE
TEACHING

Advaita (*a+dvaita* = non-duality) simply means that the Source, by whatever name known – Primal Energy, Consciousness, Awareness, Plenitude, God – is Unicity, Oneness, Non-duality. The manifestation that arises or emerges from the Source is based on duality, the inevitable existence of interconnected opposites: male and female, beauty and ugliness, good and evil. At any moment there are bound to be interconnected opposites. The sage accepts the duality that is the basis of life and is anchored in peace and tranquility while facing the pleasures and pains of life exactly like the ordinary person. The ordinary person does not accept the duality, the existence of interconnected opposites at any moment of life, chooses between them and is unhappy. The sage accepts the 'duality' of life; the ordinary person chooses between the interconnected opposites, and lives in the unhappiness of 'dualism'.

The man of understanding certainly sees preferences being made in daily living between the polaric opposites, but is totally aware of the fact that the preferences happen according to the individual programming in each case, and are not made by any individual person doing the preference. The man of understanding is, therefore, always in tune with the Source. When the final flash of total understanding happens, it is not at all unlikely for the individual to realize the unbroken wholeness of the universe and to clearly see the whole range of polaric opposites as a great illusion or a play of a feigned quarrel between lovers. The result can be an uncontrollable fit of huge laughter or intense weeping.

If only one would realize it, one's daily living is never more than a continuous choosing, comparing and judging, blaming and praising – hardly ever mere witnessing and accepting. How can there ever be peace and harmony in our daily living? There is a recollection about Neem Karoli Baba:

> *When Maharajji came out you never knew what to expect. He could do the same thing a week in a row until you'd think, 'well, he'll come out at 8:00.' Then he might not come out all day, or he might just go into another room and close the door and be in there for two days. You had to learn to expect the unexpected. One day he came out and all he said all day long was 'Thal – Thal, Nan – Nan', repeating those words to himself like a mantra. Days went by like this and somebody finally said, 'Maharajji, what are you saying?' And it turned out to be an old Bihari dialect and all it meant was 'too big, too big, too little, too little'. When he was finally asked why he was saying this, he said: 'Oh, all you people, you all live in Thal – Thal, Nan – Nan; you live in the world of judgment. It's always too big or too little.'*

Beauty and ugliness, love and hate, good and bad really do not exist until thinking makes it so. When these dualities are accepted as the very basis of life and living, preferring and judging do not happen and everything becomes clear and transparent. A child was alone in the bedroom, playing with her toys. The two-and-a half-year old was engrossed in her play, when the mother came into the room and asked whether she had spilled the face powder on the floor. The mother told her that she could smell it. The child looked at her blankly for a moment, then the word 'smell' registered. She said, "oh yes, I did fart a moment ago." The child was intuitively aware that everything happens.

In day-to-day living, one faces problems that have an astonishing range of apparent reasons and possible consequences. The interesting question, therefore, is whether there is a basic common cause that could be isolated and dealt with. Indeed, the basic cause of human conflict and unhappiness is 'dualism', as distinct from 'duality'. The core of this difference needs to be thoroughly analyzed and clearly understood. In fact, such a clear understanding could itself be the solution of human unhappiness because it would relieve the human being from the double-bind in which he finds himself in his relentless pursuit of unalloyed happiness.

The fact of the matter is that 'duality' is polaric, interrelated and, therefore, not really separate, whereas 'dualism' is opposition, separation, and, therefore, conflict. Phenomenal manifestation is a process of objectivization that basically requires a dichotomy into two elements: a subject that perceives and an object that is perceived. This is the process that is known as 'duality': all phenomena that are sensorially perceivable are the correlation of a subject (object-cognizer) and the object (the object cognized). This process of duality makes it evidently clear that without such a process there cannot exist any phenomena, and that neither of the two phenomenal objects (neither the cognizer subject nor the cognized object) has any independent existence of its own: the existence of one depends on the existence of the other.

When the basis of duality is clearly apperceived, there is no question of either any *samsara* (phenomenal day-to-day living) or any bondage for any conceptual individual for the simple reason that the 'individual' concerned is merely the psychosomatic apparatus, the instrument through which the process of perceiving and cognizing takes place. Our unhappiness, our conflict, our bondage arises as the effect of the identification of What-We-Are (Consciousness) with the object-cognizer element in the dichotomy of the whole-mind (Consciousness) into subject and object in the process of duality.

This identification or entitification as a separate independent entity (as the pseudo-subject) is the 'dualism' – the *maya* – which results as the practical application in day-to-day living of the original principle of duality, that is polaric, interrelated and, therefore, not separate. *It is this illusory entitification that causes all the conflict,* all the suffering, all the unhappiness that is collectively termed 'bondage'. The instantaneous apperception of this very fact of the illusoriness of the pseudo-subject as an independent doer-entity means the freedom from the bondage.

It is an interesting phenomenon in daily living that in the process of perceiving, there is an important distinction between our outer perception and inner perception, between 'sensing' and 'feeling'. You are in the mountains, looking at a scene that is totally different from the urban scene you are accustomed to. You look at the beautiful scene and, of course, there is the visual perception of the scene and a sense of wonderment, something you are not used to. Then a feeling of great joy and peace and harmony arises and makes you close your eyes. The sensory perception, which teaches you objectively about the outside world, is the elaboration of a mental image, reproducing by resonance, certain aspects of the outer object. Thus, although the perceived image is in the mind, it can be called the *outer* perception. But the joy that you feel is a different perception, *inner* perception, totally personal to you. If you have a friend with you, his outer perception would in all probability be similar to yours. But the inner perception of your friend could be totally different. Along with the mountains, he has also seen the surrounding poverty, and while the outer perception was similar, his inner perception would be sadness instead of joy.

The outer perception, a sensory perception, is a general structure characterizing the human being as an essential identity (like the silver cup and the silver jug) beneath the different forms. The inner perception is also a resonance but, this time, the resonance is not to the general phenomenon as a human being but to the unique programming within the human object: hence the different perceptions. The mental images thus vary between the non-dualistic outer world and the dualistic inner world: the outer or sensory perception may be called 'sensing' and the inner perception may be called 'feeling'. 'Sensing' is general; 'feeling' is essentially dualistic, based on one's likes and dislikes.

The general human structure, although based on the essential *duality* of male and female, corresponds to the universe as a harmonious unification, a microcosm similar to the macrocosm – the primordial human being, a replica of all creation. The personal structure, on the contrary, corresponds to the inner world, the 'me' against the 'other', based on the egoic identification with the body-mind organism.

The real significance of this distinction between the outer and the inner perception has been brought out beautifully by Hubert Benoit in his *Lacher Prise* (*Let Go*):
"To the degree that my physical body and my thoughts, while diminishing in opacity, lose their reality, my consciousness acquires, on the contrary, more and more reality. The more my thoughts [my thinking] become rapid, light, without importance, unreal, the more my consciousness is felt as real, important. At the same time the more real my consciousness feels to be, the

more I feel I am 'being', independently of my body and my thoughts. I could say, in opposition to Descartes, 'I do not think, therefore I am' [or, 'I am, therefore I think']... Now the more the perception of the manifestation of my 'being' becomes subtle, grows lighter, that is to say, the less I feel myself as existing, the more I have the impression of being and the more happy I feel. It is then as if my consciousness of existing personally were the inverse reflection of my consciousness of 'being': the less I feel, the more I have the impression of approaching the moment when I will have the consciousness of 'being', the moment when my consciousness will be conscious of itself."

Some time in a day of living, the thought may occur, 'what would it mean to 'die'?' The question is obviously asked by the ego. The simple answer is 'dying' means being oblivious to whatever happens in day-to-day living, not being concerned with or being bothered by whatever happens in day-to-day living. So, if we are able to die every day to the pleasure and the pain of what we know as living, dying could happen every day. In other words, if we accept whatever happens in the moment, and do whatever needs to be done in the moment, without fighting with the self-importance, the self-pity, the hatred and malice towards the other, the guilt and shame arising in memory, we could enjoy the happiness of dying every day. *This can happen* only if the thinking mind, inevitably functioning in the past or the future – never in the present moment – is really quiet and quiescent. And this can happen only if we are able to accept totally and unconditionally that every human being is only a uniquely programmed instrument through which the Primal Energy functions. In other words, as the Buddha said: "Events happen, deeds are done, but there is no individual doer thereof."

The average person cannot help seeing in day-to-day living the fact that certain few people, generally known to be 'wise' people or 'sages', seem to live their lives enjoying the basic pleasures and suffering the same pains and miseries as does the ordinary person; and yet one cannot help but also notice that deep down they seem to be anchored in peace and harmony. They seem generally relaxed not only in their own day-to-day living but also remarkably comfortable in their relationships – personal or business – with others. What is more, the average person experiences a certain kind of peace and relaxation in the sage's company and he realizes that this has rarely anything to do with what is talked about during the meeting. The very presence of the man of wisdom seems to exude peace and harmony in spite of the fact that he seems to respond to outside events with an absolutely normal reaction!

In other words, the question arises: how does the spiritual Ultimate Understanding translate itself into action in day-to-day living? The answer is that the sage is constantly aware of the 'happening' of life persistently but effortlessly, without projecting it unduly into the future. The result is that this 'being aware' keeps functioning even when thoughts, feelings, desires arise in the body-mind organism. Because they are merely witnessed as they arise and take their course, there is no involvement through the sense of personal doership about any happening.

The true understanding absorbs the realization that, like the clouds that wander through the sky, thoughts and feelings floating through the mind have neither any home nor any roots. Once Consciousness is understood as the substratum of everything phenomenal (including sentient beings and their thoughts and actions), discriminatory judging ceases because no thing is seen to have any independent existence. Then virtues and vices are not seen as opposites as such, but as polaric counterparts that negate each other when superimposed.

All action becomes spontaneous, being the operation of virtuality as latent power that exhibits itself in the miraculous fruition of plants, the formation of eyes and ears, the circulation of blood and the reticulation of nerves. Such force or power is generated without any conscious direction – it is a natural and spontaneous working force, of which, for instance, electricity (no one really knows its nature though its operation is clearly well known) is only one aspect. This is what true understanding translates itself into: spontaneous and uncontrived activity in practical matters of day-to-day living.

This miraculous natural force, the basis of which is the absence of personal volition – virtuality (which has nothing to do with spiritual powers or *siddhis*) – has been described beautifully by Lao-Tzu:
"Superior virtue is not (volitionally) virtuous, and thus is virtue.

Inferior virtue does not forsake being virtuous, and thus is not
    virtue.
Superior virtue uses no force, but nothing remains undone.
Inferior virtue uses force, but achieves nothing."

Virtuality is steeped in ordinariness and anonymity, and it is
precisely for this reason that the ordinary person is puzzled when he comes
across it in his day-to-day living. It is this same force or power that brings
out the genius in various people in various fields of life, which cannot be
explained in mundane terms through the step-by-step linear method
expressed in ordinary words. The only way it can be described – but not
really explained – is through some pointers, as did Lao-Tzu:
"When the great Tao was lost, there came (notions of) humanity
    and justice.
When knowledge and cleverness arrived, there came great
    deceptions.
When familiar relations went into disharmony, there came
    (notions of) good parents and loyal children.
When the nation fell into disorder and misrule, there came
    (the ideas of) loyal ministers."

When action is spontaneous and without the slightest hesitation
there is no room for thinking in the future. The curious fact is that the
chances of survival are best when there is not undue anxiety to survive
because the special force of virtuality is available to those who do not tire
themselves out by their anxiety. And this is seen from the number of
successful 'do or die' actions. The fact, however, that is even more curious
is that anxiety also includes the positive effort to stop the worry. All
volition, positive or negative, constitutes a drag for the simple reason that
it is the spurious non-existent individual ego with the sense of personal
doership that does the worrying either way. True understanding accepts
whatever life brings and responds to each experience without any resistance
or recoil, giving the mind freedom to think, including the freedom to
worry! Thus, speaking of the death of his Master Lao-Tzu, Chuang-Tzu
said: "The Master came because it was time. He left because he followed
the natural flow."

In other words, the senses, feelings and thoughts must be allowed
to operate in their natural way because any attempt to control them can

only result in worsening the disturbance. As Lord Krishna said in the *Bhagavad Gita*: "The man who is one with the Divine and understands the Truth believes 'I do nothing at all' for in seeing, breathing, in speaking, emitting, grasping, opening and closing the eyes, he holds that it is only the senses that are concerned with the objects of the senses." It is only through true understanding that any change may occur in thoughts, emotions and desires, and muscular effort at controlling them would necessarily be futile to a large extent because the nervous system is essentially electric circuitry and not muscle.

One of the most daring pronouncements in this matter was made by a Chinese sage, Yang-Chu:

> "Let the ear hear what it longs to hear, the eye see what it longs to see, the nose smell what it likes to smell, the mouth speak comfort that it craves, let the mind do as it will... What the body desires for its comfort is warmth and good food. Thwart its attainment of these and you cramp what is natural and essential for man. What the mind wants is liberty to stray whither it will, and if it has not this freedom, the very nature of man is cramped and thwarted."

It must be remembered, of course, that this advice is given to the seekers of knowledge who might otherwise be misled into disciplinary practices that would turn out to be a hindrance. In other words, whatever has to go must fall off by itself. Any effort at controlling thought and appetites would only strengthen them, and along with them the sense of personal doership in the ego.

The deep and clear Ultimate Understanding – not the intellectual comprehension at the linear level – of What-Is leads to true humility and the annihilation of the sense of personal doership in the ego-entity. This means, in effect, natural and spontaneous action which reflects the fact that human intelligence is not something of an outside agency implanted into the sentient being. In other words, the human intelligence – not the mind-intellect – is very much an inherent aspect of the whole organism of the phenomenal universe, which maintains the functional order in dynamic balance through the operation of the Consciousness that is the substratum of the entire phenomenal manifestation.

This balance in the functional order of the phenomenal

manifestation is maintained through the natural mechanism of polarity between apparent opposites. Therefore, conflict based on stark, irreconcilable opposites of good and evil, subject and object, 'me' and the 'other' would necessarily be not only superficial and of temporary significance, but basically unacceptable to the essential culture. What this really boils down to is that this entire phenomenal show of the universe – the *lila* – has no real purpose, and it is futile to seek a cause or a goal in life in open competition against all contenders.

Most 'successful' men would readily admit this in their heart of hearts, but the conditioning over the years is so powerful that most human beings, especially in the West, would not dare to accept it and openly admit that over the years it had been futile to seek a goal in life. And, it would be more difficult to admit that the achievement of such a goal had not really brought them the deep sense of peace and harmony that their hearts had always craved for. Of course, as soon as a goal is conceived, spontaneity is at once destroyed and the self-consciousness of the ego-entity – with its sense of personal doership – takes over. From then on, the vision is pin-pointed on the goal, thus missing everything really worthwhile in life.

The 'purposeful' life indeed misses the purpose of day-to-day living, which is to enjoy the unity in the duality and the multiplicity of life. It is only when the ego-entity realizes this fact that there springs the sense of total freedom, and then comes the floodlight of true vision, which misses nothing and enjoys everything. Then spontaneous action, not being in conflict with the natural course of events, with What-Is, enables the man of true understanding to be fully receptive through his senses to the entirety of the universe. He takes it easy in life, is relaxed and free of tension because he is not self-conscious about either the effort or the result, and he enjoys the sport of life to the full without any inhibition. He becomes the *mahabhogi*, the super-enjoyer of life and living.

An important point for the seeker is that a clear understanding of What-Is does not shut out the phenomenal world as an illusion because, then, we would be making a false distinction between the real and the unreal, between the substance and the shadow, between the Noumenon and the phenomenon. As the Buddha put it so vividly: *samsara* (life) is *dukkha* (misery), *nirvana* (the Source) is *shanti* (peace) – and they are not two.

All there is, is Reality and any illusion, any appearance, any shadow, cannot but be a reflection of that very Reality. Illusion cannot have an independent existence. The true understanding accepts the position that noumenality is at once both transcendent to and immanent in phenomenality and, therefore, all distinctions are seen to be void. In other words, nothing is seen as acceptable as real and unacceptable as illusion, with the result that a certain amount of dispassion gets cultivated through the realization that any distinction between the attractive and the unattractive only means involvement, which can only cause unnecessary unhappiness. Both the attractive and the unattractive are interconnected polaric opposites, which are the very basis of the phenomenal manifestation and its functioning.

Most important, through the understanding, what happens is that rivalry and competition in day-to-day living become a game, a *lila*, rather than a strife and conflict, leading to hatred and malice, jealousy and envy. In other words, the immediate result of a deep understanding is that man frees himself from the bondage of the world and its ills and fears and suffering and chaos, merely by seeing the absurdity of it all – 'does it really matter?!' He sees that what he had considered and labeled as desirable or undesirable, the illusory distinctions on which he had based his ideals and aims, merely constitute the diversity in the course of his day-to-day living, which otherwise would have been an unbearable bore. There is the case of the famous actor George Sanders who committed suicide; he left a note to say that he was taking his life because he had everything that life had to offer – good health, money, fame – and he was too bored to go on living!

An apperception of the basic meaninglessness of conventional values in terms of Reality lifts man out of the apparent strife and conflict of life. He now sees it as a game in which he must participate according to the rules, which he need not take at all too seriously. How can this happen? The man who has, through the acceptance of What-Is, freed himself from conventional standards of judgment, considers it stupid either to accept the unhappiness that is imposed by those very standards, or to immerse himself in what are usually considered great joys. He sees the stupidity of carrying a load of guilt and shame for actions that are merely a part of What-Is, or carrying a load of hatred and malice towards an object through which some event has occurred to cause him pain.

The man of understanding, in his day-to-day living, does not in any literal sense withdraw and hide himself from the natural world of people and events. To do so would at once mean a confession of having passed a judgment upon the world based on the same conventional values. He continues to remain within society, playing according to the regular rules, but refrains from acting out of the prevailing motive that makes the ordinary man struggle for wealth, fame and security. His mind is empty of futile ambition, cunning, desire and artifice. Cheerfully accepting whatever comes his way, accepting change as the very basis of life, as part of the totality of functioning, he remains with the underlying unity that encompasses man and nature in the totality that is the universe. He wanders through life witnessing and participating in all experiences without being attached – either positively to the delights or negatively to the sorrows – in any way. He truly seems to extend virtue and kindness to the whole world without contending with anyone.

With the surrender of the concept of an independent entity with its supposed volition, the very source of desires dries up, and simultaneously the bondage inflicted by desires and the efforts to achieve the objects of these desires, also gets annihilated. It is necessary to clarify this point: it is not that thoughts, feelings, desires do not arise in the body-mind organism as a natural, biological function. The arising of thoughts-feelings-desires in the mind is as natural and spontaneous as the arising of waves on an expanse of water. Any attempt to suppress this natural happening can only result in failure and frustration. What does happen after the dawning of the understanding is that the thoughts-feelings-desires that arise *are not pursued*. They arise, but when they are ignored and they do not get any sustenance from the volition of the ego, they can only disappear. In other words, the understanding results in mere witnessing of the process of the arising and the disappearing of the thoughts-feelings-desires without any involvement. And then, gradually, the arising of the desires itself lessens both in its frequency and intensity. The beauty of the process is that the man of understanding is truly not concerned with the process!

There is a well-known incident concerning Bhagwan Ramana Maharshi. A man from North India heard a knock on his door in the middle of the night. He opened the door and saw a *sannyasi* who asked him to go south to Tiruvannamalai and visit the Ashram, where he would get the necessary guidance in his spiritual quest. He went to Ramanashram. When he first went inside, he saw Ramana Maharshi reclining in his wide seat, talking to people. He suddenly realized that he was the same man who had knocked on his door some days ago. This made him very angry because he saw it as a confidence trick, a cruel joke. He decided to go and tell what had happened to someone at the Ashram. He was then even more shocked to hear that Ramana Maharshi had not been out of the Ashram even for a single night for the last several years.

How could Ramana Maharshi have been at two places at the same time, several hundred miles away? There have been several other recorded instances of other sages at different times being seen at two places at the same time. A fairly recent case is that of the well-known Neem Karoli Baba. Physicists take as gospel the notion that a subatomic particle can occupy more than one position or state at a time. Now they are grappling with the perplexing corollary: can a person be in more than one place at the same time as well?!

We understand that Albert Einstein used to complain that something had gone horribly wrong with Max Planck's elegant quantum theory. As Werner Heisenberg and others laid out the principles of quantum mechanics, the theory quickly took a turn for the bizarre. And the more we learn about the quantum world these days, the stranger and 'more counterintuitive' it becomes! We now know, for example, that an ocean of particles continuously pops into and out of existence all around us. If you were to take a box into the void of space and look carefully inside, you would find it is not empty after all: particles would appear in the box out of nowhere, only to vanish in an instant and be replaced by others. *True emptiness does not exist.* And now theoretical physicists seem to believe that quantum mechanics has even greater mysteries in store: more universes, even ones with other versions of you. They have the insistent belief that the principles of quantum mechanics hold true not just in the subatomic world but also in the world all around us.

And the fact remains that if quantum theory were not valid in the world around us, no one would be walking around with cell phones or palm pilots. So physicist David Deutsch wonders: "Why do so many scientists ignore the larger implications of quantum mechanics?" The 'many worlds' interpretation of quantum mechanics suggests that all of us have twin counterparts in an infinite number of other universes. But despite the unrivalled empirical success of the quantum theory, the very suggestion that it may be literally true is still greeted with considerable cynicism.

Few physicists deny the validity of these laws. The laws insist that the fundamental constituents of reality – protons, electrons and other subatomic particles – are not hard and indivisible. They behave like both waves and particles; they can appear out of nothing – a pure void – and disappear again. Physicists have even managed to teleport atoms, to move them from one place to another without passing through any intervening space. It seems totally in conflict with the world of big physics according to Newton and Einstein.

To grapple with these contradictions, most physicists have chosen an easy way out: they restrict the validity of quantum theory to the sub-atomic world. But the purists like David Deutsch argue that the theory's laws must hold at every level of reality because everything in the world, including the human being, is made of these particles, and because quantum theory has proved infallible in every conceivable experiment. Therefore, we too must exist in many states at once, even though we do not realize it. Perhaps we live not in a single universe, but in a vast rich 'multiverse'. To the purists, the most serious consequence of refusing to accept the quantum theory in its entirety would be that physicists will never advance to a new, deeper understanding of nature.

It is interesting to note that many physicists around the world, including a team at Oxford, are trying to build a quantum computer that would manipulate atoms or photons and exploit the particles' abilities to exist simultaneously in more than one state. Those quantum properties would tremendously increase the speed and capacity of the computer, allowing it to complete tasks beyond the reach of existing machines. It seems that a quantum computer could, in theory, perform a calculation requiring more steps than there are atoms in the entire universe! To do that, the computer would have to be manipulating and storing all that information somewhere. Computation, after all, is a physical process that uses real resources, matter and energy. But if those resources exceed the amount available in our universe, then the computer would have to be drawing on the resources of other universes! The results would be, to say the least, interesting!

The final question still remains: what if the quantum theory is wrong? Physicist David Deutsch answers: "I'm sure that quantum theory will be proved false one day, because it seems inconceivable that we've stumbled across the final theory of physics. But I would bet my bottom dollar that the new theory will either retain the parallel universe feature of quantum physics, or it will contain something even more weird." Whatever the prevailing theory of physics, the fact would still remain that it can refer only to the physical manifestation and its functioning – the phenomenal existence – and the unmanifest Source, the One Reality, from which the phenomenal reality has emerged would still remain a mystery to the created object, the human being, a part of the phenomenality.

In our day-to-day living we live constantly under the tyranny of time. And, yet, do we really know what 'time' is? Has anyone ever known it? St. Augustine has put it rather succinctly: "What, then, is time? If no one asks me, I know what it is. If I wish to explain it to him who asks me, I do not know what it is."

The fact of the matter is that we live in a world not of 'being' but of 'becoming', where nothing ever stands still. What happens is that in our personal experience we translate this flux into continuity, into duration. Without this sense of continuity, we could not maintain the sensation of permanence in our individual selves and live within a constantly mutating world.

According to Hindu beliefs, cosmological time is measured in terms of *yugas*, calculated in terms of humanly manageable time as well as a larger unit of divine time associated with Brahma, the Creator. While the smallest unit of time is measured as the duration of the blink of an eyelid, a human year is equivalent to one day of the Gods. According to the sage Manu, four *yugas* can be apprehended: *Krita* consists of 4800 human years, *Treta* has 3600 human years, *Dwapara* consists of 2400 human years, and *Kali* yuga 1200 human years. At the end of a cycle of four ages or the *mahayugas*, the first *yuga*, i.e. *Krita*, returns, commencing a new cycle of time.

In ancient Greece, Ouroboros, the emblematic serpent, represented time. It is shown with its tail in its mouth, continually devouring itself and being reborn from itself. The Ouroboros serpent expresses eternity and the unity of all things material and spiritual, which never disappear but perpetually change form in an eternal cycle of destruction and re-creation.

The association of time with the mystical, fascinating and compelling though it may be, undoubtedly served to hinder a proper scientific study of time for many centuries. The crucial position that time occupies in the laws of the universe did not become fully manifest until the work of Newton in the late 17th century. Newton prefaced his presentation with the famous definition of "absolute, true and mathematical time, (which) of itself, and from its own nature, flows equably without relation to anything external." Having discovered the mathematical laws according to which natural bodies move through space along predictable paths, Newton was able to calculate the motion of the moon and planets, as well as the paths of projectiles and other earthly bodies. This represented a giant advance in human understanding of the physical world, and the beginning of scientific theory as we now understand it.

It was into this world of rigid temporality that Albert Einstein was born. Newton's time had endured for two centuries and was scarcely questioned by Westerners, though it had always rested uneasily alongside Eastern mystical thought. Yet, Newton's time is the time of 'common sense': there is but one all-embracing universal time; it is simply there; time cannot be affected by anything, it just goes on flowing at a uniform rate. Newton's concept of time chops it up into past, present and future in an absolute and universal manner. But this simple view of time as rigid and absolute, powerful and common-sensical though it may be, turned out to be fundamentally flawed. Around the turn of the 20th century, the Newtonian concept of universal time began yielding absurd or paradoxical conclusions concerning the behavior of light waves and the motion of material bodies. Within a few short years, the Newtonian world view had spectacularly collapsed, taking with it the common-sense notion of time. This profound and far-reaching transformation was primarily due to the work of Einstein.

Einstein's Theory of Relativity introduced into physics a notion of time that is intrinsically flexible. It did not restore the ancient mystical ideas of time as essentially personal and subjective, but it did tie the experience of time firmly to the individual observer. Time became relative. Although Einstein's time remained subject to the structure of physical law and mathematical regulation, the psychological effect of abolishing a universal time was dramatic. In the decades that followed Einstein's original work, scientists probed deeper and deeper into time's mysteries: was there a beginning of time and will there be an end? What is the origin of our sense of the flux of time? Is time travel possible? Remarkably, in spite of nearly a century of investigation, the revolution started by Einstein remains unfinished.

Thanks to Einstein, the world has accepted the Space-Time-Equivalence. In the various chronometers, all that really occurs is a movement in space and, therefore, a movement in time. Unshifting, seamless, unfracturable, immeasurable time provides a substratum in which a movement occurs, which then is assigned a value by the prejudiced human mind. In Vedic parlance, time (or space) is the *adhisthana*, the substratum, and the chronal movements are superimposed *adhyaas*. A whale or a Titanic does not move the ocean, but the ocean in an act of condescending generosity allows you to think so.

Apart from the External Time, there are *a)* Individualistic, Inner Time, or Psychic Time and *b)* Biological Time. Silence is the best measure of Inner Time. However, some data on Biological Time are interesting. Does a rat really live 'less' than an elephant? Laws of scaling dictate that small, warm-blooded animals live at a faster pace than larger relatives. For several criteria of relative time, all animals live about the same amount, all breathe about the same number of times during their lives. The everyday experience of relative motion – a stationary train seeming to move when another moves, or the sun seeming to set when really it is we who are setting – should tell us that nowhere does time move, but the *maya* of our senses seduces us into thinking so.

Our trouble has been that we have foisted the flux on fluxless time. The whole basis of the negation of time is the need to think, in our day-to-day living of life, as such, without a sense of "hubristic hurry". The chronometrically driven faster-the-better vehicles on the roads, in the water, and in the skies have only led to wanton destruction. A story was told of four Americans being treated to dinner by His Holiness the Dalai Lama in his palace at Lhasa. The Dalai Lama was told that one Mr. Nicolson had crossed the Atlantic in three-and-a-half hours. The Dalai Lama asked the hero if he might ask him a question. The hero replied: "Your Holiness, ask me any number of questions." The Dalai Lama said: "I only want to ask you one question. I only want to know, what was the hurry about?"

The human being needs to realize that the Noumenon is the abiding Reality, whereas the phenomenal universe of events, objects and beings is a fleeting universe, orchestrated by the unseen Reality. The Noumenon, being conceptual in nature, is formless and, of course, free from the shackles of space and time, which are the very basis of the phenomenal universe. The human being is only a part of this phenomenal universe, as a uniquely designed instrument through which the Noumenon, as the Primal Energy (*Shakti*), functions and brings about every moment that which is supposed to happen. The assurance in the *Bhagavad Gita* that no one dies for no one is born has biological backing: everything, every cell, every atom, every molecule, every body co-exists, is coeval, within the cosmic ocean. A wave arises, individual and yet bound to the ocean, merging into it, once its ephemeral, phenomenal stage is over. Each is uniquely shaped by all the rest, and vice versa. The concept in the *Gita* is based on the conceptual Cosmic Law of the universe. The first human being ever is coeval with all human beings of all times, for none truly dies, for none is truly born.

It is an interesting point that one of the most difficult concepts to accept for even an 'experienced' seeker is that 'time' does not exist. One question persists: all action can only be in horizontal time – the past has led to the present and the present will lead to the future; how can one ever accept that there is no time? The answer, in a way, is simple: the past, when it was present, could only have been in the present moment. What we now think of as the past event is not the past event but the memory of it. When the future event happens, it can only happen in the then present moment. The future event, now, is only a supposition; it does not exist. The significance of what has been just stated cannot be mentally understood. The understanding can only happen as a 'flash' of understanding: only the present moment exists.

The question is similar to this question: a movie takes two hours to happen; how can one say that there is no horizontal time? The answer is that the 'movie' is the happening from moment to moment, frame by frame of the movie film. The movie, as a whole, has happened as a connected story only in the mind. To repeat, the unfolding of the movie, frame by frame, is in the present moment; connecting the frames horizontally happens in the mind. Horizontal time can only happen in the mind. The actual happening – frame by frame – is in the present moment.

The Arabian sage Monoimus said, if you want to understand God: "Find out whence it is that you fall asleep when you would rather not, that you wake up when you would rather not, that you fall in love when you would rather not..." Now comes a research report that explains "the chemicals of 'falling in love'":

"Neural evidence shows that the phenomenon of 'falling in love' is a series of chemical reactions taking place in the brain that cause mental and physical reactions. There are an estimated 100 billion neurons that make up the brain's communication network. Candace Pert, in 1999, pioneered the research that discovered neuropeptides, strings of amino acids that float around the body and attach themselves to welcoming receptors. So far, 60 different neuropeptides have been discovered and they trigger emotional reactions in the body when they attach themselves to the receivers. In other words, all our emotions – love, grief, happiness – are all biochemical. When the English scientist Francis Crick and his associates won the Nobel Prize in Medicine for deciphering the DNA code that defines genes, he stunned the medical world by saying: 'You, your joys, sorrows, memories, ambitions, your sense of identity, free will and love are no more than the behaviors of a vast assembly of nerve cells.'"

If it is possible to accept totally the concept of non-doership, that in the words of the Buddha, "events happen, deeds are done, but there is no individual doer thereof" – if, in other words, one accepted totally the significance of the words "Thy Will Be Done" – then the word 'forgive' (or 'forgiveness') would seem to have no meaning at all. In fact, in daily living, when one dares to say that he has forgiven someone for what he has done, it has to be assumed that one has not been able to accept totally that nothing can happen unless it is God's Will. If I am hurt, does it not mean that I am hurt because it was God's Will – and my destiny – to be hurt (and I cannot possibly ever know the basis of God's Will) and if it is not my destiny to be hurt, no power on earth, let alone any individual human being, could possibly hurt me. When, therefore, someone says he has forgiven someone, is he not assuming a divine function? In fact, if one does truly accept that nothing can happen unless it is God's Will – that no action is anything but a divine happening – then there simply cannot in truth exist in any vocabulary the word 'forgive'.

It is only in accepting that nothing can happen unless it is God's Will, that the whole concept of forgiveness becomes totally unnecessary. In other words, it would be meaningless to say, 'you cannot truly forgive yourself or others as long as you derive your sense of self from the past.' Indeed, time or timelessness would seem to have nothing to do with forgiveness.

It is such a shame really that in daily living today, one seems to be always looking for 'fun'. 'Fun' has become the watchword. It is a shame and a pity because each one of us has had the experience, some time or the other, of the deep, real joy of living brought about not by some thing or event outside ourselves, but some thing, which is not a 'thing' – very deep within ourselves. It seems to be unrelated to time, being in the present moment: one is almost inclined to say 'dead or alive'!

Perhaps this is related to the experience many of us have certainly had, in a life-threatening, emergency situation: there is a sudden shift in consciousness from temporality to the present moment. The 'me', based on a conceptual past and present, has given way to an impersonal conscious presence of great intensity and alertness in which the necessary response to the situation has happened with an astonishing spontaneity. There was immense joy in that moment totally unrelated to the personal 'me' and his circumstances.

I have often wondered if it is not this aspect of life – not 'fun' but 'joy' – that is the real attraction for people who engage in dangerous activities like doing stunts in movies or car racing or whatever. In fact there certainly are teachings that have, from time immemorial, directly pointed to this experience. The very basis of Zen would seem to be this very experience of walking along the razor's edge, in the present moment, when time is absent, and so is suffering.

Is there not a passage in the Gospels that speaks of the lilies in the field who need not think of the morrow. Or, again, the passages related to the kingdom of God: "Nobody who puts his hands to the plow and looks back is fit for the kingdom of God." The unfortunate thing is that in the frenzy of daily living, no one seems to think that they have any relevance to actual living.

In practical daily living, a human being hardly ever lives alone – yogis living alone are rare and scarce. In life, there is usually an intimate relationship. Such relationships, which seemed perfect for a while, when the two are 'in love', somehow quickly turn into love-hate relationships as arguments and conflicts begin to occur with increasing frequency and intensity. The end result can usually be easily foreseen. Each one may feel that the next relationship would certainly be better, but in the end hope turns into frustration.

The fact of the matter is that the intimate human relationship is basically not any different from any relationship between 'me' and the 'other'. And avoiding any kind of relationship in life is just not feasible or practical, and is just not the answer. The answer is to be sought in seeking the basis of any and every relationship, intimate or otherwise. The basis of a relationship with an office colleague, or a bird or dog that visits you regularly, is truly not different from any intimate relationship. The basic reason for the relationship going sour is the same: the 'other' does something that you do not like, and likes and dislikes must necessarily be different in different people.

In other words, the only way a relationship – formal or intimate – can continue smoothly in peace and harmony is when both the persons concerned are able to accept that the other person – the other persona – does not exist, cannot exist, except insofar as the programming in the body-mind organism allows it to be. The persona, the personality, is severely restricted by the positive and negative aspects of the genes, and the conditioning in the body-mind organism, which itself is restricted by the geographic and social environment of the person concerned. The only way any relationship with the 'other' (whomever it might be) can function smoothly and harmoniously is for both the partners to understand the unavoidable limitations of the genes and environmental conditioning in both body-mind organisms. In practical terms, what this means is that each 'me' must be able to accept that the 'other' truly has no control over what he or she seems to be 'doing'. His 'thinking' is based on the programming (genes plus environmental conditioning) and his 'doing' is based on his destiny, or the Will of God, according to a conceptual eternal Cosmic Law, the basis of which no human object can ever possibly understand.

Life being what it is, difficulties must and would arise on the surface of life, but if the understanding in both cases were fairly deep, these superficial problems would soon be accepted with amusement, rather than resentment. When someone investigated a truly wonderful relationship between a man and his wife, with sincerity and compassion, he found that the husband thought he did whatever his wife would want him to do, and the wife thought she always did what her husband would want her to do!

In daily living it is such an unfortunately common habit to see differences in the way of living and, thereby, create unnecessary hatred and resentment among one another. This starts as differences in cultures, differences in countries, differences in religions on a fairly large scale. And, in a way, it is truly amusing that they narrow down to states in the same country, down to areas in the same state, down to various cities in the same area and, amazingly, down to various pockets of society in the same city! Needless to say, such differences become the cause of serious misunderstanding and conflict.

Basically physical, cultural and social differences are no more than the variety in the magnificence of God's creation, and should really be seen as such – there is neither anything good or bad about it, just different, interestingly different. In some cultures, it is considered rude to look a person in the eye; in others, it is rude to avoid looking a person in the eye. At times it is polite to keep a distance when meeting and talking: in some cultures the correct way is merely to bow from a certain distance, in others to join one's palms in a *namaste*; in yet others to shake hands, while in

Arab countries, a tradition values savoring the fragrance of a friend's breath, and any attempt to keep a polite distance could be construed as a sign of aloofness.

A few years ago there was a report of a meditation course arranged by Mahesh Yogi, of 100 people participating together in meditation for a certain length of time every day for 90 days, in a small Midwest town in America. It was found at the end of the period that crime in that area had suddenly come down very substantially, and the Chief of Police could find no apparent cause for the phenomenon. There was, therefore, a certain justification to assume that the sharp and sudden fall in crime in the area was the result of the intensive meditation course undertaken by the meditators.

The phenomenon was also likened at the time to the rain-making dances of the native Americans who could produce rain on a day when there was bright sunshine without a single cloud. At the end of the dance several clouds would gather without any apparent reason, and rain would start falling. At that time, I remember thinking that the basis of both of these phenomena was probably the same behind the *yagnas* performed for a specific purpose like producing a good monsoon or a good harvest or for victory in war or whatever.

Now there is a report of a remarkable experiment conducted by a team of researchers from the Institute of Noetic Sciences and the Global Consciousness Institute, just before the Millennium in 1999. They set up 40 devices around the world, called Random Number Generators (RNGs), that fed back into a computer at Princeton University in the USA.

These random number sequences were created to detect synergy of mass consciousness. When a specific event became the focus of mass consciousness (a significant mass of people thinking about the same thing at the same time) the numbers would become ordered and less random. On New Year's Eve, 1999, what they discovered was that as the time-line swept across the world heralding the year 2000, and huge populations in each geographic area were celebrating together, the numbers indeed became more ordered and less random.

The equipment remained in place. In September of 2001 something remarkable happened. After the horrific events in New York and Washington D.C. on September 11, the team was astonished after studying the input from the 40 RNGs around the world. What they found was that not only was there a massive blip on September 11, but the blip actually started to occur two days earlier. Late in the day on September 9, the numbers began to appear less random and more ordered. There were several peaks on September 10 and, by September 11, it was off the scale!

From these data, they made an incredible conclusion: human consciousness knew on some level what was about to happen! This was more evidence proving the existence of the hologram – that we are not separate, we are intimately connected, and we are all a part of a fundamental whole. They now believe that this program can be used as a predictor for significant world events.

There are earlier data that support the fact that it takes a very small portion of a population to shift consciousness. In fact, it has been shown that the square root of 1% of a given population becomes the quality of consciousness for that population. What this means is that in a population of 1,000,000 people, the square root of 1% of that population is only 100 people.

This means that a total shift of mass consciousness can occur if 100 out of every one million people align their thinking. It takes a very small number of individuals seeing the world in peace to create the peaceful existence we have always wanted here. As Margaret Mead said: "Never doubt that a small group of thoughtful committed citizens can change the world." The horrific thought is that the same applies to both the opposites: a small group of committed people could bring about another September 11, or worse!

It is reported that at the age of 32, historian Arnold Toynbee visited Turkey to study the Greco-Turkish War. He first observed conditions from the Greek side, then the Turkish. He placed particular emphasis on listening to the side that was "the more in danger of not being given a fair hearing". Witnessing the massacre and suffering of Turkish refugees, he felt outraged that these atrocities went totally unreported in the West. Putting down facts exactly as he saw them, he wired them to the *Manchester Guardian*. The editor of the paper courageously published them in full in the paper. The article made a deep impression on the Turks: it was the first time that their side of the story was conveyed to the world; so far it had been the "unspeakable Turk". On his return to Britain, Toynbee was forced to resign from London University because of his support of the Turks, and for the next 33 years he had to make his living writing reports on international issues for the Royal Institute of International Affairs.

It is necessary for all of us to wake up and realize that we are all creatures of the same Creator, and no one is a creature of a lesser God. In the absence of such a clear understanding, all that we do is to create for ourselves an awful load of hatred and malice which grows day by day. Worse, still, we create for ourselves a heavier load of guilt and shame for perpetrating this hatred and malice. It is undoubtedly this massive load on the mind that the Buddha referred to as "*dukkha* in *samsara*" – suffering in life.

The only way to look at life is not only to see all mankind as creatures of the same God, but to see clearly that life itself can only happen as the Will of God operating every moment through every human being. And each human being is used as a uniquely programmed instrument, through which God produces whatever is to be produced as a happening according to a conceptual Cosmic Law that applies to all Eternity. It is this very understanding that is the basis for peace and harmony in day-to-day living.

When spiritual seeking
happens naturally, intuitively,
it is very simply merely wanting
to be close to God, wanting to be
comfortable with oneself and with others.

CHAPTER 7

THE SPIRITUAL SEARCH

One might surmise from the frustration expressed by so many visitors at the morning talks, that the apparent plight of the spiritual seeker has continued unchanged, unabated for centuries:

> *Why, all the Saints and Sages who discussed*
> *Of the Two Worlds so learnedly, are thrust*
> *Like foolish Prophets forth; their Words to Scorn*
> *Are scattered, and their Mouths are stopt with Dust.*
>
> *Myself when young did eagerly frequent*
> *Doctor and Saint, and heard great argument*
> *About it and about: but evermore*
> *Came out by the same door as in I went.*
>
> *With them the seed of Wisdom did I sow,*
> *And with mine own hand wrought to make it grow:*
> *And this was all the Harvest that I reaped –*
> *'I came like Water, and like Wind I go.'*
>
> – Omar Khayyam, *Rubaiyat*

In dealing with the spiritual search in day-to-day living, the question that often gets buried under the avalanche of words and emotions is the one that comes from a sincere ordinary person: "I am quite content to lead my life as I have always done, in a law-abiding manner, with an attitude of reasonableness towards all others. I am, in other words, a nice, ordinary, unregenerate person. Why should I concern myself with enlightenment or any spiritual search? What will it get me in this life that I do not now have?"

This is a valid question and to give an answer, such as, that life is not a bed of roses and that a succession of illnesses or failures in life would make him think of God would really mean nothing but a sort of spiritual blackmail. The only genuine answer would be: "You are right. There is really no apparent reason for you to seek enlightenment. But are you sure that underneath the apparent satisfaction of the surface of your day-to-day living, you are not carrying a load of guilt and shame, a load of hatred and malice towards others, which is in fact burning your heart out, and prevents you from being anchored in peace and quiet? Are you sure you are at all times comfortable with yourself, comfortable with others, comfortable with your Creator? This is the real reason behind the spiritual search for your real nature." This is the answer that will make a genuine seeker out of the ordinary person in day-to-day living.

The basis of spiritual seeking is very often misinterpreted as regimens and disciplines, denying the body any kind of comfort, suppressing all desires, fasting for days at a time, forcing oneself to meditate for long hours. The result is very often a state of frustration and depression – a kind of dark night of the soul. The pity of it all is that the unfortunate seeker interprets the absence of any result as want of adequate effort!

It is necessary to realize without any doubt what the spiritual seeking is all about. One would be astonished if one could really notice how much pride and arrogance lies behind the asceticism and discipline of some spiritual seekers. What is actually sought, whether or not it is consciously realized, is the *pleasure* of achieving something inwardly that is infinitely more superior to the kind of pleasure sought by the ordinary man.

When spiritual seeking happens naturally, intuitively, it is very simply merely wanting to be close to God, wanting to be comfortable with oneself and with others. Then when the result happens – not something achieved – one is truly grateful for the divine gift of being anchored in peace and tranquility, the "*shanti* of *nirvana*", as the Buddha said, while living in the "*samsara* of *dukkha*" (the life of pain and pleasure).

It is often seen that an ordinary person is not unconcerned with the essential nature of things. An ordinary person is more concerned with the 'meaning of life' – the spiritual quest – than is generally believed. How can this not be the case? The 'ordinary person' is truly none other than the Source or Consciousness – which is all there is! – now identified with a particular body-mind organism as a separate entity. And the identified Consciousness would naturally be seeking its own source or its 'true nature'.

What happens, however, is that this natural curiosity of the ordinary person in seeking his true nature is often stifled by the overeager *Guru* who is more concerned with showing off his own learnedness than with rendering any help to the spiritual seeker. An undue familiarity with the key words, phrases and formulas of the supposed *Gurus* would have the effect of frightening off the ordinary seeker in the very beginning, or of leading him up the garden path until, after a time, his spiritual search leads him into deep frustration and depression. The genuine and sincere *Guru* speaks from his own experience and relies as little as possible on the stock words and phrases in the many traditional writings. But it is not every spiritual seeker who can intuitively sense the greatness of a genuine *Guru* like Nisargadatta Maharaj or Ramakrishna Paramahamsa. This is undoubtedly the point behind Lord Krishna telling Arjuna in the *Bhagavad Gita* that among thousands of beings there is only one seeker, and among thousands of seekers who think they are seekers, "hardly one knows Me in principle."

If one examines one's own life in an honest objective way, does not one find that one's day-to-day living is in fact a sorry, shoddy, shabby affair – full of conflict and struggle, ambition and competition, guilt and shame, hatred and malice? Man realizes this state of affairs at odd intervals in the mad rush of day-to-day living and asks himself if this is all that life is supposed to mean. Man *knows*, deep down, intuitively, that there simply has to be something beyond what one sees as 'life' with all its suffering and chaos and disorder, something beyond the very concept of time, something untouched by an experience, pleasant or otherwise: something unchangeable, immutable, pure and sacred. Indeed, man *knows* deep down *it is there* for the simple reason that in odd moments it has descended upon him unasked, and spontaneously made him one with the universal pulsing. The stillness and silence of these moments has been frightening with its unfamiliar immensity and intensity that has totally destroyed one's sense of individuality.

In spite of the frightening aspect of such an experience of Oneness, man has been seeking this Absolute Reality because of the realization that this experience meant a total absence of the usual load of guilt and shame, hatred and malice. This seeking for the Oneness with the Source produces infinite frustration because the Source, which sought, seeks its own Source! The result of this frustration is that thought creates the concept of God as the Creator and gives Him various attributes like 'all-knowing', 'all-powerful', 'all-merciful', etc., so that man himself could seek Him as an ally against the vicissitudes of life. But God still remains a concept, and thought, which created the concept, finds itself forced to ask the question, the nagging question, 'if God created the universe, who created God?' Indeed, that is precisely the question any intelligent child asks the adult.

What has happened is that man has conceptualized God *in the image of himself*, attributing to it the noblest sentiments and qualities that he himself lacks. Frustration arises because in reaching *That* which is beyond God, intellect is powerless because That is the very source of the intellect. That which is timeless cannot have any path leading to It for the simple reason that a path can lead only to something fixed and immobile. That-Which-Is, the source of all thought, can only be the Potential Plenum throbbing with the impersonal Primal Energy that is present everywhere, and not at a single point.

The very possibility that there must exist the Divine Ground, totally apart from the conceptual God acting as the Chief Executive Officer of the multinational Universe, is difficult for the intellect to comprehend. There is a beautiful Sufi story that illustrates this point admirably.

> *A banquet is being given in honor of the King. All assembled guests are seated according to rank and only one chair remains vacant, awaiting the formal arrival of the King. At this point a raggedly dressed Sufi fakir walks in, marches straight to the chair reserved for the King, and sits in it very comfortably. The Chief Minister cannot believe his eyes, angrily approaches the fakir, and the following dialogue takes place:*
>
> CM: *'How dare you sit in that chair? Are you an important minister, senior in rank even to me?'*
>
> Fakir: *'No, I am more than that.'*
>
> CM: *'You are certainly not the King.'*
>
> Fakir: *'No, I am more than that.'*
>
> CM: *'You are certainly not the Prophet.'*

165

Fakir: *'No, I am more than that.'*
CM: *'Then are you God?'*
Fakir: *'No, I am more than that.'*
CM *(horrified)*: *'How can you say that? More than God,*
there is nothing.'
Fakir: *'Yes and I am That NOTHING, which is everything.'*

In day-to-day living, even those who are genuinely and sincerely interested in the Divine Ground as the formless Reality would find the very bottom knocked out of their existence and find themselves being thrown into a pit of sheer, impenetrable darkness, when they are told with great seriousness by a sage that the individual is a mere fiction and, therefore, without any real independence to act on his own initiative and volition. This may be pure *Advaita* (or non-duality), but most seekers would find it extremely difficult to let go of their individual identity with a very definite sense of doership and responsibility. They would much rather, as spiritual seekers, think of their individuality as something that they would have to merge with the Absolute Reality, and accept that this should need a great deal of persistent effort from them.

The basic cause of all human misery, often underlying the spiritual seeking, is the one single fact that man disidentifies himself from the subjective perceiving center, which is the subjective functioning aspect of the Source, and identifies himself with the objective psychosomatic apparatus (or body-mind organism) through which the perceiving takes place. In other words, man forgets that 'he' is in fact sentience, which is the functional aspect of the Consciousness that is our real nature (indeed, Consciousness, the Source, is all there is), and mistakenly believes that he is a separate entity represented by a particular psychosomatic mechanism. It is necessary to find out how this comes about, first in a general theoretical way and then in the practical details of everyday life.

The subjective center must be clearly distinguished from the objective center because it is the confusion between the two that makes one stop in one's tracks and ask: 'What am I doing in the world? What exactly am 'I', other than this physical frame that is born and after a time must die?' We may ignore these questions and brush them aside whenever they arise, but they persist and cannot be denied. There is a clear distinction between the subjective center that is intuitively referred to when each one of us says 'I' – the ultimate symbol of *what we are* – and the tri-dimensional phenomenal object that we identify ourselves with when we say 'I' but actually mean 'me'.

A deep apperception of this very real distinction, between the subjective perceiving center that *we are* and the objective operating center that *we think we are*, provides not only the answer to those persistent nagging questions about our real nature but, more importantly perhaps, saves us from considerable misery and unhappiness that man has unnecessarily made himself heir to. The mistake that occurs is that we identify ourselves with the objective operational center (the mechanism) and forget that we are the subjective functional center which is beyond phenomenality. Indeed, it is this subjective functional center that provides the original Primal Energy (as consciousness and sentience) to the millions of mechanisms known as sentient beings – not merely human beings – which, without that Primal Energy, are only 'dead matter'. It is a little like mistaking ourselves for the electrical gadgets rather than the electrical energy that functions through the electrical gadgets.

This 'mistake' is understandable and indeed not illogical because all operations of the psychosomatic apparatus are directed from this objective center. And this objective center is thus mistaken for the subjective center (sentience) – the switchboard is mistaken for the power station. In actual fact, however, the objective operational center is only psychic just as the heart or the liver is somatic, purely phenomenal and entirely devoid of any subjective noumenal aspect – and, therefore, obviously without any volition or autonomy or independence in regard to any choice or decision.

The distinction between the subjective functional center and the objective operational center clearly shows us how the identification with a supposed autonomous entity with volition arises. The mistaken identification of what we noumenally are with the operating psychic organ in the psychosomatic apparatus, our body-mind organism, thereby assumes a pseudo-subjectivity, a supposed 'self' or 'ego' with supposed independence and choice of action. The condition that brings about this situation is known as 'dualism', a consequential aspect of the process of duality, which is a basic, necessary condition for the Absolute Noumenon to objectify Itself as phenomena. In the classic instance of the rope being mistaken for the snake, the perceiving of the rope is the primary delusion; that of the snake, the secondary delusion.

Every time an object is seen, it is really the perceiving of its pseudo-subject, i.e. the Subject in its objective manifestation, because every object (sentient or otherwise) is really a mirror reflecting That which is seeing. Objects can have no existence other than as appearances, sensorially perceived and interpreted, which means that what is perceived can only be a reflection of what is perceiving – perceiver-object is only an object and what is perceiving is truly the Subject.

The difficulty in understanding this obvious fact arises because the perceiver-object is regarded as an entity with independent existence. In fact, he is only a phenomenal apparatus or object with certain characteristic reactions – the real perceiver is the perceiving itself, the subjective functional center. In short, perceiving as from the subjective functional center (sentience) is true perception whereas perceiving as from the objective operational center (the entity) is imperfect or split-mind perception.

An aspect of true perception is to perceive that any object or event perceived has its existence only because one of our senses has cognized the object or event, and has interpreted it in the subject-object duality. The object or event, therefore, cannot have any existence independent of our perceiving of it as an appearance in our consciousness. In other words, objective existence – whether physical or psychic, whether an object or a thought – and the subjective perceptive faculty are naturally dependent in an object-subject relationship. It is only in the total negation of both these aspects that Totality occurs. All thoughts and all phenomena are based on the concept of space-time, and since space-time is not some perceptible or cognizable 'thing', it must obviously follow that the perceive-*ing* and cognize-*ing* – and indeed, all functioning in general – must be noumenal. As the sage Jnaneshwar has put it, Subjectivity and phenomenal functioning are like "sky and space, or wind and movement, or flame and light".

The essential element in true perception is the fact that there really is no perceiver/perceived relationship in the phenomenal manifestation. What exists is the function-*ing* of the whole-mind of Consciousness, and this objective functioning is conceptualized by the split-mind as subject perceiving the object: there is really neither any objectivizer nor anything objectivized. The sentient human being makes the cardinal mistake of viewing the phenomenal world as something separate from himself, whereas he himself is an intrinsic part and parcel of the *totality* of manifestation, which is the objective aspect of the unmanifest Absolute Subject.

Phenomenal manifestation has not taken place *separately* in order that human beings may perceive and cognize it. Sentient beings came into existence as part of the totality of manifestation, simultaneously and concurrently with the entire universe. A clear understanding of this position makes it obvious that the perceiver and the perceived object are both objects in the phenomenal manifestation, that each of the two sentient objects (the two human beings) becomes the perceiver when the other is the perceived object, and the subject and object are thus interchangeable and interrelated concepts. In other words, the perceiver cannot perceive the perceiver and the perceiver-cognizer is in effect only the act of perceive-*ing* and cognize-*ing*, the thing cognized being its counterpart. In other words, there is no object, only the one true Subject, the entire manifestation being its objective expression. This is the transcendence of the subject-object dualism, the total phenomenal absence that is the Potential Presence, the turning back of the mind from the outward objectifying (which is what perceiving in dualism means), back inward to its wholeness or the non-objectivity from which objectivity arises.

In daily living, perceiving things or objects – animate or inanimate – is a fact that is taken for granted. In fact, daily living has come to mean perceiving and reacting to things. But an analysis of this everyday fact of life leads to interesting inferences. What happens when one consciously perceives an object is that one is attentive to it. This means that the object is perceived not in its totality but only as a mental representation that is built up as a result of the eye, as one of the senses, responding to its object. This usual, ordinary perception is based on the fusion of subject and object, by an identification. In other words, the perception, as it usually happens when one perceives the object, is not total but only a partial one because of identification. The total perception of the object, as a manifestation of the Absolute Totality, does not occur because of the individual perceiver's identity – as an individual self as opposed to the outer world! The usual view necessarily creates an antagonism between the individual perceiver and the outer world on the basis of 'me' and the 'other', the subject and the object.

In the usual perception, one sees oneself as conditioning one's own realization and using the outer world merely as an instrument for this conditioning. Perfect attention would be that by which, in response to the outer world, one *awaits* the total and spontaneous awareness of the outer world and oneself as the Totality. The perfect perceptive attention is prevented because of the dichotomy between one's separate 'self' and the object: there is no awareness of the central identity between the apparent subject as the 'self' and the object as representing the 'other'.

The 'self', the subject, only allows the outer world to come to him in order to grasp it like the spider's web captures its prey. Such a situation creates tension in the individual 'self', and the usual 'suffering' was noted by the Buddha as the intrinsic part of *samsara* or daily living. The perfect perception – without the opposition of the subject and object, 'me' and the 'other' – would be illumination; the imperfect, divided perception becomes darkness, false interpretation, *maya*, ignorance. The disruptive dualism does not primarily exist, as the individual 'self' believes, between the self and the outer world. It exists entirely in the restrictive nature of the identification with a particular name and form as the individual 'me', separate from the 'other', as the individual doer, opposed to the other doer. When the true perception or understanding happens that the 'me' and the 'other' are both objects through which the Source, as the Primal Energy, or God functions every moment, the *maya* and the ignorance disappear, and the perfect perception happens, with no opposition between the seer subject and the seen object. One then becomes the spectator of the spectacle of life and living. Perception becomes total and impersonal perceiving.

In the *Bhagavad Gita*, Arjuna asked Lord Krishna how to recognize the one who is anchored in the wisdom of the Ultimate Understanding, how does he live, how does he behave, how can we know him? Lord Krishna replied: "What disturbs the inherent peace and harmony is the attraction for the objects in the outside world." He explained that as soon as the understanding happens, that the attraction for the outside objects arises in the programmed body-mind organism as a biological reaction to the senses meeting their respective objects, and that there is nothing that the ego can do to achieve anything, then the disturbance subsides and does not affect the inherent peace and harmony.

The sage understands that whatever happens is the Will of the Source and the individual ego is not the doer of anything. With this understanding – that every apparent action is actually a happening that has to happen according to the Will of the Source, according to a Cosmic Law, and not the action or doing of any individual ego – the sage, anchored in the wisdom of the Ultimate Understanding, accepts whatever pleasure or pain life brings in the moment as his destiny and the Will of the Source. Therefore, his peace and harmony is never disturbed. Just as the full moon, in giving out its illumination, does not make any distinction between the good and the bad, the high and the low – the sage, knowing that there is no individual doer of any action as a good man or a bad man, treats everyone in the same way making no distinction, and his compassion extends to all. His sense of equanimity is never disturbed in spite of the momentary arising of the biological reactions in his body-mind organism. When life brings pleasures, the sage enjoys them to the fullest (and is, therefore, known as a super-enjoyer, a *mahabhogi*) but he does not pursue pleasure. When, as a matter of his destiny, life brings pain, he suffers it with courage and does not go into a depression.

The sage's attitude towards life is thus quite different from that of the ignorant aspirants who try to suppress their desires by trying to control their senses, but the seeking of the pleasures continues in their minds. The sage lets life happen to him according to the Will of the Source. Therefore, whatever appears in the moment as a biological reaction – anger, fear, pleasure, pain, compassion or any other thought or feeling or whatever – does not disturb his equanimity and he continues to live anchored in peace and harmony. In other words, with the total acceptance that whatever happens is not the doing by anyone, either himself or anyone else, he never carries the load of pride and arrogance on the one hand, and the load of guilt and shame on the other, regarding any actions happening through his own body-mind organism. Nor does he bear the load of hatred and malice, or jealousy and envy towards others. He is, therefore, always comfortable with himself and comfortable with others. And, leaving everything to the Will of the Source, he is always comfortable with his

Creator. In other words, while the ordinary person suffers shame and guilt during his waking time for his own actions and carries the load of hatred and malice towards others, the same waking time for the sage means the peace and rest of deep sleep even when living his life during the day, accepting with equanimity whatever life brings.

Many people want to know if there can be one particular simple point to remember in day-to-day living that could make living simpler and less stressful. I would think that there is one such simple thing: don't complain. Complaining is sheer waste of energy, especially when it is in effect little more than whining or self-pity. If one analyzes the complaining, one finds that the complaint means the presence of something one did not want or the absence of something one did want. Also, the complaint refers to something about which one can do something or something about which one can do nothing. With this analysis, it would seem clear that it is useless to complain about something about which one can do nothing. If there is something one can do, why not do it? Why complain or whine?

Very often a complaint refers to something that one's colleague has done or failed to do, in spite of repeated instructions or suggestions. Here again, if it is done or not done deliberately, then complaining or whining only encourages the person concerned. If it is not done deliberately, then complaining only creates avoidable ill will. A very successful executive has this to say about his own experience in such a situation: "If I find that someone has done an act of commission or omission that should not have been done – and I know that this is not deliberate – what I do is to put the matter right myself or send for the person concerned and repeat the instructions again in the most civil manner. This practice produces excellent results."

In daily living in modern times, perhaps too much importance is given to dieting and discipline. While both are necessary, it is often forgotten that in any society, tradition has not ignored these factors but has not given an undue importance to them. The famous saint, Baba Neem Karoli Maharaj, for instance, while not giving any special importance to diet for the usual meals, did suggest that we "eat simple foods". And he also advised people to eat food that was indigenous to the area. This is obviously good advice coming from a saint. It would be stupid to expect a Scandinavian person, in his extremely cold climate, to eat *satvic* vegetarian food. Neem Karoli Baba also gave specific instructions to some devotees about diet, advising one to forego wine, meat, eggs, hot spices, "because they lead to an impure heart". Yet he said to other devotees: "What is this concern with what is meat and what is not? When you can live without meat, well and good. When you cannot live without it, then you should have it."

Then there is the matter of prayers; if undue attention is given to the narrow confines of discipline and routine, the very purpose of a prayer would be defeated. Prayer is indeed the spontaneous utterance, with or without the spoken word, of what lies deep in our hearts. It is the longing of the heart to break free from the narrow confines of the individual self to find the universal Impersonal Self, from isolation to communion. But when the disciplinary guideposts are mistaken for the destination, when the means are confused with the end, when the finger is mistaken for what it points at, then prayers can only become empty words, rituals, mere routines and the spiritual seeker becomes a slave of habit. Nizamuddin Aulia, the renowned Sufi saint, is reported to have said: "The observance of rituals and the performance of spiritual practices are like the spices in a cauldron; the real thing is the meat. If there is no meat in the cauldron, then there can be no stew and the spices are of no use."

It is one's everyday experience that the moment of one's deepest pleasure is not the positive enjoyment of something but the removal of a great pain. Unless one has experienced a bad migraine headache or an intense pain in the tooth, one can never know the pleasure that is close to ecstasy when the pain finally stops completely. In other words, it is one's everyday experience that the opposite energies always go together and that one cannot exist without the other. And yet, living in dualism, our energies seem to be constantly directed towards attaining one or the other and to be constantly directed to one or the other – happiness or frustration.

It is very interesting to see how a *bhakta*, someone who has taken the path of devotion, as opposed to that of *jnana* or knowledge, comes to realize the Oneness of life as a whole. Perhaps, the most revered *bhakta* in modern India was Ramakrishna Paramahamsa. I was, therefore, most deeply impressed by the words of Ramakrishna about the Oneness in the universe.

"Now our Master is weeping tears of pure love: '*It is all Her Play, Her delirious Plan. Om Kali, Om Kali, Om Kali.*' For a moment, we expect the Great Swan to disappear into one of the many dimensions of Divine Ecstasy... Now the Paramahamsa surprises everyone by regaining crystal clarity on the plane of human conversation.

Ramakrishna: *These apparently opposite energies – knowledge and ignorance, positive and negative – are simply God's unitary play. I clearly see that Mother has become the sword, the wielder of the sword, and the sacrificial animal. There is no duality. We appreciate glorious light as well as dense darkness. They enhance one another. When spiritually mature, one can appreciate as sheer divine manifestation both happiness and misery, which depend upon each other to be fully experienced. Some suffering is good. It helps one to find the path to Truth and make actual progress. The cosmic conflict between good and evil is an integral part of Mother's Drama, Her testing of souls. Could you enjoy the sweet golden mango pulp if the bitter green skin did not also play its role? The green skin called ignorance, the instinctive grasping of the life force, enables the delicious fruit of awakened mind to grow and ripen. Appreciate the bitter skin of ignorance as maya, Mother's magical projection. But do not bite into it. The golden pulp of knowledge is also Her magical projection. There is the maya of ignorance and the maya of knowledge. Each is integral to the functioning of the other in this theater of mahamaya. As timeless awareness – Nitya – Mother abides far above, while incarnating fully as lila, Her Cosmic Play.*"

When the seeker has advanced well enough to accept that the individual human being is in fact nothing more than a programmed instrument through which the Source or Primal Energy functions in phenomenality, the question that pops up frequently for the seeker is: is there a particular type of programming that is more open to the happening called 'Self-realization' or 'enlightenment' than others? From the astonishingly wide range of cases where enlightenment has taken place in different parts of the world in different times in the history of mankind, it is clear that Nature or Totality does not restrict the occurrence of enlightenment to any particular type of human being. The term '*dharma*', used so effectively in the *Bhagavad Gita* to denote the cardinal characteristic, the innate nature of one sentient being which clearly distinguishes him from another, is considered the basis of his very being, the *raison d'être* for his active life. To this extent, the *dharma* of an individual provides, to a reasonable extent, the basis and reason for the way in which he is expected to live his life.

According to the Hindu tradition, there are three paths to salvation. A natural propensity towards externalizing emotions would make one almost naturally take the path of devotion to a personal God (*bhakti*), with its inherent component of universal goodwill accompanied by charity and compassion towards all sentient beings. The path of action (*karma*) would obviously suit an individual with an abundance of physical stamina and energy that makes him to be 'on the go' all the time. Similarly, the path of knowledge (*jnana*) would be clearly marked out for an introvert or an intellectual. The three paths to salvation are purely conceptual and are very rarely so exclusive as to keep out the other two. Indeed, to consider and approach the Source or God in a particular, restricted manner is to invite a distorted view of both the Totality and the Reality, and would mean considering the matter purely from the viewpoint of the individual and not from the viewpoint of the phenomenal functioning as a whole.

The real question is: is there a common ground in the various cases of enlightenment that happen in the widespread spectrum of the human personality – whether inclined towards *bhakti*, inclined towards *karma*, or inclined towards *jnana* – overlaid profusely with the many different shades of the other two types? It is thinking along these lines that is likely to give us an insight into the happening of Self-realization or enlightenment, which transforms the human being from phenomenality to noumenality.

There is indeed such a common ground for all the three types, and innumerable combinations of the characteristics of each type. And that is the effacement of the 'me' or the 'self' as the individual doer in the various happenings in day-to-day living, which the human beings misinterpreted as their actions. This has been made amply and beautifully clear in the words of the Buddha: "Events happen, deeds are done, but there is no individual doer thereof." This annihilation of the 'me' or the 'self' as the individual doer cannot be 'achieved' because the one who wants to achieve this is none other than the 'me' or the 'self' as the 'ego-seeker-doer'. The seeker-doer cannot destroy himself.

The mind asks: "If and when I have the Ultimate Understanding, how should I, as a sage, act and behave?" Intellect tells the mind that such a question is 'mundane sophistry'. The answer – also, of course, 'mundane sophistry' – is that the sage has become the sage because there has occurred the Ultimate Understanding that no individual does any action, that all action is a divine happening according to a conceptual Cosmic Law. Therefore, there simply cannot be any 'sage's action'.

Then the mind asks: "Well then, if I do not at present have the Ultimate Understanding, and I still consider myself the individual doer, should I not have certain approaches that could be set out for day-to-day living, even if they may be difficult to practice?" This is a valid demand. Various answers have been proposed by way of contemporary therapies and by specialists in human behavior.

An answer which should be very seriously considered has been provided by an expert in human relations and management, Shivdas Balsekar, in his book, *Life and the Management of Suffering*. He has given several suggestions.
"We need to try and cultivate:

1. Highest possible level of integrity and values, despite an unethical world;

2. Self-confidence but not over-confidence, to be able to action your intentions;

3. Courage to tackle the complexities of life while being as open and honest with people as practicable;

4. Total honesty with yourself through constant awareness of your real motivations, strengths and deficiencies, and facing facts even if they cannot be shared with others due to circumstances;

5. Humility, through dignity for all work and adequate enough to acknowledge your own mistakes and to forgive others theirs;

6. Practice in resolving issues since the world does not beat to your rhythm;

7. Moderation, since extreme positions are rarely justified or necessary;

8. Care and compassion for, and empathy with, people by trying to put yourself in the position of the other;

9. Action to be taken only after:

a. Maximum clarity of purpose;
b. Fullest acceptance of responsibility and accountability;
c. Total commitment to an effort of the highest quality;
d. Detailed objective analysis of alternative options based on facts and opinions and not purely on hearsay;
e. Necessary consultation and appropriate mix of logic, intuition and conscience.

10. Eagerness to learn from every single experience life provides, and especially if difficult or troublesome.

We need to try and avoid:

1. Pride and arrogance because our inherent qualities are God-given, no achievement occurs singly; you believe you are unique which is never so and Time ultimately erases all memory of human action;

2. Greed for power and wealth, and temptation and lust for gratification of sensual organs, because it inevitably involves you in corruption, it leads to your glorification, losing your sense of balance and linking you to a minuscule segment of society with abnormal lifestyles and out of touch with reality;

3. Anger, hatred and malice when things go against our wishes, leading to loss of self-control and words and deeds which hurt or harm others, because no retraction is ever possible and no apology ever adequate to restore personal relationships once spoiled;

4. Envy and jealousy, when others are or do better, unfortunately almost a reflex with humanity, because each of us is allotted happiness or suffering as our role in life decrees;

5. Worry, anxiety and fear of the future, not yet with us, as also regret for the past now unchangeable, because it is an undiluted waste of precious energy;

6. Superstitions and irrational action based on them either to ensure things going in our favor or to prevent them from going against us, because events are not influenced in this manner;

7. Prejudices and intolerance for different kinds of behavior because they prevent a correct assessment of people and adversely affect relationships;

8. Expectations from people in return for whatever you might have done for them; and giving advice unless they are close enough not to misunderstand;

9. Taking people into confidence without being extremely selective since it is almost impossible for humanity to keep secrets;

10. Criticizing and complaining about people or events especially if you can do nothing about it, because it is utterly useless and only leads to frustration all around."

This is one of my favorite incidents about spiritual seeking. In the case of most smaller communities – sub-sects of the main Hindu religion – each one has its own *Guru* who is venerated and revered by the members of that particular community. In one such community, a few months after a new young *Guru* was initiated and appointed, his mother went to visit him. When she saw him, she noticed that he had lost a certain amount of weight – he looked thin. She expressed this fact to him, obviously as a mother with her own feelings. The young *Guru* advised her, obviously in the role as a *Guru* of the community, in response to her expression of concern: "You must give up attachments." Promptly the mother replied: "*Guruji*, it is not I who have taken *sannyas*."

The man of
understanding does not have
any problems in his day-to-day living,
because the very understanding comports
the surrender of the sense
of personal doership to the Will of God.

CHAPTER 8

*𝒯*HE
UNDERSTANDING

It was a lazy, hot afternoon in late August – a Sunday holiday –
and Ramakrishna Paramahamsa was napping in his surprisingly breezy room
after the noon meal. An account of the gathering was retold:

"The visitors place their foreheads on the fragrant floor of
the Master's room, prostrating with awe before this *rishi* of the
present age, who so clearly manifests the stature of a world teacher.
Yet the Master dresses like a simple villager. Just the previous day,
a new visitor found the Master strolling through the rose garden
carefully examining the blossoms, and mistook him for one of the
Temple gardeners. The Calcutta gentleman called peremptorily
to pick him a rose. Bruising his tender fingers, the selfless sage
quickly and quietly complied.

We now observe Ramakrishna as he enters the mood of
teacher. The child of the Divine Mother mysteriously disappears,
and we encounter the lion's roar of a fully awakened Buddha.

Ramakrishna: *The objectless, subjectless insight into the
essential nature of Consciousness – or atmajnana – is radically
investigated and unfolded only by a small group of Vedanta scriptures,
such as the Ashtavakra Samhita [or Gita]. Not many seekers will be
drawn to this most uncompromising discipline of direct knowing. Persons
qualified for this path of knowledge feel completely comfortable and joyful
when renouncing all notions of separate, substantial self-existence
[renouncing all sense of personal doership]. They are the true
proponents of Advaita – non-duality – because they genuinely understand*

that they do not exist apart from the Supreme Reality: the knower and the known are simply not two [there is only knowing]. *Reality alone shines: neither two nor even one – beyond description or calculation.*

Your very life-breath must become the conscious timeless affirmation of Reality: So'Ham, So'Ham – I am IT. Only the dualistic imagination perceives some separate practitioner who makes this primordial affirmation, So'Ham. To lose completely any notion of separate self [as the doer], *no matter how subtle or instinctive, is the true definition of sannyasa, renunciation. Non-duality is renunciation* [self-doership is what is renunciated]. *As long as one imagines oneself to exist independently as initiator or recipient of various actions – either as actor, agent, subject or object of any kind – then one has not renounced completely... As long as one holds exclusively the personal view – 'Such is my responsibility and I must perform it, because if I do not take the initiative, it will never get done' – one is not ready to engage in Advaita Vedanta.*

Nonetheless, regardless of differences in the capacity to understand, the fact remains that this same Truth holds for every conscious being... When the practitioner is consciously identified, not with any expression of awareness but with the living principle of awareness – breathing So'Ham, So'Ham – there remains no sense of intrinsic involvement with polarities such as good and evil, virtue and vice, self and other, existence and non-existence. However, when one identifies with activity rather than with principle, manifesting an ego that claims to generate various chains of events, then the tensions between polar opposites split that person's consciousness, creating various forms of obvious and subtle suffering.

My dear friend, Krishnakishore, a radical Vedantist on fire with the most intense renunciation, affirms with total conviction and authenticity: 'I am the principle of empty space, within which and by which all phenomena transparently manifest'. This great practitioner is not a monk. He attends skillfully to his social and family responsibilities in the same effective way that space permits various phenomena to be displayed. This is an advanced level of realization, an inward sannyas, not a mere intellectual position that any student of Ashtavakra Samhita might claim.

Once one has received the initiatory transmission of Advaita Vedanta from an illumined sage, not simply from a textbook, it becomes fruitful to practice the radical attitude that one is free from individuality, free from particularity, free from any imaginable limits. One can sense when this attitude is approaching true atmajnana – omniconscious knowing, without any veils of knower or known, totally beyond mere playing with words and intellectual posing. How? Just as one easily distinguishes a ripe mango from a green mango.

Then, one unconsciously affirms with every breath, every heartbeat, every intention and action: 'I am freedom from every limitation. I am the principle of timeless awareness.' On the other hand, the function of conventional identified consciousness – in the personal sphere, the social sphere, the religious sphere – is to proclaim various limits, barriers, partitions, distinctions, definitions and frontiers, and then to submit to these abstractions, gradually becoming entirely enslaved by them. In effect, this means constantly repeating, consciously or unconsciously: 'I am not free. I am bound up in all these categories of thought and perception.' Such a conditioned person obsessively and even instinctively repeats: 'I am worthless. I am superficial. I am incapable of transcendent insight. I am irrevocably immersed in family, career and political concern.' This is not a mere verbal repetition but a routine ritual invocation of limited existence by the entire body-mind organism of the falsely isolated individual, identified consciousness. This state of illusory bondage becomes increasingly vivid and convincing. Choose instead, to affirm with your whole being: 'I know that Supreme Reality alone exists, and this transcendent knowing is itself that Reality.' How can such non-dualistic awareness ever become limited by notions such as bondage, impurity or imperfection?"

A very sincere seeker went to Ramana Maharshi, and with tears in his eyes, confessed that he was a simple man and learned discussions went over his head and his confusion remained. He requested, with much emotion, that the Maharshi would very kindly tell him in very few, simple words what he should do as spiritual effort. Ramana Maharshi told him: *"Just relax – and let go!"*

The wisdom of *Advaita* in daily living is clearly seen in the actions of the sage, inasmuch as there is no clear separation between understanding and action. Such happening is also seen in the case of an ordinary person on such occasions when it is generally said that he is 'in form'. One's performance at any job is said to be 'in form' when his movements are seen to be smooth and efficacious – effortless: effortless because there is no 'me' wanting to succeed in what he is doing. There is only the working mind functioning smoothly and efficiently in the present moment without the thinking mind functioning in the future, worried about the results.

All action of the sage in his day-to-day living follows his true understanding, without the hesitation and doubts of the thinking mind, because the sense of personal doership has been totally eliminated through the Ultimate Understanding. In other words, all action that follows true understanding would necessarily be spontaneous, natural action in which the individual 'me' as the doer would be not only absent, but actually irrelevant.

The principle is that if nothing is prevented or obstructed from going its own way – 'doing its own thing' – the established harmony of the universe would not be disturbed because all the processes in the universe are interrelated. This may shock people. It may be taken.to reflect Kropotkin's anarchist theory that a social order will emerge of itself, even from a possible anarchy if people are left alone to find for themselves what pleases them and are allowed to follow their nature and bent of mind, because individuality is intrinsic in the community and the order of nature is not a forced order. The individual would certainly not accept this principle because he thinks in terms of his own individual happiness, whereas the principle is based on the totality of manifestation and its functioning. The individual would refute the argument and would certainly press the point that such an argument would lead to chaos in the world. Whenever someone did put up this argument, one Master's dry comment would be to ask what is the condition in the world today when things are not allowed to have their own natural way and there is quite some regulation all around!

It is said that the Buddha was not in favor of setting forth a system of philosophy that would be consistent enough to satisfy intellectual curiosity on conventional lines. When He was pressed for answers in such situations that He considered irrelevant from the point of view of actual experience, He would 'maintain a noble silence'. Ramana Maharshi, too, would look over the shoulders of a visitor into the distance when the visitor kept repeating questions that the Maharshi had earlier indicated as being not relevant and, therefore, of a distracting nature.

There is the most interesting story of the Chinese sage, Hui-Neng, who is said to have had his first *satori* when, even as a boy, he happened to hear someone reading the *Vajrachhedica*. He was so overwhelmed by the experience that almost without any further thought he set out for the famous Hung-Jan's monastery for a formal initiation and spiritual training. He was at the time known to have been an illiterate peasant. When Hui-Neng arrived at the monastery, Hung-Jan at once recognized the depth of Hui-Neng's insight and at once put him to work in the kitchen area, perhaps fearing that the majority of the scholarly monks in the monastery might reject him because of his humble origins. In due course, Hung-Jan announced that he was in search of a successor and that he would form his judgment after each monk had submitted a poem based on his understanding. It was generally assumed that the office would go to the chief monk Shen-Hsiu and so no one really attempted to compete.

The chief monk posted the following poem on the board in beautiful, flowing brush strokes that clearly proclaimed generations of culture behind them, but he submitted his poem anonymously with the intention that he would claim authorship only if it received the approval of the Patriarch:

"The body is the Bodhi Tree;
The mind like the bright mirror standing,
Take care to wipe it all the time, and allow no dust to cling."

When Hui-Neng was passing by, he noticed the poem, read it, and spontaneously added below in his rough unlettered hand the lines:

"There never was a Bodhi tree,
Nor bright mirror standing,
Basically, not one thing exists,
So where is the dust to cling?"

The Patriarch, who had kept an eye on the board, came out and read both the poems. He knew who the authors were, knew also the amount of careful effort that must have gone into the chief monk's poem (and the reason for submitting it anonymously), and also the utter spontaneity and conviction with which Hui-Neng had carelessly dashed off his words.

The Patriarch sent for Hui-Neng quietly that night, and conferred the office of Patriarch on him by handing over to him the traditional robe and begging bowl (said to have come down from the Buddha himself) which were the official insignia. Then he told Hui-Neng to flee into the mountains because when the news was known, the powerful chief monk, Shen-Hsiu, would do him harm. It is said that Shen-Hsiu did pursue Hui-Neng, overtook him at about mid-day, and tried to pull the robe and bowl from his hands. Hui-Neng quietly put them down on a rock beside the path, and said to him: "These are only things which are no more than symbols. If you want the things so much, you are welcome to them." It is further said that when Shen-Hsiu eagerly tried to grab them, he could not even move them because "they had become heavy as the mountain". Then he fell at Hui-Neng's feet and said: "Forgive me, I really do want the teaching, not the thing." Hui-Neng made him sit by his side on the rock and told him gently: "It is really very simple. Stop thinking this is mine and this is not mine – and then tell me, where are you? Tell me also, what did your face look like before your parents were born?"

A friend of the Chinese sage went to visit Chuang-Tzu in order to offer his condolences on the death of his wife, and found him sitting with his legs stretched out, pounding on an inverted tub and singing lustily. When he expressed his displeasure at this unseemly conduct, Chuang-Tzu said:

"When my wife died, do you think I did not grieve like anyone else? Then I looked back at her beginning and the time before she was born; not only before she was born, but the time before she had a body, not only the time before she had a body, but the time before she had a spirit. In the midst of the confused jumble of mystery and wonder there was a change and she had a spirit; a second change and she had a body; another change and she was born. Now there has been a further change and she is dead. It is exactly like the progression of seasons – spring, summer, autumn, winter."

Some time or the other, in the course of day-to-day living of many people, the urge arises to have a reliable person as a 'spiritual' guide. It may be a sudden crisis in life, or just a persistent feeling that in the absence of a reliable anchor in life, the day-to-day living appears empty of purpose. So one finds oneself guided by friends or relatives to someone they consider their *Guru*, whom they meet regularly for *darshan* and advice. Very often, unfortunately, one finds oneself in the presence of someone who has great familiarity with the key words, phrases and formulas, and repeats them indiscriminately and considers the repetition to be the end in itself.

How many pseudo-pundits and pseudo-saints and pseudo-*gurus* have we not come across or heard of, who pride themselves on their ability to recite the entire *Bhagavad Gita* or other classics? The only danger, of course, is that the real significance behind the key words and phrases is more than likely not only to be pushed into the background, but even totally ignored. The danger is that the formula ($E=MC^2$) might be taken to be the comprehensive Theory of Relativity.

Actually, the birth of the several formulas in the *Advaita* philosophy could easily be imagined in a scene in the hoary past, at the end of a series of really enlightened talks and dialogues and discussions among a group of highly trained and intuitively gifted aspirants. The ancient, enlightened sage would be most respectfully requested by the disciples to condense the entire teaching in one sentence or formula that could at once rekindle the joyous spark of understanding or at least empty the mind into a state of vacancy. Thus could have arisen the inspired formula like *Tat Twam Asi* – That Thou Art. But what happens very often is that what must have emerged as the crowning glory of a very deep lesson in mysticism, the *mahavakya* (the great sentence) is now treated as the starting point, without the substantial content of preparation that must have originally gone into it. The result very often is a superficial familiarity with the formulas, which breeds "a kind of reverential insensibility, a stupor of the spirit, an inward deafness to the meaning of the sacred words".

The essence of the teaching primarily concerns the one Divine Reality substantial to the totality of the phenomenal manifestation, the *One* without which no manifestation would be possible, let alone the perceiving and cognizing of it: the Universal Consciousness, or as the Chinese philosophers called it, the Mind. Consciousness is all there is, the manifestation and everything therein being an appearance within the Consciousness. Human beings – and all the sentient beings, the worms and the animals – are in fact mere appearances forming a part of that total phenomenal manifestation and, other than that, they have no autonomous or independent existence. This is the Truth, whether human beings like it or not, whether they are able to accept it or not. Indeed, the apperception of this Truth is all the Self-realization or enlightenment that can be expected to happen. Such understanding, the Ultimate Understanding, of course, must be not merely on an intellectual basis but it must be an apperception in sheer depth and utter conviction.

The most pertinent point is that such apperception can only take place in a mind (the content of Consciousness) that is not already cluttered up with fears and hopes of the individual self concerning the phenomenal sensual world, in a mind that is, therefore, in a vacant or fasting state and thus receptive to such apperception. Such a vacant mind (not only not an idiot's mind but an extremely keen and alert mind) is what is described by the Sufi poet, Jalaluddin Rumi, as one equipped with the moral "astrolabe of God's mysteries". The ordinary sensual mind is only concerned with the moving, changing process of *becoming*, whereas That-Which-Is is the perennial state of Being. The individual self can be concerned only with the process of becoming, changing from one to the other. It is only when the individual entity with the sense of personal doership or volition is annihilated that the state of Being can be apperceived and realized in noumenal dimension.

The other basic point concerning the apperception of the Divine Ground is that this state, being basically unchangeable, is not to be 'attained' or 'achieved'. All that is necessary is for the conditioning of becoming or changing, which has superimposed itself upon the perennial state, to be removed. The process – if it can be called that – is not one of creating or achieving something by positive effort by an individual entity, but truly the negative one of removing the obnubilation or covering – *maya* – that has imposed itself on the original state, through the negative functioning of an understanding in depth. *Understanding is all.* As Meister Eckhart has put it: "The knower and the known are one. Simple folk imagine that they should be able to see God as if He stood there, and they here. This is not so. God and I, we are one in Understanding." God alone Is.

The futility of making positive efforts to grasp Reality has been beautifully expressed by Young-Chia Ta-Shih:
"It is only when you hunt for It that you lose It;
You cannot take hold of It, but then you cannot get rid of It;
And while you cannot do either, It goes on Its own way;

> You remain silent and It speaks;
> You speak, and It is dumb;
> The great Gate of Charity is wide open,
>   with no obstacles before It."

Over the years, an unnecessary mystery concerning the essential nature of things has been made by those who have not realized the Truth. Those who have, say how simple the whole thing is, the only condition being the tremendous intensity of the longing for it. Indeed, that is the only irony and mystery about it: you cannot see It, you cannot feel It, only because you really do not want to. You do not want to, because you are either too busy enjoying the many 'good' things of life or too busy feeling sorry for yourself at the sorrow and unhappiness which many 'bad' things of life are causing you. All you really have to do is to be quiet and silent, and you cannot but feel It. Without It – Consciousness – you would be a dead body. Even when Consciousness is in abeyance – as in deep sleep – you are not aware of either the world or anything in it. In fact, *you are Consciousness* if you want to see Reality as Unicity. In fact, Consciousness is at work all the time, directing the subtle physiological intelligence to work the ceaseless processes of breathing, assimilation, etc.

What can it be but Consciousness that causes the insignificant seed to develop into a fully formed fetus or a mighty tree? One does not have 'one's' consciousness. The fact is that Consciousness has the many sentient beings – "the ten thousand things", as the Taoist says – as its manifold physical mechanisms through which it functions and operates the world and the rest of the manifestation. The totality of the functioning of the manifestation is Consciousness, perceived and cognized by Consciousness through the many psychosomatic mechanisms known as human beings and other sentient beings. This is the *lila*. A person who has been able to see this fact is bound to see that the Consciousness or "God" in Meister Eckhart's phrase, the Creator and perpetual re-Creator of the universe "becomes and dis-becomes" in the totality of the phenomenal functioning, that it is the Divine Ground in which the entire phenomenality is rooted. All that is necessary is to be able to discard the sense of a separate entity with independence of choice and action.

To a certain extent, the simple truth gets shrouded in mystery because of the very severe limitations of the word and the language. Language is like a single beam of light that is used to light up an enormous scene, and then it can only be shown piece by piece. It is, therefore, repeatedly asserted by the Masters that Reality can only be apperceived by a sudden flash of lightning. What the artist visualizes as the finished piece of sculpture, the ordinary man can only see as a piece of stone. It is only by removing the unnecessary portions of the stone that the sculptor produces the final image.

In an extremely apt and lovely extract, the 5th century author known as 'Dionysius the Areopagite' explained the situation thus:

"For this is not unlike the art of those who carve a life-like image from stone, removing from around it all that obstructs clear vision of the latent form, revealing its hidden beauty solely by taking away by a scription, for we ascribe attributes to Him when we start from universals to particulars; but going up from particulars to universals we remove things from Him in order that we may know openly the unknowable which is hidden in and under all things that may be sensually known."

In dealing with the subject of the Divine Ground or Truth or Reality or God – or whatever – the question that often gets buried under the avalanche of words and emotions is the one that comes from a sincere person who says: "I am not particularly interested in spiritual concepts or religious tenets. And I am often told that I should be interested in deeper things, other than the material things in life. Why should I be concerned with, say, the Ultimate Reality?"

If the answer happens to be, "to know God or one's true nature or whatever is the basic and ultimate purpose in life", the question would again be asked in all humility and sincerity, "why?" The question is valid and must be faced with equal sincerity. The point really is that the personal individual or self is, for all practical purposes, certainly entitled to lead his life in perfect freedom to identify himself with almost any number of possible objects: food, drink, sex, wealth, power, fame; wife and children, friends and relatives; hobbies, collections; clubs, profession, politics, ambitions; pains, illnesses, hopes, fears or any number of combinations of these things. Why should a nice, ordinary contented person be expected to be interested in the meaning and purpose of life – or in God or Reality?

The genuine answer to this valid question could only be: "You are quite right, there really is no need for you now to concern yourself with religion, God or Reality or whatever. If the need arises in the future, you can then deal with it." There is a base for this genuine answer, founded on certain inalienable facts of life: *a)* The individual entity – the ego – simply does not exist and can, therefore, have no real problems other than what the mind might conceive. Hence, the answer of the Masters to the seeker, "produce your ego and I shall personally smash it to bits for you"; *b)* When in the totality of the phenomenal functioning there is need for an ego (fictitious though it be) in a particular psychosomatic apparatus to think in terms of God or Reality, it is the ground of all being – Consciousness – by whom the mind will naturally be translated into appropriate thought-pattern and necessary action; *c)* Since there is no such thing as an individual self or entity with autonomous or independent choice of action, the very question of an individual self seeking union with Reality is ludicrous; *d)* All that exists is Consciousness functioning in totality through the mechanisms of multitudinous sentient beings. All events – 'good', 'bad' or 'indifferent' from the viewpoint of the fictitious ego or the split-mind – are part of the totality of functioning by the Source or Energy or God according to a Cosmic Law, of which the intellect of the human being could not possibly have any understanding in a million years.

In other words, the individual entity or ego is a purely fictitious creation of *maya* or the divine hypnosis that arose when the Universal Consciousness identified itself with the individual psychosomatic mechanism, so that interhuman relationships could happen to form the basis of 'life' as we know it. It is Universal Consciousness, the energy immanent in all sentient beings and in everything that is phenomenally manifested, which truly functions in totality. And, therefore, a particular 'individual's' thought will turn towards God and Reality only when the Totality feels the need of that happening, not a moment earlier, or later.

This – the purest *Advaita* – that the individual being a mere fiction and, therefore, without any independence to act on his own initiative independently, is not generally acceptable to many people because for them free will and volition comprise the very basis of their life. Those who are genuinely and sincerely interested in the Divine

Ground as formless Reality cannot and do not dispute the inescapable logic behind the illusoriness of the ego or entity, but they just cannot 'let go'. And this is easily understandable because it is the ego itself which is supposed to let go, which is supposed to annihilate itself. And this is truly impossible.

It is for this reason that the Masters from time immemorial have been repeating ceaselessly that it can only happen, that it is only the deepest understanding, the deepest conviction – the apperception – that can bring about the sudden transformation. This apperception cannot be of the same dimension of the space-time intellect, which is merely the split-mind of subject-object that came about when Consciousness identified itself with the individual body-mind organism for the specific purpose of perceiving the manifestation as the perceiver perceiving a perceived object. Apperception is of a totally different dimension – timeless and spaceless, the whole-mind of the Universal Consciousness. And such apperception, being timeless, happens suddenly and spontaneously in the flash of the moment, and the individual sense of personal doership gets annihilated in the ego.

How difficult it is even to understand intellectually the concept of sudden enlightenment in which the fictitious ego cannot possibly have any active part, can be seen from the manner in which the concept has been understood – or misunderstood – even by well-known and sincere contemporary thinkers. One famous philosopher-writer dealt with "*metanoesis*", a happening that he described as a "sudden convulsion or complete revulsion of consciousness", and said that it is the "realization of a 'no-mind' state, free from an intellectual attachment to the ego principle". The author then went on to say that this 'no-mind' state exists, as it were, "on a knife-edge between the carelessness of the average sensual man and the strained over-eagerness of the zealot for salvation". To "achieve" it, he continued, you must walk delicately and to "maintain" it, you must combine tremendous determination with "a total submission to the promptings of the spirit".

Thus, what is in fact a *happening* is often described as a prescribed process of 'conscious' discrimination between the personal self and the Self that is Brahman, between the individual ego with volition and the Universal Mind. One might well wonder, with considerable frustration, 'who' is to do this conscious discrimination! These proponents of enlightenment understand – and speak – from the viewpoint of an individual understanding something with the object of achieving something. The sage speaks from the viewpoint of the understanding as such – it *is* the understanding, the apperception that is speaking, and not the individual.

Meister Eckhart, the German mystic, has stated the matter this way:

"A man must become truly poor and as free from his own creaturely will as he was when he was born. And I tell you, by the Eternal Truth, that so long as you desire to fulfill the Will of God, and have any hankering after eternity and God, for just so long you are not truly poor. He alone has true spiritual poverty who wills nothing, knows nothing, desires nothing."

With the totality of the phenomenal functioning as the perspective, difficulties cannot arise, but when anything is considered from the viewpoint of the fictitious individual, difficulties will never cease. With the dawning of apperception, the ego is exposed as the empty myth that it is, and by the very exposure is instantly annihilated. If the enlightenment is a happening in totality and not something which the spurious entity achieves – the individual psychosomatic apparatus being merely the phenomenal instrument for such a happening – in what particular circumstances does enlightenment occur? Although enlightenment could occur anywhere at any time, Totality, or the Source, is not bound by any laws or regulations of space-time duality. It can be seen, however, that wherever enlightenment has occurred, the ground has already been prepared for it, although in certain cases this fact may not be easily apparent.

In the day-to-day living of the common man, religion as such has its basis – whatever the religion – in a search for God by an individual entity for its own personal betterment in this world or the conceptual world beyond. Religions variously prescribe the progress of the entity from a lower plane of existence to a higher one in an ascending scale, at the top of which is God, the highest entity who eternally controls the manifest universe. Such a scheme naturally envisages the progress from the lower plane to the higher plane only through hard, intensive personal effort until the entity reaches the very top, close to the supreme entity. Everything is associated with a divine entity, prayers are personified and His Grace is considered essential for material and spiritual prosperity.

During the course of this spiritual history there have been occasional rare instances throughout the world – but more so in the East and especially in India – where an intuitive approach to the Truth produced a radical vision of transcendence. In such transcendent vision, Reality became transported into a different dimension wherein the manifested appearance was seen as illusory and the absent unmanifest was perceived as the Reality. Such were the mystics and sages who intuitively understood that what they had apperceived was truly exceptional and could not possibly be understood by the average person who was too deeply involved with himself as an independent entity with volition or choice of decision and action.

Such a separate entity could not possibly have even a glimpse into the mystery of transcendence and Unicity, which for some divine reason the sages were privileged to apprehend. Indeed it could well be that the sages found that any inclination they had of sharing this mysterious knowledge with others would not only be an exercise in futility, but could unnecessarily get them into serious trouble both with the traditional religious leaders and with the law of the realm. So it was that these sages continued to live their lives quietly without any fuss among their neighbors, and some might have even preferred to live as hermits away from human society. However, whenever they found kindred spirits on the threshold of this transcendental knowledge needing their guidance, they undoubtedly did their best to help them. Those who received such help would naturally regard the sage as so superior a person that they would consider him as the very personification of Truth. It is undoubtedly in this way that the extraordinary relationship of the *Guru* and the disciple came into being in India, and which seems to be beyond the logical comprehension of the Western people: that one human being could hold another apparently ordinary human being in such obvious reverence, far beyond just respect!

The basis of the transcendental way is the very antithesis of the traditional religion, inasmuch as the individual entity is considered to be a fiction, totally non-existent. And the 'knowledge' that such an entity is supposed to acquire is considered not different from ignorance, as both knowledge (information) and ignorance are interrelated opposites of a polarity. And finally, the ultimate attainment is the realization of the Unicity, which is tantamount to the total annihilation of the separate entity that was doing the seeking! This view of Reality has undoubtedly prevailed under different names, of course in a very limited way, over the last several hundred years in different parts of the East – the more well-known being *Advaita* in India, Chan or Tao in China and Zen in Japan. The essential characteristic in all of them could be termed 'Self-inquiry' – 'who or what am I?', or something similar. The basis of such Self-inquiry naturally is the understanding that 'I' am not the psychosomatic apparatus, the body that is generally considered to be the symbol of man's individual existence; and, *ipso facto*, the image of God as the supreme entity has had to undergo a revolutionary change.

Xenophanes, in the 6th century B.C., criticized and ridiculed the prevailing tendency of personifying God in man's own likeness, of considering the essential Beingness not as the infinite Intemporality but as a projection of man's own ego: "While the Thracians would give their gods blue eyes and red hair, the Africans would make their gods snub-nosed and give them a black complexion." As C. M. Bakewell has cited in his *Source Book in Ancient Philosophy*, Xenophanes said: "If oxen and lions had hands, and could paint with their hands and fashion images as men do, they would make the pictures and images of their gods in their own likeness; horses would make them like horses, oxen like oxen."

It was undoubtedly in order to wean man away from this anthropomorphic representation of God that the Buddha is supposed to have ignored and even discouraged questions about God. Of course, because of this there has been a misconception through the ages that the Buddha was an agnostic. Actually, all that the scriptures could do was to point the way to the existence of the Higher Power or the Self or the *Paramatman* or Tao or any other name, and so various myths and symbols have been used to make this process of pointing easier. But, unfortunately, this fact has been generally ignored and the pointing signboard – the symbol – has been mistaken to mean God: the map has become mistaken for the territory.

It is certainly for this reason that many a Master has enjoined absolute faith in and total surrender to 'God', though, of course, the real basis of the *Advaitic* teaching has been that God as such is merely one of man's concepts. In fact, however, there was no inconsistency – the inconsistency, if any, has been in the understanding. For anyone who could conceive of the essential Unicity as the totality of the unknown Potential, the Plenum, from which emerged the totality of the manifested known (and which would ultimately merge with the Potential), it was easy to apprehend that God as an entity, even though all-powerful, was merely a concept. The ultimate goal in any case is the annihilation of the ego, of the identification with a separate entity with the sense of personal doership, either through intuitive understanding or through intellectual surrender depending, of course, on the respective programming in the body-mind organism.

Self-inquiry is essentially an inquiry into the nature of man because, whatever man may think or conceive of God as the Creator, all of it would be conjecture and conceptualization. The only Truth, the only thing of which man can be certain, the only thing he *knows* is that he exists, that he is alive – I AM. In deep sleep, he is quite unaware of the world, and yet when he wakes up again, he knows not only that he is alive but that he was alive even during the period of his sleep, because the impersonal Awareness of I AM was there even in his sleep.

It cannot be gainsaid that abstraction is certainly necessary for communication between people. The word 'tree' brings about a comparatively communicable basis for exchange of information between two individuals; otherwise a whole lot of description would be necessary every time one talked about what is known as a 'tree'! But the fact of the matter is that abstractions and conventional signs and symbols are necessary for comprehending events one at a time on the 'spotlight' basis. Nevertheless, such a method is likely to be not only inadequate but misleading when one talks about day-to-day living in a universe in which events are happening not only all together at one time but with incredible rapidity. Only a powerful floodlight with a wide periphery would function in such circumstances for any comprehension to be possible.

Trying to understand day-to-day living within the working of the universe in terms of linear thought and verbal concepts is a little like trying to see an enormous mural by Michelangelo in the dark with a single dull ray of a pen-light! The working of the human body seems frighteningly complex to a medical student because he tries to comprehend it in bits and pieces, one at a time, whereas to an experienced physician or surgeon it is a comparatively simple matter: his experience has turned his spotlight into a powerful floodlight. Indeed, the success of the expert in any field depends on the extent to which he keeps the central, conscious thought in the background and is able to permit the general intuitive, unconscious thought to take over. This is precisely what the spiritual Master means when he repeatedly urges his listeners to listen totally: to ignore the individual words which distract attention and allow the deepest meaning in those words to penetrate into their very being, that kind of meaning which would lose all significance if any effort were made to communicate it to someone else – or even to oneself – by linear thinking, by verbalization. In other words, it is most necessary to allow the intuitive understanding to take root without any obstruction so that it can flower and blossom. Again, true understanding of Reality cannot come about by "cumbersome calculations of theology, metaphysics and logical interference", which only serve as obstructions.

It has been my experience during my morning talks that a fairly simple point (from my viewpoint!) was easily grasped by a fairly simple-minded person, but escaped the apprehension of someone else renowned for his academic achievements. This caused a certain amount of confusion among the visitors, too. The simple answer is that in such situations the academic mind produced a peculiar kind of thought pattern, which prevented the apprehension of a subject that was not based on a purely scientific and dialectic approach to problems that occurred in one's day-to-day living – problems that usually did not have specific clear-cut distinctions! In other words, problems in our day-to-day living do not present a clear demarcation between black and white but do present a very large grey area. Apparently, an identical kind of difficulty prevented the older, theoretical physicists from clearly understanding the principles of subatomic physics while the newer, younger breed of physicists in their twenties took to the new physics like ducks to water.

Another real difficulty in regard to the communication of Reality in relation to day-to-day living is that the use of the transitive verb with a subject has become so unavoidable that the use of the passive tense without the subjective 'who' immediately gives rise to a certain amount of suspicion that something is being deliberately hidden. When the Master explains that 'thinking' happens or 'doing' happens without any individual 'doer', the mind-intellect finds it extremely difficult to accept. One generally expects the verb 'know', for instance, to have a subject who knows and an object to be known. In other words, the subject-object-verb convention prevents the clear perceiving of the fact that our phenomenal world is more a collection of processes rather than entities; day-to-day living, and the things and human beings in this living, are in fact events or happenings rather than 'doings' by individual entities. Then again, for instance, we can at once understand that the sun shines on the various objects in the world, but it is not so easy to comprehend that it is the process of shining, rather than the sun, which is the more important of the two, that shining is the very nature of the sun rather than a deliberate doing by the sun.

Another very real difficulty in facing problems in day-to-day living is the fact that every human being is forced to adopt, in the process of living together in a community, several conventional roles. This involves an enormous amount of conditioning concerning law and order, ethics, conduct according to social rule and regulations, etc. The difficulty operates at every step to such an extent that it is almost impossible to live one's day-to-day life without a *personal identity* in some role or other – husband or wife, father or mother, white-collar worker or blue-collar worker – apart from the roles depending on a variety of hobbies and clubs.

The result is that we are so accustomed, so deeply conditioned, to think in terms of the individual. Therefore, it becomes almost impossible even to think in terms that do not specifically include and involve the individual as a separate entity with autonomous choice of decision and action. It is this conditioning which makes a clearly 'intelligent' human being ask the question: "I understand, at least intellectually, the basis of that eternal state which we all seem to seek, but why is it that, however perfect that state may be, I myself would not have chosen, if I had the choice, to give up my existing state?" This query from an intelligent person shows the depth of the conditioning about the individual entity, though the point of the query is another matter. The point is that the individual entity that seems so clear, so specific, so substantial, is in absolute fact, nothing but a concept, a convention, an inference made up of certain selected memories over a certain past period. And, most importantly, what in fact exists is nothing more than a three-dimensional object which, together with billions of other objects, constitutes the totality of phenomenal manifestation. The interesting fact is that this seemingly specific entity varies not only as different people see it and evaluate it, but also changes accordingly as the impressions of that particular entity about itself keep on changing!

When one's understanding reaches the higher level, there is the persistent problem of how to live at the practical level of day-to-day living with its continuous problems of decision-making and human relations. The problem specifically boils down to this question: will not the acceptance that the supposed entity is merely an illusory concept, without any kind of real volition or independence of choice and action, upset and weaken the process of living life effectively in day-to-day matters? The problem is very real indeed. The devious answer that the problem itself does not exist for one who is established in the understanding is not easily acceptable to the average seeker. The average seeker is liable to interpret the response as an effort at evasion if he is told: 'establish yourself firmly in the understanding and then see if there is a problem.'

Certainly it is necessary to consider the problem as a real problem for the seeker. For one perspective let us see what Lao-Tzu had to say about this problem, particularly because he did not deal with the principles of any kind of philosophy, but was essentially concerned with practical results, at a time of serious troubles when war led to more wars, treachery was answered by more treachery, and as armies from different factions roamed all over the land and "thorns and brambles grew". He came to the firm conclusion, based not on any religious tenets but on firm impeccable logic and actual experience, that "he who acts harms, he who grabs lets slip." What this means is that where human relations are concerned, force can only defeat itself because every action must produce a reaction, every challenge a corresponding response in a never-ending cause-effect relationship. This would seem to apply to every object and every arrangement, and in all walks of life, whether in personal relationships or business or politics.

I am tempted to narrate an incident that is so apt in this regard, concerning a bank executive I knew personally who was endowed with a more than ordinary powerful ego and, of course, with the intrinsic sense of volition, personal effort and achievement. Whenever he succeeded, it was his personal achievement; whenever he failed, it was the fault of others. He had never realized that he had a job because there were customers, and there was enormous pride and arrogance, particularly because he came from a very poor background. He came to know that a particular customer, whom he had not only neglected but had often insulted and antagonized, had suddenly come into a position of prominence. He knew that he would lose a lot of business if he did not approach this customer himself, which all the other bankers would do. So he arranged with the bank's popular Public Relations Officer (PRO) to do the job. The PRO succeeded in persuading the influential customer after a lot of difficulty, and arranged for him to call at the bank. An appointment was fixed, and the PRO warned the haughty executive of the consequences if he failed to keep his temper in control while dealing with the customer this time. On the day of the appointment, everything seemed to go well, the executive had welcomed the customer with unusual warmth and unaccustomed humility, and the PRO, with a sigh of relief, went to arrange for refreshments. However, by the time he returned after a few minutes, he could hear angry voices inside the room, and almost immediately the customer came storming out of the room, threw an accusatory glance at the bemused PRO, and left without saying a word. When the PRO went into the room he found the executive mopping his face with his handkerchief, muttering, "I certainly did not intend this to happen." How often have we not heard this heart-rending plea! Volition, then, would seem to be merely an illusory inference, and what works always is the programming in the body-mind organism and the destiny of the people concerned – the Will of God.

The problem of how to live effectively at the practical level really does not exist for the man of understanding for the simple reason that he does not see himself as 'doing' anything. With the absence of conceptualizing about the consequences, the 'soft' attitude of the man of understanding – actionless action – succeeds by *being* rather than *doing*, by attitude rather than action, compassion rather than compulsion, by humility and tolerance rather than force and aggression. In the words of Lao-Tzu: "To yield is to be preserved whole... Because the wise man does not contend, no one can contend against him." In other words, simply, day-to-day living for the man of understanding is simply not a problem!

The man of understanding does not have any problem in his day-to-day living because the very Understanding comports the surrender of the sense of personal doership to the Will of God. This results in all action becoming spontaneous action – actionless action – action without tension,

tension, personal responsibility or guilt. Thus, in this abiding in our true nature, peace and serenity will arrive in the acceptance of What-Is as the Will of God, according to a Cosmic Law or a Natural Law. Our 'true nature' is the Universal Consciousness, the impersonal sense of Presence – I AM. It is this Universal Consciousness that the saint Tukaram addresses as God, and sings: "Wherever I go, you are my constant companion, leading me by the hand; taking over all my responsibilities and worries, you provide constant support for me."

When we discuss problems in our day-to-day living, they do not include any problems concerning our basic needs of food, clothing and shelter. To those below the poverty line who, very unfortunately do have such problems, any word would be adding an insult to injury. So, for our usual problems in day-to-day life, we should be aware that such problems concern some kind of knowing or understanding. Here again, in such problems, a very real difficulty exists in our linear type of thinking which includes the grammatical convention that a transitive verb like 'know' must have a subject and a predicate: there cannot be 'knowing' without someone who knows and something to be known.

Our identification with this convention is so powerful that we cannot grasp the fact that there can be 'knowing' or 'understanding' as such without the knower and the known. This inability to put down the ghost of the individual entity – a creation of *maya* or divine hypnosis – shows the extent to which we let conventions and concepts rule our lives. This is indeed the basis of the persistent obsession, 'what will happen to me when I die?' The obvious answer to this question would seem to be, 'you will be precisely what you were before your parents were born.' The question, in other words, is as misconceived as the question 'what happens to my lap when I stand up or to my fist when I open my hand?' If nothing else, let us hope that our mental conditioning would be weakened at least to some extent by remembering the summary of the Buddha's teaching in the *Vishuddimagga*:

"There is suffering but none who suffer,
There is the event, but no doer thereof;
There is nirvana, but no one seeking it,
There is the path, but none to travel it."

The only certain thing in life is death, and obviously death is the end of everything. This was the perspective in which death was viewed in the West until the early 1970s: death meant the end of everything, so what was there to think about, except perhaps that one must make the best of one's opportunities in this life to achieve whatever it is that one wanted to achieve. The basic view in the East, by and large, was different: life and death have, since time immemorial, been viewed not as separate events but as a series of connected events in the flow of time.

In the 1970s, there was a sudden explosion of interest in the West about the phenomenon of death and the process of dying, mainly because of a series of studies made by several psychiatrists, physicians and scientists concerning the process of death. These 'near-death' studies have focused the attention of the Western man on the nature and significance of the phenomenon of death, and have thus brought the East and the West together in regard to the question of individual survival after death. The most important point, however, which has been ignored in these near-death studies is the fact that all near-death experiences can only be movements in Consciousness and, therefore, can only be of the *nature* of dreaming and, therefore, conceptual and illusory. Near-death experiences can happen only to the ego, and it just cannot be denied that the ego has no real existence: the ego is purely a concept, an illusion, and it is only when the ego gets totally annihilated that real Beingness can come into being. *Being* is cognized as *That* which, by its very nature, can never be non-being.

In most cases, the interest in this subject is not to know the process, as such, and the principle behind the phenomenon of death, but to find the key to survival of the individual entity, the key to achieving the security that will provide such survival, the immortality of the individual personality. In this incessant search the basic question that is forgotten is: who or what is this individual entity that is afraid of insecurity?

The key to the problem – and the search – is the deepest possible understanding that no individual as such can pull himself out of the perennial stream of life, that he is an inseparable part of the whole manifestation, and that death and life are the inseparable and interrelated duality of an essential whole. And it really is a truism that such deep understanding cannot come out of an intellectual comprehension but only out of a totally different dimension. Intellection is part of phenomenality and the required dimension of apperception must be other than phenomenal, that is to say, it must be noumenal. In other words, the individual comprehension must lose itself and merge itself into noumenal apprehension or apperception in which the individual no longer exists as such and the ego is annihilated.

When existence is accepted and apperceived as an impersonal sense of being alive and present HERE and NOW, the concept of space-time disappears, and the individual entity with his mind and sense of doership gets annihilated. All seeking becomes irrelevant, and all that remains is Impersonal Consciousness, our true nature as the imperishable birthless and deathless Infinity and Intemporality, the purely Subjective 'I'. The only way such apperception can arise is through the acceptance by the mind-intellect (the ego) of its inherent limitation – mind cannot locate its own source – so that mind-intellect gives up its search for meanings and totally surrenders itself. Then the mind becomes a vacant, fasting mind that can lay itself open to the arising of that intuitive apprehension which may be called 'apperception'. Such apperception cannot be 'achieved' for the simple reason that in such efforts it would necessarily be the individual mind that is concerned, and the individual mind is a split-mind divided into subject-object, separated into the 'self' and the 'other'. It is beyond the capacity of one individual wave to understand its true nature; it is only when it subsides, surrenders and merges into the ocean that it is the ocean.

Deep down, man has always known with intuitive conviction that he really is immortal and it is for this reason that he has always been seeking – consciously or otherwise – for his true nature. And this search is bound to be futile until the realization happens that the ego – the split-mind – cannot possibly find the answer to its own source until he gives up the search in total surrender; the mind cannot transcend mind, the eye cannot see itself.

Self-knowledge is not something to be acquired through a process, as is generally misconceived. Self-knowledge is something to be experienced in the moment when the mind is silent and, therefore, extremely alert; in that alertness of the mind lies a certain motionless silence, that is itself Self-knowledge. Self-knowledge, therefore, is not something apart from day-to-day living. Sometimes, in the midst of the day-to-day activity, a sudden quiet awareness of the activity of the mind happens – a passive awareness of the hopes, fears, wants and joys of the thinking mind of the self, a quiet awareness of the craving of the mind. In that awareness, free of the chatter of the thinking mind, lies the Self-knowledge, the Self-awareness. It must be very clearly understood that this quiet, passive but alert awareness is totally different from self-observation by the mind and investigation by the ego. In other words, Self-knowledge cannot be an intellectual understanding.

The Ultimate Understanding means the end of the questions, the end of the search for knowledge, which means the end of worry and vexation. The spiritual seeker, at a certain stage, understands and accepts that when the Ultimate Understanding suddenly happens, all doubts and questions about the seeking cease altogether. But what happens to the ego, after this happening, during the course of the normal life? Does something happen perhaps gradually? The answer is 'yes'.

The sage realizes that the programming somehow gets mellower: the reactions to the outside world in the body-mind organism have become fewer and less intense. Witnessing becomes more and more obvious with the lessening of the mechanical reactions. For instance, the imminence of a calamity like a war, which did produce at one time a real reaction, now really does not seem such a calamity that may not happen at all, or if it does happen, will take its course and affect everyone according to the destiny of each one. It certainly seems rather amusing that such a thought did at one time create, even for an instant, any concern. Perhaps this is what the Zen Master had in mind when he pronounced that Awakening is always "sudden", while deliverance may take time.

It is an interesting fact that *Advaita* is generally considered as something meant for a retired person to take to in order to fill the vacant time. Some time ago, my nephew, Mahesh, a well-know pediatrician, took me to his colleague, a heart specialist, for a routine check-up. Mahesh mentioned that I have been giving talks on *Advaita* for a number of years. His colleague promptly brushed aside this piece of information with the remark that he was only 52 and that there was plenty of time for him to think about the subject when he retired. Mahesh looked at me and smiled. He told his colleague that most of my visitors were less than 50 years of age and almost everyone wished that he had known about me 10 years earlier! He also added that he himself had found in his own experience that the principle of *Advaita* had been of tremendous help in keeping the stress and tension in day-to-day living under control.

The understanding of *Advaita*, or non-duality, is that the manifest universe is only an appearance that arises in Consciousness, the Source, and, therefore, the Source and the appearance in it are not two. The arising of the apparent universe is not independent of the human beings, nor is it because of the human beings. Both the universe and the human beings therein appear together spontaneously and concurrently like in a dream. It is only Consciousness (like the dreamer) that perceives and cognizes the universe through the instruments of the sentient human beings. There is nothing other than Consciousness: the appearance of the manifested universe and everything therein is the static aspect of Consciousness while sentience (by means of which phenomena are perceived and cognized through the senses in the physical bodies) is the dynamic aspect of Consciousness.

A clear understanding of the nature of the universe, and the human beings therein, would make it clear that the individual human being is essentially a mere phenomenal appearance that is 'being lived' in this dream-manifestation. Thus, the process of being lived totally excludes the idea of any individual volition whereby the human being could decide and pursue what he wanted. In other words, volition – choice, independence of decision and action – can never be an effective factor in phenomenal life.

What has to be realized, in fact, is that every human being is the dreamer who is asleep, who can only witness the dream and everything that happens in it, and can take no active part in the dream. The dreamer is as real as Consciousness, the dreamed character only an illusion like the entire dream. How can the dreamed character play any part or role other than the one that has been assigned to it? When this is clearly apprehended by the human being, such apperception – Self-realization – bridges the separation that was created by his identification with a separate entity with volition and choice of action. And, thus the sense of oppression and fear resulting from the earlier separative aggression gives way to a sense of freedom, an acceptance of What-Is. Absence of fear means a love that can never be the result of any commandment, but only the result of a deep understanding of the Oneness of non-duality.

In other words, with the new understanding of non-duality, that all human beings are merely physical instruments through which the Source or Consciousness functions, and not independent entities with choice of action, life becomes a relaxed, effortless non-volitional living. Such natural living – effortless because of the absence of the illusory sense of personal doership – actually results not in a lazy or wasted living but in a healthier, more meaningful living because of the absence of fear and tension that had earlier sapped our energy in wasteful pursuit of imaginary goals with perverted values.

A really important aspect of the non-volitional living is that the absence of the sense of personal doership leaves the mind open and receptive for the direct, intuitional promptings which must necessarily be far more effective than the working of the limited human intellect. Every renowned scientist, musician, artist, writer, athlete, dancer has confessed that his best performance has been the result of spontaneous and intuitional inspiration – the ego can only recoil and restrict, never expand or create. Finally, the Ultimate Understanding is that there is no one to understand anything.

*Once we have
made a decision,
whatever happens thereafter
has never, ever, been in our control.
No individual can alter
the inevitable flow of life.*

CHAPTER 9

HAT-IS

For I remember stopping by the Way
To watch a Potter thumping his wet Clay:
And with its all-obliterated Tongue
It murmured, 'Gently, Brother, gently, pray!'

For has not such a Story of Old
Down Man's successive generations rolled,
Of such a clod of saturated Earth
Cast by the Maker into Human mould?

– Omar Khayyam, *Rubaiyat*

Life is one perspective and day-to-day living is quite another. It is because of a lack of this discrimination that our day-to-day living has become out of alignment with the movement of life. This lack of discrimination results in many of our frustrations and dissatisfactions. This is precisely the difference between the ordinary person and the man of understanding. What is not realized is that life is like a wide and deep river, flowing incessantly, continuously, always in movement, whereas the day-to-day living for most people, seemingly out of choice, is a preference for the security and stagnancy of little pools beside the river.

In day-to-day living what is generally sought is not the flow of life, the inevitable processes of life – What-Is – but the illusory security and permanence in wealth and status and the observance of ritual and tradition in one's outlook and behavior. The result is that day-to-day living for most people has become insensitive and fearsome. The only answer is a transformation in one's basic understanding of life and living: no individual can alter the inevitable flow of life.

It has always seemed to me that perhaps the greatest wisdom is simply to be surprised at everything. As Chesterton has put it:
"In heaven I shall stand on gold and glass,
Still brooding earth's arithmetic to spell;
Or see the fading of the fires of hell
Ere I have thanked my God for all the grass."

The sense of wonder expresses itself in gratitude; it also expresses itself in humility and humor. The essence of humor lies not in seeing what is funny about other people and things, but what is funny about oneself. Indeed, humor is really the simple art of seeing oneself – the human being – in true proportion with the universe. Laughter is the reaction which gushes out with the realization of the utter insignificance of human knowledge and wisdom and power before the might and the mystery of the cosmos. And, this does not refer only to the great, vast cosmos which the astronomers explore, but also the equally mysterious cosmos which is vast in its littleness, which can be discovered in pools of muddy water and powerful organisms invisible to the eye.

Our lives are surrounded with such mysteries and it surely behooves us to be boundlessly grateful for such a feast, instead of busying ourselves in a lot of pettiness of the mind. It is truly a matter of actual fact that a moment's contemplation of even the smallest piece of God's magnificent handiwork could make hours of pain worthwhile. It is indeed in this way that we learn the art of having a great deal of gratitude even for a very little good. We learn to be grateful to God for the suffering that he has bestowed upon us when we realize how much infinitely worse it could have been.

It is this sense of wonder and gratitude that sets us free, which opens up for us the gates of a great wide universe in which we have the tremendous privilege of being able to explore and enjoy, to look all around us and see on every side a divine mystery. This divine mystery would, of course, include the many terrible things that we can suffer. And then we would see God's mysterious universe in which all the pettiness of the mind would be blown aside with "a great rollicking wind of elemental and essential laughter".

There is an older man, Subbarao, who calls me on the telephone fairly regularly and grumbles about the slow progress in his spiritual seeking. He puts up a problem or a query; I give him my answer. He agrees, but puts up another query beginning with, "yes, but..." This goes on for some time, and my wife grumbles about this conversation later. My answer to my wife is that obviously the gentleman is suffering a great deal, even if it is mostly of his own making; talking to me relieves him of some of this pain. Should I grudge him the time during which I talk to him?

In one of the recent conversations, he asked me about 'prayer'. I told him that, for me, a prayer is not a begging – it is a prayer of gratitude for what I do have. Promptly Subbarao asked me, "you mean I have to thank God for my suffering?" I said, "yes." He could not believe he had heard me right. So, I repeated that he must thank God for his suffering which is much, much smaller than the suffering which many, many in this world are now suffering at this moment, for instance, the many villagers in India and Ethiopia and elsewhere where they do not have enough to eat! For a while, there was no response from Subbarao. Then, quietly, he replied, "I see what you mean" and put down the telephone gently.

To ask if there is an easy way to live one's life is to miss the point altogether. To choose an easy way is to accept that there is a difficult way that you wish to avoid. The only way to walk freely through the day-to-day living is to obey the nature of things in phenomenality – to accept one's own nature and that of others. That is to say, all actions happen through the various body-mind organisms according to the respective programming (genes plus environmental conditioning). The totality of all the happenings through all the body-mind organisms, at any moment, is What-Is in the moment. There is nothing one can do to alter What-Is in the moment because that is what is supposed to be in that moment according to a conceptual Cosmic Law, or according to God's Will. Any action that happens in that moment is part of What-Is in the moment. To accept even the world of senses and concepts totally, without disliking and rejecting anything, is indeed true enlightenment. To set up goals and strive to achieve them is the way the foolish and ignorant individual doer fetters himself into frustration.

It was many years ago, but I still remember a particular incident. My friend and I were going some place. He promptly hailed a taxi, and when the taxi stopped he waved me in, but before he himself got in, he stretched out his hand and put down the little flag indicating that the taxi is occupied. The taxi driver smiled his thanks, and I envied my friend, his easy confidence in dealing with life. Being envious meant unhappiness – unnecessary unhappiness. Then it struck me that my friend also perhaps envied several different attractive traits in my natural programming, causing him unnecessary unhappiness as well.

The cause of unhappiness is non-acceptance of What-Is. Does it mean, then, that one should not try to improve oneself? The answer is that there is no reason not to do so. But there is the distinct possibility of adding frustration to the existing unhappiness, in case of failure to add something that is not an integral part of one's nature. I remember two instances. In one case, a friend of mine always seemed disgruntled in spite of reasonably comfortable circumstances in life. When I visited his place, I found he had a huge collection of 'self-improvement' books! In another, when I was invited by a different friend to his place, I found that he had a huge collection of books on how to invest money for profit. Then his wife whispered to me that he had lost a fortune in speculation! Pursuing something alien to one's nature, and perhaps contrary to one's destiny, could be a sure cause of unhappiness.

You cannot prevent the flow of living from putting you in a situation where you cannot but be in competition with someone. The problem in this situation is that when pitted against petty people, you begin to think that you have to act at their level and, what is worse, you think you were forced to do so and find justification in the fact. But is there a way you can compete without the stress and strain of the competition? The answer could lie in whether or not you expect the result to depend entirely on your own efforts. Everyone's personal experience has been that one's best efforts, including some shortcuts totally against one's principles, have not always resulted in the anticipated good results. Sometimes, on the other hand, one has been able to stick to one's principles and not stoop to the level of the competitors, and yet one has been pleasantly surprised by the results. Very often one has been compelled, against one's reason, to accept the concept of 'destiny'.

If one is able to accept the very strong possibility that everyone's entire life has already been decided by God or fate or whatever – and this is proved by the intuitive wanting to know one's future through astrology or any other means – it could prove a very strong deterrent to falling a victim to our temptations, especially by way of corruption. It would prevent our blaming ourselves for any failure because we did not stoop to the level of our .competitors.

A recent news item reported one author's discovery of popular maxims that pertain to 'being decent in a mean world'. According to the report, Kent M. Keith, a Rhodes Scholar, had written what have come to be known as 'paradoxical maxims' as a student at Harvard University more than 30 years ago. These paradoxical maxims are:
> "People are unreasonable, illogical and self-centered. Love them anyway. If you do good, people will accuse you of selfish, ulterior motives; do good anyway. If you are successful, you will win false friends and true enemies. Succeed anyway.
> The good you do will be forgotten tomorrow; do good anyway.
> Honesty and frankness make you vulnerable. Be honest and frank anyway.
> People favor underdogs but follow only top dogs. Fight for some underdogs anyway.
> What you spend years building may be destroyed overnight; build anyway.
> People may need help but may attack you if you help them; help people anyway.
> Give the world the best you have and you will get kicked in the teeth. Give the world the best you have anyway."

The ultimate message of the paradoxical commandments is the wisdom of being a good citizen, a good neighbor, regardless of returns. But the bottom line is that you will be able to accept these paradoxical maxims only if they truly appeal to your 'true nature' or your natural 'programming' – genes over which you had no control plus your up-to-date environmental conditioning, which includes your upbringing, education and experience in the relevant social and geographical environment. In addition, in spite of your programming, whether or not *in the moment* your action conforms to these paradoxical maxims would depend on your destiny, that is to say, on what is God's Will, according to a conceptual Cosmic Law, which would be impossible for any human being ever to know.

The essential reason why day-to-day living seems to be such a heavy burden is because, for a thousand years and more, one has been conditioned to think constantly in terms of activity – personal effort and activity. And the basis of activity is to choose to accept or reject one thing or another, and in so doing, we are unable to see the true nature of phenomenality. All apparent actions are not the activity or doing of any individual entity, but the happenings brought about through the relevant body-mind organisms, according to their nature or programming, by the one functioning element, the Primal Energy.

And the real cosmic joke is that as soon as you try to stop the activity to achieve passivity, the very effort constitutes your activity. The only answer is: accept What-Is in the moment and be at peace in the Oneness of things. And then comes another cosmic kick: even that acceptance can only *happen* in the Oneness of things. The more you think and talk about it, the further away you wander from the Oneness of things.

The *karma* yoga as in the *Bhagavad Gita,* for the ordinary human being in his daily living, has deep down always created a sense of resistance. What is prescribed, as is generally understood, is a system of ethics focused on unselfish actions: "That activity which is selfish is immoral and that which is unselfish is moral; work is never the cause of misery, selfishness is." Can we not understand that this advice is not generally accepted with enthusiasm? Why does the ordinary human being work? Obviously he works to earn his livelihood, to provide for his family and, incidentally to contribute to the needs of society in general. Is this 'immoral'? Also, in the absence of 'motivation', admittedly a selfish aim, how can an ordinary person persuade himself to work at his best? This is the general reaction to the *karma* yoga – and, therefore, it is generally relegated to that human being who is content to have, as the aim in life, enlightenment or the search for *moksha,* liberation from the cycle of birth and death.

My interpretation of what the *Bhagavad Gita* says is slightly different. To begin with, what the *Bhagavad Gita* suggests is not a prescription but a description of what happens in life. The *Bhagavad Gita* says that the proper action – which will make us happy – is to do our duty according to our *svadharma,* our individual nature. This clearly refers to what I am inclined to call one's natural 'programming'. The important fact is that none of us has had any control over the programming, either our genes or our environmental conditioning. And yet this is our individual nature. It is also a simple fact of everyone's experience that if one has been fortunate enough – if it is our destiny or God's Will – to have an occupation that suits our nature or programming, one is certainly more likely to have a much better life than one would have if forced to do work in life that does not suit our nature or programming. This is what the *Bhagavad Gita* obviously means when it says: "Better is one's own *dharma* though imperfect, than the *dharma* of another better performed. He who does the duty ordained by his own nature incurs no sin." (VIII/47)

There has been also a considerable amount of misunderstanding about the verses in the *Bhagavad Gita* that say:
> "You have the right to perform your prescribed duty (*svadharma*) but you are not entitled to the fruits of your actions. Never consider yourself the cause of the results of your actions, and never be tempted to not doing your duty. Perform your duty with equanimity, O Arjuna, abandoning all attachment to success or failure, and be equanimous in all conditions." (II/47-50)

This is where the gross misunderstanding arises: how can anyone be expected to work without motivation, without demanding the fruits of one's actions? The obvious advice is not to expect that success will always attend your good actions; if you do, you will feel disappointed and frustrated if, as it is not unlikely to happen sometimes, your actions do not bring you your expected success.

If only one analyzes one's own individual personal experience, one must surely realize that when one means to do any action all that one really can do is to decide to do some action. Our everyday experience is that: *a)* sometimes our actions result in the anticipated results, yet quite often, the anticipated results do not happen – in which case we are likely to feel that life is not fair!; or, *b)* sometimes our decisions do not result in the anticipated actions for reasons beyond our control. In other words, it is everyone's experience that all one can really 'do' is to make a decision, and that thereafter, nothing is really in our control. The decision may or may not result in action, depending upon our destiny or God's Will.

And, the action, even if it does happen, may or may not bring about the desired results, again, depending upon our destiny or God's Will. This is our everyday experience. Once we have made a decision, whatever happens thereafter has never, ever been in our control.

This obviously means that if we are able, by the Grace of God (or our destiny) to accept this situation – that neither the happening of the action nor the resulting consequences have ever been in our control – then we shall be saved the disappointment and frustration if we do not get our desired 'fruits of our actions'. Nor will we feel any pride and arrogance if the actions do happen and bring about the desired results. This is the simple, direct explanation of what happens in life, in the *Bhagavad Gita*. It is not a prescription.

Sex is one of the big problem areas in day-to-day living for many people. Many of the problems based on supposed love relationships often have their origin in sex. Sex is a fact of human biology, part of What-Is. It is certainly acceptable that many of our problems are of the mind, that it is the thinking mind that creates them, but it is a matter of fact that sex is of the body. Therefore 'witnessing' or 'passive awareness', which could certainly dissolve many of our usual problems, would not work where sex is concerned.

It is a fact that sex is very often regarded negatively, as subversive of the spiritual life. But Ramana Maharshi and many others did not think so. Ramana Maharshi made it perfectly clear that *Brahmacharya* has no connection with celibacy as is generally understood. He said, '*Brahmacharya*' means 'living in Brahman', being one with Brahman. Again, he made it perfectly clear that celibacy is not a necessary condition for enlightenment or Self-realization to happen. It may be a requirement for yoga and what yoga stands for. It may even be one of the many aids to realization, but it is not essential. He made it quite clear that married or unmarried, a person can realize the Self because it is here and now! When it was mentioned to him that at Sri Aurobindo's ashram there was a strict rule that married couples could live there only on condition that they abstain from sexual intercourse, Ramana Maharshi promptly asked: "What use is that? If it exists in the mind, what use is there in forcing people to abstain?"

One is appalled by the violence that some *sannyasins* in India –

and those of similar cults elsewhere in the world – perpetrate upon themselves (and upon other people) in vainly trying to overcome their sexuality. They are totally unaware of the basic fact that sexual desire is essentially biological and, therefore, natural. Sex is not the product of thought in its basic essence. To the extent that the mind is involved, to the extent that it is a remembrance, strengthened by horizontal thinking, passive awareness of the fact would certainly be of considerable help. But whereas sex is basically biological, it would really be monstrous to punish oneself through the mortification of the body. Surely, self-torture through renunciation cannot in any way take one very far towards Self-realization. Surely, basic bodily requirements as passion and sex have to be understood and accepted as part of What-Is, and not either suppressed or sublimated.

Is there not, in the moment of the sexual act, besides the pleasure, great tenderness, delight, self-forgetfulness, self-abandonment, a total absence of the 'me', the self, usually absorbed in fear and anxieties of life? The problem, as such, arises only later – "thinking about it afterwards" as Ramana Maharshi put it – when the experiencer-ego, who was necessarily absent in the moment of What-Is, comes into the picture wanting a repetition of the pleasure, or thinking about the experience as the committing of a sin.

Sex as an expression of love usually does not present any problems. Problems do arise only when sex and love do not coexist and they are separated by the thinking mind. What creates problems when sex and love do not coexist, is to imagine or pretend love in order to get sex, or hope to get through the mechanical process of sex the imagined satisfactions of love such as tenderness, companionship, security or whatever. And this is how problems arise in day-to-day living when the What-Is is not accepted and the thinking mind goes on a rampage imagining and wanting what is not.

One single fact that one is likely to forget in one's day-to-day living, in What-Is, is that one does not feel the slightest change in the 'me' over the years. I was the same 'I' 50 years ago or 500 years ago or even before Time ever was, and I shall be the same 50 years hence or even after Time ceases to be. This is not a play on words, it is the firmest possible conviction when the thinking mind of conceptualizing does not intervene with its reason and rationality: 'I' remain changeless while time passes by – the body may change but 'I' do not change. This conviction grows further:

while I may superficially think that I am an entity that is living my life, in actuality I am 'being lived' as an infinitesimal – yet highly significant – part in the functioning of the totality of universal phenomenal manifestation. I am not now thinking in terms of any conceptual father-figure as an overlord God with his heaven and hell. I am thinking clearly and purely on the basis of day-to-day personal experience.

When I was born I had no choice, no control. When I am faced with death I expect I shall have no choice either: I shall not be able to tell death to come back after two days as I have still some unfinished work to complete. In between the two phenomena of birth and death, I have considered myself the master of my own destiny. I have read a number of books on the power of positive thinking and allowed myself to be brainwashed by 'miracles through will power and mind control', and yet I found that at every stage in my life almost every significant thing or event has had an enormous element of 'chance' or 'coincidence' in it. If something turns out to be successful, we consider it the result of our concentrated effort; if not, we blame it on bad luck or lack of adequate 'influence in the right quarters'.

Nothing in life seems to have any stability. My own experience with day-to-day living has been, to say the least, interesting. Quite early in life my mother, a voracious reader, told me that my propensity to eat small meals at fairly frequent intervals was supposed to be a bad habit and that medical opinion was quite clear on the point that the stomach must be given adequate rest between a limited number of meals. I tried the system and found that it did not suit me – it made me feel ill – and so I went back to my unhealthy ways and kept quite fit. Many years later, medical opinion veered round to the system of smaller and more frequent meals because the stomach was then spared the strain of digesting heavy meals.

Then, I was told that I would come to a bad and early end if I continued to ingest aspirin at regular intervals for my hereditary migraine headaches. While I tried every available system of medicine – over periods long enough in all conscience – I could not possibly have given up aspirin and still continued to put in my usual long day at the office. And now, for the past several years, aspirin is, I believe, prescribed in regular doses for certain heart conditions. And it has so happened that my migraine headaches happened to be ultimately cured by the manipulations of an osteopath! This has clearly shown me that each one of us is to a certain extent different from every other human being. Every fingerprint is different from all other fingerprints, and the biologist tells us that every leaf on the same plant is different in some respect from every other leaf.

Thus, from my day-to-day living, I have learned to admire the miracle that is Nature, which provides such diversity and multiplicity in what is really Unicity. The mystics have been talking to us about this Unicity in the universe from time immemorial, and the subatomic physicists have recently demonstrated this same Unicity in their laboratories. I have learned from my day-to-day living that I must never forget that I am an intrinsic part of the manifested universe, and at the same time, as a separate individual in the multiplicity of the universe, I must not accept anything generally advised without carefully considering whether what is generally recommended suits me as an individual. This would refer to all areas of human existence subject, of course, to the law of the land and the basic social courtesies towards others.

Acceptance of What-Is in daily living as the flow of life, is one thing; accepting death also as an inevitable part of What-Is, creates for many, a perpetual snag. One morning I had an unusual visitor. She had read a couple of books and wanted to meet me. She had a good understanding about what the spiritual search was about. She was in a comfortable position in life. She was aware that life meant sometimes pleasure, sometimes pain; that there was an air of the unreal about life itself; that there was nothing particular she wanted in life; that there was considerable gratitude in her for what life had given her. One could see the peace of a deep understanding in her face and attitude. Then, suddenly, she confessed that there was a fear of death. When I asked her whether what she was afraid of was the phenomenon of death or the process of dying, she confessed that she was not sure – perhaps it was only the process of dying that she feared.

This confusion is widely prevalent: the phenomenon of death is not the same as the psychosomatic process of dying – the latter is only a minor aspect of the former. The fear of death is totally different from the fear of the possibly painful process of dying: the former is concerned with the loss of one's individuality, the latter only with the physical pain that the process might involve. The fear of death is the fear of the unknown and the unknowable, whereas the fear of the possible pain in the process of dying is known and recorded in memory.

The only way to transcend the fear of death is to be able to accept both the inevitability and the 'unknowability' of the phenomenon of death. Such acceptance is totally useless if it is based on helpless frustration. It is effective in getting rid of the fear of death if the acceptance is the result of a clear understanding of the mechanics of phenomenal appearance and disappearance. Such acceptance comports the surrendering of the illusory ego to the Absolute Reality, of the insignificant fictitious 'me' to the real 'I' – the giving up of the fictitious part and being the whole Unicity.

A simple glance at the phenomenal manifestation in the correct perspective should be enough to bring home to us the utter unreality of the process of life and death. We attach so much importance to the well-being and comfort of our individual bodies and to the necessity of providing security for 'ourselves' in the time to come. If we would but think of the normal activities of man during the span of 15 minutes or even less, we could be shaken out of our identification with what we call our 'selves' as against 'others'. Are we *essentially* in any way different from the billions and billions of 'beings' that get created and destroyed continuously during the very normal activity of breathing, eating, digesting, reproducing? – billions and billions of microscopically small 'beings' endowed with the same animating consciousness that we are endowed with? While we may have a comparatively longer duration of life (even this duration becomes insignificant from the perspective of a million years), are we any more important in the Totality that functions as phenomenal manifestation?

Every sentient object begins to die from the moment it is created. Should it be so difficult to see clearly What-Is, and to accept it with a depth of understanding that would get translated into sweet surrender to that What-Is? If we were able to see and accept the What-Is without the intervention of our thinking mind of conceptualizing, and surrender our fictitious but selfish individuality, then we would begin to enjoy life as it happens – both the 'good' and the 'bad' (conceptual criteria that keep on changing according to circumstances) – with a sense of wondrous anticipation. 'Living' then would become free, natural and, therefore, noumenal when the fictitious phenomenal 'me' stops intruding.

What it all amounts to is that in order to understand this strange unknown thing called 'death', which is so starkly inevitable, we must understand 'life'. No doubt, man has always been thinking and dreaming of the day when he will be *physically* immortal, but he must find out the real significance of death before he can consider physical immortality because one could come to the conclusion that death is not all that unwelcome after all! Living and dying necessarily go together because they are not two separate things but the beginning and the ending of the process we call 'life'. And, it is while we are still living that we must consider the matter of death without sidetracking into a discussion about rebirth. One thing is very clear: there is no question of finding out the meaning of death after the death has occurred. And whatever thought can tell us about death is a mere concept. To think in terms of rebirth as some continuity would be nothing more than conceptualizing. What we must find out is what we are NOW, other than a form to which a name has been given by people who have told us that they are the 'parents', other than the conditioning that the form has received, and other than the experience of pleasure and pain that it has undergone over a period of time and on which would be based whatever thinking and conceptualizing we do.

The fact of the matter is that the permanent soul (if you happen to believe in rebirth) or the permanent entity that you think you are is in fact nothing other than the illusory thing that thought and memory have created as a result of recoiling from the movement and insecurity which is the very basis of life, this dream-life. So the whole problem of finding out what death really is, boils down to this: if there is truly no entity as such at all, who then is really concerned with death?! This is the stage of confrontation where the thinking mind – which has all along been the villain of the piece – finds itself exposed and must, therefore, slink away in disgrace. Whatever we are – call it Consciousness or Awareness or Witnessing or God or by any other name – then remains in the NOW, totally free from all conceptual problems and questions.

In fact, that is death – dying to every moment, every experience. That is Eternity. That is Immortality. And the actual event of death (and the process of dying) is a minor formality because apperception of the Truth means dying every moment to your present attachments, your past experiences and guilts, your future fears, hopes and ambitions. Then you forget about both life and death, and live – or, more accurately are lived –

with love and humility, accepting what comes every moment with willing surrender. In this way, one becomes a little child again with its sense of Unicity and its universal Oneness with all that is seen, heard and felt.

The sage is not afraid of dying because he is not afraid of living. He is not afraid of living because he has been able to accept, without the slightest doubt, that nothing can happen unless it is the Will of God – or, it is according to a conceptual Cosmic Law which it is impossible for the mortal man ever to know. Therefore, he knows there is absolutely no reason for him to be either ashamed and guilty or vain and proud about anything that has happened through his body-mind organism. In other words, the sage finds himself divested of all the superficial trappings of a sense of personal doership or volition and, therefore, free to immerse himself in the natural flow of the river of life and live without any stress. The important fact is that being in the flow of life means actually living without the slightest fear of death: living and dying must go together. In other words, the sage thinks of death as a perfectly natural happening and not the ultimate obscenity when, as Shakespeare put it, we "die in cold corruption and rot". Be content with each moment of eternity and be willing to follow the flow – then there will be no cause for joy or grief, only peace and tranquility.

The human being is at some time or the other confronted with the problem of death and dying. In a way, the core of this problem was ironically presented by Woody Allen when he said, "I am not afraid of dying, but I do not want to be there when it happens!" The concept of death in its development through the ages provides a perspective to consider the problem that the phenomenon of death presents to us. To the primitive man, death was not really a problem: he would have been perplexed if he were to be presented with a truism that 'all men are mortal'. Life to him was a perpetual affair unless he was killed by a natural phenomenon or in battle either with his enemy or with a wild animal. In other words, to the primitive man, death was part of living and those who were not killed continued with their living.

Death becomes a problem for the modern man in day-to-day living because he is stunned by the sudden 'disappearance' of a loved one who is dead, and whose death brings home to him, at least at that moment, the undeniable fact that he himself will have to die one day. Actually, the problem that is posed for him is this: *my* organism, the physical body will disappear, but what about the 'me' who used to own the body and preside over its functions before breath and consciousness left the organism?

The fact of the matter is that the problem is a problem because on the one hand man sees himself as the presiding principle – the functioning element – in the physical organism manifested in space-time. But what he does on the other hand is that, instead of keeping this functioning element as the Intemporal Source, distinct from the physical apparatus, he personalizes it and conceives it as being endowed with a perpetual duration. In other words, instead of correctly conceiving the functional element (or the Self or the Soul) as Intemporality itself, he conceives it incorrectly *as an entity* separate from the psychosomatic apparatus but, nonetheless, existing in space-time perpetuity whose end is pushed back into an infinity within the temporal duration. Thus arises the problem: where do 'I' go after death? In order to understand this problem in total clarity, it is necessary to examine the structure of the human being in totality, and not merely as a phenomenal manifestation, a physical appearance.

'Infinite dynamism' is how the totality of the cosmos could be described with reasonable accuracy. All phenomenal manifestation is the ceaseless play of the Primordial Energy, wherein things appear and disappear, integrate and disintegrate continuously but all within the eternal stability of the Absolute Intemporality. Indeed, the entire cosmos is an illusion appearing within the Consciousness when it is in movement, an illusion that disappears and merges into Consciousness when the movement of energy ceases and Consciousness goes into its eternal state of rest. In its state of illusory movement, the cosmos presents a picture of innumerable phenomenal objects (which appear and disappear continuously) that form a holistic hierarchy from the initial hydrogen (atom) to the human being gifted with intellect – all together forming wholes of more and more complex, and more and more individualized organization, within the total hierarchy.

While in perspective, this phenomenal hierarchy may present in its functioning a certain continuity, a closer view would reveal two definite quantum jumps, the first being the distinction between the inanimate and animate things (the presence of sentience) and the other consisting of the appearing of intellect (its manifest expression being the physical world) which differentiated between the sentient human beings and the other sentient animals. The important point in this analysis is that in spite of this notional distinction, the various phenomenal objects are not basically different. The animal (and the vegetable) are inanimate matter plus something more which makes them grow and live; man is both inanimate matter and animate matter plus something more by way of intellect.

The sentient object – the living thing – is an unstable equilibrium (as opposed to the relatively stable equilibrium of the inanimate object), being the combination of the two opposing metabolisms, one of disintegration and the other of integration. Every living thing is a whole composed of various sub-wholes, individual cells which are in a continuous state of altering, disappearing, and being replaced by new cells. In fact, this polaric duality is the very basis of what is conceived as 'life', of the very appearance and existence of the universal manifestation – the integration and disintegration represented by the Vedantic *Purusha-Prakriti*, and the Chinese representation of *yang* and *yin*.

The third category, differentiated by the appearance of intellect as manifested by the 'word', is represented solely by the human beings. It is through intellect that man has evolved to the higher plane of general ideas – pure ideas, symbols – which go beyond the things symbolized by comprehending them. Not only does man perceive things like the sentient animal, but *he is aware of that perception* and is able to think about such perceptions. While the animal is a sentient being like the human being, it cannot, in the absence of intellect, perceive the functioning of his individual or personal consciousness. The individual consciousness certainly functions in the animal as the 'me' in opposition to the 'other', and the animal consciously divides the other animate things as friends and foes. But the mind is not aware of this duality of feeling or emotion because this consonance and dissonance, this affinity and antipathy, are intuitive and in-built. It is the conditioned reflexes of the animal that regulate its behavior and not reason or rationalization. The animal, therefore, does not have to face the kind of problems which oppress the human being and which are created by the operation of the intellect.

Man's 'will to live' becomes, with the appearance of the intellect, not an end in itself as in the case of the animal, but the means to a totally different end, that is to say, '*to be*', as totally different from 'to live'. The result of the comprehension and evaluation by the intellect of the consonances and dissonances of the reactions of the physical organism to the outside world is that man longs for perfect harmony, which he has only conceptualized but not actually experienced. This is the perpetual problem of the human being in his day-to-day living from which he cannot free himself.

Indeed, this is man's 'bondage' from which he seeks 'liberation'. The real cause of this gap is the fact that conceptualization of the ideal state is based not on the actuality of the interrelated dual aspects of joy and suffering, but on the entirely illusory aspect of unalloyed joy in this very phenomenal existence as a phenomenal object. Underlying such conceptualization is the basic fact that, instead of *being* the universal Consciousness, man endeavors to *become* something – the result of a complete misconception. Thereby, instead of realizing that he is merely one object among "the ten thousand things" (as the Taoist says) representing the objective Noumenon, man considers himself to be an independent, autonomous entity, the subject of his objects. In a word, the *Beingness* of Absolute Reality is confused with the 'becoming' in the relative duality. Man is not prepared to surrender the relative 'me' in order to become the Absolute Subject. It is like the case of a drowning man who is not prepared to let go of his heavy hoard of gold. Man is not prepared to accept death as the final welcome disintegration of the object 'me' so that he could be the eternal and only Subject 'I'. He wants and expects death as a temporary disintegration that would bring for the 'me' unalloyed and perpetual phenomenal joy and happiness!

In other words, death poses a persistent problem but, in point of fact, the problem is truly not a problem at all, because this 'problem' is based entirely on false and illusory conceptualization. When a man witnesses the death of another, what he sees is that the organism stops functioning. And because his intellect tells him – and his deep-rooted intuition convinces him – he *knows* that it is the body that will be dead and that he himself, the one who was there a hundred years ago and who will be there a hundred years hence, cannot die. But he cannot envisage the possibility that *That* which has always been eternally present does not need a form, because he cannot give up the idea of a separate entity as a 'me', opposed to the 'other'. His instinct of eternal presence is indeed true, but his intellect cannot give up its conditioned reflex to personalize that eternal Principle. The result is that he sees the eternal Principle as a 'me', leaving the existing body on death but continuing to 'exist' phenomenally somewhere else, perhaps in some other world. In other words, he cannot give up the idea of space-time representation for the 'me', and he asks, where does one go after death? Thus the problem is based on false and illusory conceptualization. There is truly no 'me' as an individual entity to go anywhere. Indeed, a deep understanding of this fact itself would constitute enlightenment or Self-realization.

The fact of the matter is that the 'me' is only an appearance in Consciousness that totally disappears in deep sleep when Consciousness holds itself in abeyance. All the 'me's' are part of the total manifestation which is the objective expression of the subjective 'I'. Since What-I-Am is the subjective Absolute Reality, the question of what happens to an appearance in Consciousness, which is all that the 'me' can be as a phenomenal object, when it disappears (dies) is ridiculous because any happening can only be in relative duality, and What-I-Am – what we all are in Reality – is Intemporality. Seeking stability and permanence of *Being* in the state of relativity – the very basis of which is incessant movement – is what the problem amounts to. Death is only part of the series of movements that began with birth, the last change which marks the disappearance of one phenomenal object among millions of them.

Considered in this manner, the problem does seem indeed absurd, but the question is, why does the problem, so very real, arise at all? The answer is that it is our memory, which plays a trick by giving events a sense of continuity, a beginning and an end, the appearance and disappearance of a phenomenal object. We know that changes keep on happening to every body from birth onwards during the process of 'growing'. All the cells composing a body are in the continuous process of dying and being replaced – the process of disintegration and integration – and in this process the new cells group themselves in the same old plan. *The regrouping of cells in the same plan is what gives the sense of continuity* and the illusory impression of permanence underneath all the changes. Once in every 12 years or so, the entire body has changed itself: the body now is not the body that was 12 years ago, and yet we think of it as the same body and the same 'me'. Every tree in the forest will have died and been replaced over a period of time, but the forest will continue to be regarded as the same forest with the same name; the water in the river keeps flowing all the time every moment, and yet the river continues to be regarded as the same river with the same name.

It is, therefore, clear that the 'reality' and 'permanence' of a phenomenal object that one imagines until that object dies or is annihilated – the basic permanence within the apparent impermanence of changes – is truly entirely illusory. The 'reality' (and the basic sense of permanence that goes with this reality) of any object – as near as a chair or as distant as a star, whether animate or inanimate – is nothing but an image in mind, which is the content of Consciousness. An object is 'sensed' or 'perceived' in mind because of an impression that gathers body and form by incredibly quick repetitions. Each repetition is a separate quanta and a series of such quanta constitutes what is known as 'time'. Thus what we imagine as the reality of an object is nothing but a continuous series of impressions in a succession of quanta that we consider a duration in which 'changes' take place. It should be clear, therefore, that integration and disintegration take place so incredibly quickly that we are in fact dying all the time, that both the reality and the permanence are both totally illusory and, finally, that all phenomenal manifestation is 'mind-stuff'.

It is not possible to arrive at the root of the problem as such: the problem of death and what happens to 'me' after death. One can only have a concept of what happens in deep sleep. One can witness the approach of sleep until the very last moment but one cannot actually have the knowledge of deep sleep; it is only someone else who might time the very moment when one actually fell asleep. It is only when one is awake again that one can say one had good sleep. So it is with death: one can only see someone else's death. This is the root of the problem inasmuch as the problem is purely conceptual, entirely imaginary and illusory. It is only the illusory ego, the 'me' who is concerned with the problem of death. Where indeed is the 'me'?!

What happens when I 'die'? I shall obviously be back where I was before I was 'born', back where the sound goes after it disappears. A form that had appeared in the Consciousness and was perceived by the mind has disappeared. Who is 'dead'? What is all the fuss about? The 'me' who was never here is not concerned about what happens to the money and property left behind. Let the other 'me's', who do not exist, be concerned about it!!

Writing about the death of his master, Lao-Tzu, Chuang-Tzu said:
"The Master came because it was time for him to come.
He left because he followed the natural flow of events. Be content
with each moment of eternity and be willing to follow the flow.
Then there will be no cause for joy or grief. In the old days this
was called freedom from bondage. The wood is consumed but the
fire burns on, and we do not know when it will come to an end."

Apart from the persistent problem posed by false and illusory
conceptualization concerning 'death', still, for most of us who are reasonably
comfortable in life – certainly well above the poverty line – it is an undeniable
fact that many of us are not as contented with life as we should be. We tend
to compare ourselves with some others who are better off in life than we are
– 'I have only one car whereas he has three cars, including a Mercedes
Benz!' – and thus quite unnecessarily make ourselves miserable. This is
more prevalent than what we might imagine and, therefore, we see so much
jealousy, envy, discontentment, and even hatred and malice merely because
we compare ourselves constantly with those who have a better destiny at
least as far as material possessions are concerned. Very rarely indeed do
we compare ourselves with those who are far less fortunate than ourselves.
Thus, we generally see people being more discontented than otherwise.

There is a very pertinent story about an ancient king.
The king found himself one night in bed, not able to fall asleep.
He started to think about his own life. He thought how very kind God
had been to him. 'What do I not have?', thought the king, and found
himself composing a verse:
'Queens of unrivalled beauty
and law abiding citizens
Men of unparalleled sincerity
and soft-spoken servants
Armies of trumpeting elephants
and wind-paced horses...'
And then the fourth line simply evaded him. He kept repeating the first
three lines but the fourth line kept evading him. He was now considerably
agitated.
It so happened that there lived in the city an impoverished poet.
That same night, he too could not sleep because he was hungry. Seeking
food, he sneaked into the king's palace; groping in the dark, unknown

corridors, he found himself in the king's chamber. He soon sensed that the king was awake, mumbling to himself; so, very quietly and silently, he moved along the ground, went underneath the king's large bed and lay himself down, waiting for the king to fall asleep so that he could help himself to the luscious fruit he could see in the bowl on the table beside the king's bed.

The hungry poet waited for the king to fall asleep, but the king kept tossing and turning in his bed, repeating the first three lines of his poem. The poet could not help listening to the lines. When the king stopped at the third line, the hungry poet under the bed could not stop himself from saying out loudly: '...I have then all which turn to nothing when the eyes do close.'

The words had slipped out spontaneously from the poet's mouth. The king, excited at the fourth completing line, jumped out of the bed, looked for the poet, found him and dragged him out of his hiding place. 'So, I have caught a thief', shouted the king. 'No, sire', said the poet, 'I am not a thief. I am a poet whom poverty has compelled to be a thief.' The king took pity on him, and for the fourth line, he gave the fellow-poet a large sum of money.

Beautiful and bountiful though the king's possessions were, they were not eternal. The king happily recited his poem:

'Queens of unrivalled beauty
    and law abiding citizens
Men of unparalleled sincerity
    and soft-spoken servants
Armies of trumpeting elephants
    and wind-paced horses
I have them all
    which turn to nothing when the eyes do close.'

This too shall pass!

"We all walk on very thin ice", said the British author, William Boyd, during an interview with the *Financial Times*. "We all pretend we don't, but we know how easy it is for our present happiness to be shattered", he added. Anyone who touches wood (or his head!) in the middle of a sentence when referring to a happy or lucky event would know what Boyd was talking about: whether as tumors, or strokes, or tax raids, or freak accidents, the world seems to abound with constant threats to our 'present happiness'.

Psychologists constantly remind us that every day hundreds of human brains are injured. Through accidents or disease, people's brains – and, in turn their minds and their way of experiencing the world – are altered in a flash. Floyd Skloot, the poet novelist, in his essay, *In the Shadow of Memory,* said: "Nothing prepares us for this; nothing equips us to cope with it except the very thing that has been damaged: the brain and its particular mesh of signals and switches that comprise our individual selves."

Floyd Skloot should know what he is talking about. He used to manage the budget of a $400 million state construction agency until disaster struck. A viral illness punched large holes in his memory. Nothing made sense to him any more. He was lost in time and space. He felt himself, his mind, to be incoherent and his world to be in fragments. He said: "One of the strangest aspects of living with certain kinds of memory loss is knowing that the forgetting is happening. I know I am not going to remember things that I desperately want to remember and have only limited success in using special encoding techniques to hold on to what matters."

The basis of the whole problem of the possibility of losing something one values most, whether it is the self itself, the memory of oneself, or any other material possession or personal relationship, is the sense of possessiveness. And the problem of the fear of losing one's possession, whatever it be, can never be solved unless one is able to accept absolutely totally that everything must pass (and, therefore, 'this too will pass'). In the words of the poet-saint Kabir: "We came into this world with our fists closed and we shall leave with our hands open." Nothing can last.

It is only when one is truly prepared to lose everything that one can be free of the fear of losing something one cherishes: everything will be as it was before I came into this world, when I leave this world – why worry about my possessions? And the real joke is that our lives will continue to happen exactly as they are supposed to happen according to the Cosmic Law, irrespective of whether or not we continue to hang on to our fear of losing our most valued possession!

Fear of loss, the fear alone, often motivates fervid prayer. Or, when a great disaster happens, involving a large number of people being injured or dead, it is a natural reaction for most people that they pray for the well-being of their near ones, and a great feeling of gratitude arises when the news of their well-being arrives. Such prayers for help or gratitude are, of course, usually addressed to a personalized God. When there is a deep understanding it is quickly recognized that the emotion is a natural reaction in the body-mind organism, along with the realization brought about by that understanding that whatever happened would be the Will of God and so accepted as such.

Personalizing God is such a common thing in one's day-to-day living that there are quite a few jokes about it showing the extent to which the human mind could carry it. One such joke from the internet appeared in a local newspaper on the occasion of 'International Women's Day'. It is as follows:

One day in the Garden of Eden, Eve calls out to God, 'Lord, I have a problem!'

'What's the problem, Eve?'

'Lord, I know you created me and provided this beautiful garden and all those wonderful animals and that hilarious comedic snake, but I am just not happy.'

'Why is that, Eve?'

'Lord, I am lonely and I'm sick to death of apples.'

'Well, Eve, in that case I have a solution. I shall create a man for you.'

'What's a man, Lord?', asked a puzzled Eve.

'Well, man is to be a flawed creature with many bad traits. He'll lie, cheat and be vain; all in all he'll give you a hard time. But he'll be bigger, faster and will like to hunt and kill things. He will look silly when he's aroused, but since you have been complaining I'll create him in such a way that he will satisfy your physical needs. He will be witless and will revel in childish things like fighting and kicking a ball about. He won't be too smart, so he will also need your advice to think properly.'

'Sounds great', says Eve, with an eyebrow raised ironically. 'So, Lord, what's the catch?'

'Well..., you can have him on one condition.'

'What's that, Lord?'

'As I said, he'll be proud, arrogant and self-admiring. So you'll have to let him believe that I made him first.

Just remember, it's our little secret..., you know, woman to woman.'

Books have been written on how the individual can find peace and harmony in his life, but hardly does any book specifically mention that an individual is not likely to find lasting peace and harmony in his life unless there is a very clear understanding of the very simple fact, a fact of What-Is, that 'men and women are different'. In the absence of this clear understanding, the peace and harmony is not likely to remain very long. This is because in the absence of a very clear understanding of this fact, tolerance cannot happen, the tolerance that is the very basis of peace and harmony.

Men and women are different. This does not mean better or worse – just different. The fact of the matter is that, for all practical purposes, the only thing that is common between men and women is that they belong to the same species. Men and women live in different worlds, different mental creations, with different values and, therefore, different sets of rules. How can peace and harmony prevail if the male and the female constantly argue over each other's beliefs, attitudes and behaviors?

Extended research in scientific, medical, psychological and sociological studies clearly points to one conclusion: men and women are different. The difference cannot be explained away by social and environmental conditioning. As one report put it:

"Until recently it was believed that when a baby was born its mind was a clean slate on which its teachers could write its choices and preferences. The biological evidence now available, however, shows a somewhat different picture why we think the way we do. It shows convincingly that it is our hormones and brain wiring that are largely responsible for our attitudes, preferences and behavior. This means that if boys and girls grew up on a deserted island with no organized society or parents to guide them, girls would still cuddle, touch, make friends and play with dolls, while boys would compete mentally and physically with each other and form groups with a clear hierarchy.

The wiring of our brain in the womb and the effect of hormones will determine how we think and behave... Our instincts are simply our genes determining how our bodies will behave in given sets of circumstances."

Peace and harmony can prevail in a family only when the male and the female positively acknowledge that they are biologically different and neither expects the other to live up to one's own expectations. Much of the stress experienced in relationships essentially comes from the mistaken belief that modern education has ironed out the differences and that now both men and women have the same desires, drives and priorities.

Men and women are different. It is only when one truly and deeply understands the origins of these differences that one would be able to live in peace and harmony in the family, not only accepting the differences but actually cherishing them too. The Frenchman was right: "Vive La Différence"! Long may the difference live!

Until comparatively recent times, the common man, in his day-to-day living, found it difficult to follow exactly what the mystic wanted to convey. For instance, the inexorable causality – cause-effect relationship – the average intelligent man could understand from his dualistic and limited viewpoint, but the mystic saw things with the noumenal, universal, all-embracing vision which does not admit any viewpoints at all. Nor could the mystic's vision bear any close analysis as such, with the result that there was always an almost unbridgeable gulf between what the average person in all sincerity tried to understand and what he got from the mystic. And, of course, even if the average person was prepared to accept his own ignorance, but could accept what the man of science said, that did not take the mystic any further because the scientist had no more inkling of what the mystic was talking about than the man in the street. That was the position until comparatively recent times.

Now, science has come to the aid of the mystic. The subatomic physicist, after probing the behavior of subatomic particles, has come to the conclusion of quantum mechanics which puts the matter of causation completely in the background. The quantum theory of Planck – the new Law of Indeterminacy – replaces causality, and is now accepted where the microcosmos is concerned, and it seems that there is really no reason why it should not apply to the macrocosmos because size must be taken to be as relative as anything else.

So long as the manifestation exists, there must be an *apparent* cause for any event to occur. For the large number and the vast variety of people to exist in the world at a particular time, there must be specific causes. For the Theory of Relativity to 'occur' to an Einstein, which would lead to the most revolutionary theoretical and practical aspects of atomic and subatomic physics, there would have to be an *apparent* cause. For a Jesus Christ and a Hitler to be born at specific points in time, there must have been an appropriate cause, but that would be only from the point of view of the totality of the functioning from a conceptual Cosmic Law, which the individual human intellect could not possibly know or understand in a million years.

For the *lila* of 'life' as such to happen, there must be a script and the script must bring in causes which lead to certain effects which in turn could become causes for yet further effects in future. Such causes and effects must, of course, function through individuals as the characters in life's drama. But such functioning can never even be understood and appreciated by the individual human intellect. It is for this reason that, when the great Einstein objected to the Theory of Uncertainty with the remark that he could not accept that "God plays dice with the universe", Neils Bohr had to explain that God does not play dice with the universe, but the human being thinks so because he does not have the "full information" which God has! In other words, the individual human being simply cannot have the volition or independence of choice and action: "Thy Will Be Done".

The quantum theory, while passing the supreme test of any scientific theory that it 'worked', had three very peculiar features which irked and irritated many scientists of the day, including, as mentioned above, the great Albert Einstein. They were:

a) The theory does not predict unique outcomes but only states *probabilities*;

b) To add insult to injury, as it were, it accepts "uncertainty not merely as an irritating headache but as something one must live with: the uncertainty is accepted as an intrinsic feature of the subatomic world";

c) It comes to the fantastic conclusion that the observer and the object he observes cannot always be considered as separate and distinct (which is precisely what the mystic has always been saying).

The scientists of the day, in other words, labored under metaphysical dogmas of the day and could not grasp the idea of Divine Spirit as being at once transcendental to and immanent in the manifested universe. Werner Heisenberg, on the other hand, averred that the quantum theory excluded a totally objective description of nature based on the premise of a physical world existing independently of the human observer. The new vision of the universe thus gives up the long-prevailing view of it from a materialistic viewpoint, and now seems to approximate the Eastern vision of not a physical reality but a metaphysical reality. The new formulations of physics in ordinary language, devoid of the mathematical jargon, are translogical and, therefore, seem more like the paradoxical aphorisms of the *Upanishads* or the riddle-like koans of Zen Buddhism. For instance, Sir James Jeans describes the phenomenal universe as a cosmic sphere, the inside of which would seem to be made of "empty space welded to empty time".

The debate whether the 'realist assumptions' which seemed self-evident and apparently worked in the macro-world were in fact true, was for several years on a more or less academic level. But in the 1970s the instruments for actual experiments became available, and in 1980-81 an experiment took place at the University of Paris which may radically change man's view of the 'reality' of the physical world. In this Paris experiment – exceptionally well-designed and scrupulously executed – two subatomic particles, emitted by an atom, flew apart not unlike the fragments of an exploded shell. According to what the 'realists' held to be the common sense view, the two subatomic particles, now apparently distinct and separate, should have had no influence at all on each other. But they did! The interpretation of this fact clearly meant that either a signal had passed between the two subatomic particles which traveled faster than the speed of light or, that the two particles, although apparently separate were never really distinct entities but had remained integral parts of a greater whole.

This new vision of the universe is based mainly on two essential elements which take modern science very close to the Eastern mystical in-seeing:
1) What were mutually exclusive opposites have had to be accepted as a pair of polaric, interrelated complementaries. In nuclear physics, continuity exists along with discontinuity. All at once, particles are destructible and indestructible; energy and matter interchange; probability pattern makes it impossible to state specifically whether in a given place a

particle exists or does not exist. Nuclear physics basically deals in potentials and tendencies. Eastern mystical literature is full of such apparent paradoxes, usually expressed in negative statements (*neti, neti*; not this, not that) trying to transcend the pairs of opposites.

Contemporary physics would seem to have arrived at the definite conclusion that no 'event' in the universe is exclusively separate but that it is involved with almost every other event. The Mach Principle (of the physicist Ernst Mach) states that the inertia of a celestial body or system depends upon its reaction with all the rest of the universe. This was the principle that perhaps prompted the postulate of Einstein that the presence of matter and energy actually "curved" space-time. Compare this with the mystic's view of the whole universe as his objective body, a conceptual rather than a material construct mirrored in Consciousness within, and without any outside support: in other words, a mere reflection – 'mind-stuff'.

2) A most important implication in the postulations of the new physics – and the one that takes science even closer to the very basis of *Advaita* – is the bridging of the gap between the subject and the object, between the observer and the observed object. The mystic has always held that all there is, is a sort of relationship in which there is know-*ing* – the knower and the known being like the poles in a magnetic field, and not two separate opposites – the knowingness (sentience or Consciousness), the eternal One Subject.

What the quantum theory says, in fact, that any division of any object-particle, atom or whatever, is purely a mental construct: it is a whole whose parts are sub-wholes in themselves and those parts can be discovered only when the wholeness of the object is destroyed. For instance, the neutron does not 'consist' of proton and electron; the proton and electron are 'created' when the neutron is destroyed.

Similarly, the universe as such is not 'constituted' of the millions of its 'parts' or objects like human beings or stars or whatever. It is only in the eyes of the apparent observer that the division takes place – a fact that has always been apprehended by the mystic. As Einstein has put it, in the new physics *the field is the only reality*, and there is no place in it for both the field and matter. Every thing-event or event-thing exists only in relation to all others. And what is the sub-structure behind this field and its physical existence, or more 'stuff' or the mystic's consciousness? It is the totality of the potential in which the totality of the actual appears, in which particles are spontaneously produced and destroyed or reabsorbed, in which matter appears and disappears. It is the 'void' (actually the fullness or Plenum) of the *Upanishads* or the Tao or Chan, which cannot be sensorially perceived but only intuitively apperceived – and, therefore, constitutes the ultimate impenetrable barrier between science and metaphysics.

It would seem that such a view of the universe vitiates the basic 'law' of cause and effect. But it could very well be that the notion of causality is merely one way of looking at an event by connecting the various stages in which the event could be broken up, not as mere stages but as a chain of cause and effect; the only single event is, in fact, the spontaneous manifestation of the phenomenal universe. For instance, when a train comes out of a tunnel, we could as well say that the engine is the cause and the guard's compartment the effect. Lack of rain in an isolated community would mean *ipso facto* starvation, but it could be broken up into a cause and effect chain like lack of rain causes drought, drought causes famine, and famine causes death. Then again, I win (or lose) money because I place a bet. Could it not be that I am destined to win (or lose) money and that is why I placed the bet? So, causation or destiny are merely descriptions of an event broken up analytically into convenient parts. Wouldn't it be better not to chase the shadow of causation and accept that in this *lila* all event-things are interconnected?

We can only conclude that what exists is a unified field and the 'multitude of things' are not different things or entities but merely differentiations or forms. As the sage Jnaneshwar has put it so poetically in his *Anubhavamrita*, when *Prakriti* (manifested energy) found that her lord *Purusha* (the unmanifest Absolute) was without any form, she felt so ashamed that she clothed Him in millions of forms which kept on changing every instant. Or, to quote Chuang-Tzu:

> "The knowledge of the ancients was perfect – so perfect that at first they did not know that there were things. This is the most perfect knowledge: nothing can be added. Next, they knew that there were things, but did not yet make distinctions between

them. Next, they did not yet pass judgments upon them. When they proceeded to pass judgments, Tao was destroyed."

There are times in daily life when one feels 'out of sync' with the flow of life, perhaps bothered by a dull, nagging headache; the answer is simple – one takes a couple of aspirins. Or, one is bored, and one goes for a walk or uses the exercise machine, or goes to the club. But the situation is different when one is bothered by a dull, nagging feeling of uncertainty, worry, anxiety. Reading a book does not help; nor does going through a magazine, or playing a solitary game of cards. The feeling gets worse, of an impending disaster. Then one almost gets into a panic and wishes there were a kind of anxiety pill.

And there is one – always available, right in the present moment. Try it: just sit comfortably, close your eyes, and imagine yourself to be anchored in the Self. You are not *doing* anything. If a thought comes, watch it, do nothing, and it will go away. Then another – watch it and it will go away. Just remain relaxed; consciously relax all your muscles and stay relaxed. This is not a difficult exercise if you do not think of it as an exercise that needs a certain minimum length of time. Indeed, forget time and stay 'anchored in the Self'. It may be 3 minutes, 5 minutes, and occasionally, you may surprise yourself when you find that you had dropped off for 10 minutes or even longer. And, the important thing is that the mental fatigue has disappeared.

There is a beautiful phrase for this in the Sanskrit language, for 'stay anchored in the Self'. It is '*Swa-stha*': literally, 'anchored in the Self' – sit anchored in the Self and your mental fatigue will disappear.

*Peace and harmony
can prevail only when
the individual is able, in the
present moment, not to be uncomfortable
with others.*

CHAPTER 10

ℐHEER
JOY OF
BEING

When I was about 12 years old, I loved movies that showed a lot of fencing – fighting with swords. The famous stars of these 'action' movies were actors like Douglas Fairbanks Sr. and Jr. and other famous names. I have forgotten all about those many movies but there is one I think I shall never forget and, curiously, I remember nothing about the plot of this movie except that there was, of course, a hero and a villain, and a lot of fencing. But what I do remember, very vividly, is one scene: the living room of the hero, perhaps a Count. It was an enormous room with a large stone fireplace, above which was mounted an iron shield with the engraved family motto: 'This Too Shall Pass'. Somehow those words seemed to remain impressed in my consciousness. Nothing remains forever. Everything is subject to creation and destruction, growth and decay.

The human mind is somehow accustomed to think of change in terms of a lateral or horizontal growth, but our experience would seem to be that the change is more in the nature of a cycle: in the existing cycle of birth and death, creation and dissolution, in the rise and fall of political systems and civilizations, and in the inevitable cycles of happiness and unhappiness by way of gains and losses in the lives of individual entities. Everyone has experienced these cycles of good and bad, up and down, as judged by the mind. Yet the mind refuses to accept the inevitability of such cycles, and this refusal means frustration and unhappiness. It is this kind of frustration and unhappiness, and not the actual pain or pleasure of the moment, that the Buddha referred to as the *dukkha* of *samsara* – the suffering in life.

Acceptance of the existence of these cycles simply means accepting a fact of life and not a 'fatalistic' attitude. Such acceptance of the cycles of creation and destruction, gain and loss simply means witnessing them as an inevitable part of life and not getting mentally involved in them. 'This too shall pass' is an excellent attitude in life that prevents unnecessary frustration. Even one's physical energy is subject to these cycles. It is everyone's experience that the level of physical energy and mental zest sometimes is highly active and creative while at other times, for no apparent reason, one feels stagnant and physically and mentally depressed. All one can do is to accept each situation and know that this too will pass. In other words, not going with the flow of life means unnecessary frustration.

Going with the flow does not mean being indifferent to what the moment brings. It does not mean 'detachment'. It simply means enjoying fully the pleasures of the moment for the very reason that they will not last; it also means dealing with the pains of the moment as best as one can, again knowing that they will also pass. Going with the flow simply means not pursuing the pleasures, nor avoiding the inevitable pains. The remarkable fact of accepting life and going with the flow is that the pleasures seem to bring more pleasure and the pains bring less pain. In other words, going with the flow means an inner state of peace and harmony, grace and ease. Perhaps that is what is meant by the words 'Peace of God' – the sheer *Joy of Being*.

Masters have repeatedly told seekers that Self-realization in fact simply means 'being in the present moment', not letting the thinking mind get you involved in what exists in the present moment. What this clearly means is that involvement of the thinking mind is in horizontal time, which prevents the seeker from being in the present moment and accepting What-Is in the present moment. The very essence of 'being in the present moment' means the absence of a sense of personal doership, accepting whatever is in the present moment as the very essence of Beingness. And, yet, the sense of personal doership is so deeply entrenched in the ego that the ego-mind always is in search of a methodology – 'how to': how not to get involved.

It is rather interesting that Aldous Huxley, at one point in time, became deeply interested in spiritual seeking and even went to the extent of trying certain drugs to get 'the experience'. He wrote a book, a novel called *Island*, which tells the story of a man shipwrecked on a remote island, cut off from all civilization. When he is awake, he senses something different about this island. Then he notices the colorful parrots in the trees all screeching out the words, "Attention: Here and Now. Attention: Here and Now." He later learns that the islanders had taught them these words so that they would be continuously reminded to remain in the present moment. In any such methodology, the constant danger is that the very repetition of any words, any *mantra*, could take the mind away from the import of the *mantra* and, thereby, get involved in horizontal time!

The 'me' that gets involved away from the present moment is only the 'me' who considers himself the doer of one's actions and considers the 'other' as the doer of his actions. In other words, the very basis of involvement is the interhuman relationship based on relative doership. Therefore, the only thing that will keep the ego anchored in the present moment is the total acceptance that all action is a divine happening and not something done by anyone.

In the happening of life, one thing should be very clear to us. Our lives are individual lives. We most certainly have to live our lives in a society that has its own regulations and laws. Subject, of course, to these social regulations and laws, each individual must necessarily depend on himself for the peace and harmony that he is basically looking for in his individual life.

What the individual has to decide for himself is what he finally expects to get in life that will truly satisfy him. It is quite obvious that he must have adequate means to satisfy the basic needs of food, clothing and shelter. But, assuming that one does have these minimum needs satisfied, the question to ask oneself is: am I satisfied with doing whatever I can in the present moment to satisfy my *reasonable* needs? Am I always in pursuit of short-lived pleasures of food, drink, sex, fun, thrills and excitement – and, therefore, always seem to live in the future which never happens? Am I always pursuing something which I do not have but which others seem to have? Do I really believe that my life will be 'better' if I have more of what I already have by way of material possessions? Why have I lost the very zest for living – no freshness, no vibrancy, no time to appreciate the simple things, the wonder of God's creation? Am I really happier than my dog?!

It is important to realize, sooner than later, that I have really no control over my life, that swimming against the flow of life merely drains my energy, that the future can never provide an escape from the present. In other words, I must take stock of the situation at once. What do I want most in life? Is it not peace and harmony as an anchor while I must necessarily face life and accept whatever the present moment brings? I must at least give some thought to a fresh approach. Could it not perhaps be best to go with the flow, to be in the present moment, to do whatever I have to do in the present moment to provide for the future, and then let the future take care of itself (since I have never had any control over it anyway)?!

Life could present enough problems without our adding to them through the negativity based on the past that is dead and the future that may or may not happen. In one's daily living, one does not realize how much of one's suffering is truly unnecessary. Most of the strain and stress of life caused by fear of what might happen in the future could be eliminated by paying more attention to the present moment. It is a matter of simple understanding that the 'future' as such is beyond anyone's control and, therefore, after having done in the present moment whatever is possible (even assuming that one does have free will), it is absolutely futile to let ourselves fall prey to unnecessary unease, tension and anxiety.

Similarly, one has truly no idea of the amount of suffering one bears in daily living simply because one forgets that the past is dead and one continues to think about what might have been! Sadness, bitterness, resentment, grievance, guilt and regret – all these are based entirely on the concept of the dead past and on the concept of personal doership.

The only difference between a sage and an ordinary person that could quite clearly be noticed is on this very plane. While the ordinary person is weighed down most of the time by the dead past and the uncertain future, the sage lives in the present moment, believing totally that nothing can happen unless it is God's Will (and no one could possibly ever know God's Will) and, therefore, does not carry any load of personal guilt or shame, nor any load of hatred and malice towards anyone. This leaves the way open to the sheer Joy of Being.

In day-to-day living there is often great frustration because one is not able to control anger or gluttony, and yet you may see anger arising quite frequently in a sage or a sage eating quite heartily. When anger arises, it means the brain reacting to an event according to the natural programming in the body-mind instrument. The same event may produce not anger but fear or compassion in another, if the programming is different.

The essential difference between any reaction in a sage and in an ordinary person is that the sage merely witnesses the anger or fear arising *in the moment* and is not involved with the phenomenon personally, as is the ordinary person. One moment the sage shows anger, but in the very next moment he is free to be amused or show great compassion. In other words, the sage does not react with a sense of personal doership to the natural or biological reaction in the body. There is anger in one moment but compassion in the next – there is no personal involvement in the anger, no wanting to control it, no frustration if he is not able to control it in horizontal time.

It has been the experience of each one of us, at some time or another, that surrendering to the present moment – accepting What-Is in the present moment without any inner resistance – has suddenly created an almost visible feeling of relaxation in an extremely tense atmosphere. The word 'surrender' in daily living has negative connotations, implying defeat, failing to rise to the occasion. But, in reality, true surrender is surrender to the present moment, deeply accepting What-Is in the moment as something that could not possibly have been otherwise.

Accepting What-Is in the present moment does not mean putting up with all of life's situations without doing anything about them. Surrender means, simply, surrendering the resentment to the present moment: yielding to the flow of life instead of opposing the flow of life. Surrender truly means relinquishing the negativity to the present moment. It is an inner phenomenon that does not prevent you from taking any action that you think necessary in the present circumstances. Things keep changing every moment.

In other words, non-resistance does not mean doing nothing. Indeed, it is the very basis of the Eastern martial arts: yield in order to overcome. In Taoism, there is a term '*wu wei*' which is pregnant with wisdom. It is supposed to mean 'activity without action'. It is totally different from inactivity, which arises from indecision, inertia, fear. It means 'non-action' in which there is no involvement of the ego. It means action not happening through the conditioned mind and a tense body, really and truly a natural action, very much a part of the present moment. Perhaps this is what is truly behind the lovely words of Jesus: "Consider the lilies of the field, how they grow; they neither toil nor spin."

There have been recorded cases of prisoners waiting for execution in the death row, when suddenly, inexplicably they realized the deepest inner joy and peace. There have been recorded cases of prisoners in Hitler's extermination camps, while standing in a row waiting to be led to the gas chambers, suddenly laughing loud and hard, joking with the armed guards who, of course, thought that tension had driven them to insanity, yet deeply recognizing the miracle of surrender to the present moment. They were no longer afraid of death because they had already died to the present moment: they had surrendered to the present moment. Consciousness released Itself from the confines of a three-dimensional human object.

It is an interesting phenomenon that all ideological concepts are necessarily based on psychological time, whether it is a religious system like the Taliban or a national concept like socialism or communism. This is because the concepts are based on the implicit assumption that what is expected as the highest good for the community would happen in a mind-conceived future, that the conceived means would bring about a conceived end in some future.

It is estimated that more than 50 million people were tortured and murdered in the cause of communism in Russia and China – and other countries – with the professed aim of creating a better world in the future. It is for this reason that Masters like Ramana Maharshi often asked individuals who asked questions about these national and international 'causes' to stick to the present moment, to do whatever they wanted in the present moment, and to leave the national and international causes to the Creator who created the world!

The individual, with his limited span of life, finds it difficult to live in the present moment. And yet, he really knows nothing about the future in which he lives most of his life with uncertainty and misery. He does not realize that any sudden success or increase in wealth, for instance, does not and cannot provide what he truly wants most in this life in the present moment: peace and harmony in his life. Any sudden increase in wealth is not going to change his conditioned way of living, which has never brought him anything but suffering, guilt, animosity and resentment towards others.

Peace and contentment and harmony can only happen in the present moment with the complete realization of the fact that, in the words of the Buddha, "events happen, deeds are done, but there is no individual doer thereof." Peace and harmony can prevail only when the mind is not all the time seeking reason to find fault with himself, leading to a feeling of guilt and shame, or with others, leading to a feeling of hatred and malice. In other words, peace and harmony can prevail only when the individual is able, in the present moment, not to be uncomfortable with others. And this means being able to impersonally witness every happening as a divine happening, in the present moment – the sheer Joy of Being.

One cannot help thinking of 'time' as something objective, although it is perfectly clear that space-time is not some thing. The following quotation from St. Augustine (*Confessions, Book XI*) in this respect is most interesting:

"It is in my own mind, then, that I measure time. I must not allow my mind to insist that time is something objective. I must not let it thwart me because of all the different notions and impressions that have lodged in it. I say that I measure time in my mind. For everything that happens leaves an impression on it, and this impression remains after the thing itself has ceased to be. It is the impression that I measure, since it is still present, not the thing itself, which makes the impression as it passes and then moves into the past..."

In actual fact, what happens is that the mind creates time by performing three functions: expectation, attention and memory. What becomes of the present moment? If we analyze the functioning of the mind, we shall find that we are conscious only of the past, of things in the past. The functioning of the mind is a stream of thoughts, a flow of events in the mind from the past to the future, from memories of the past to the expectations of the future, so that the present moment is always excluded from it.

The state of mind is like a pendulum swinging between the backwards of the past and the forwards of the future, excluding the most important present moment. Real living, however, is in the present moment. In other words, wanting to be happy in the future, and only remembering the happiness of the past, one misses the genuine happiness of the present moment. The genuine pleasure or happiness of whatever is happening in the moment is lost in thinking of such pleasure in the past or in the future: the moment there is the thought 'this is the life I want', the happiness that led to the thought was already over. The real happiness or peace or joy of the moment lies in the interval between two thoughts, and to become focused upon such intervals – to be in the I AM – is the real joy of meditation.

Particularly among spiritual seekers, there is always a persisting curiosity of what happens to the daily living of the one who has awakened. Anchored in the present moment, how does a sage live his life? The sage lives his life with the total understanding that life lives itself through his own body and through those of all others in this universe. The sage experiences life like any other person except that he *knows* that there is no one doing the experiencing.

The sage lives his life with the absolute conviction that 'he' and 'you', and everyone else, are waves that are separate only as waves, but in fact rise and fall on one great sea of Being. He knows that when the mind is still, the Reality that is experienced is devoid of all separateness of the phenomenality. He has embraced the profound emptiness and silence. He goes with the flow of life. He is usually seen to be free from anxiety and frustration.

The sage responds when his name is called, but *knows* that 'That' which does the responding is Consciousness, that is all there is. He is quite happy to be forgotten by the world.

The sage lives his life, witnessing life as it happens, with the constant understanding that the past and the future are abstractions and that this moment is the only reality. Thus, the sage lives his life to the fullest accepting all experiences, unrestrained by the thinking mind, like 'piling fresh fruit in a basket without a bottom'.

He is seen to help anyone going to him for help but people seem to be barely aware of his existence. He truly seems to extend virtue and kindness to the whole world without contending with anyone.

The sage lives his life letting spiritual practices happen when they do, fully aware that they will stop when the time has passed.

The sage lives his life outwardly in the world of good and evil, yet without thinking of the good and the evil. He is kind to the kind and the unkind alike; he is faithful to the faithful and unfaithful alike. The sage lives his life, being a conscious but passive witness of the miracle of the unfolding of phenomenal existence in all its divergent unicity and ordinariness.

It is interesting to know what someone like Ramakrishna Paramahamsa had to say about this very aspect of living, how a sage lives his life. This is retold from an account by someone who spent many days in the company of Ramakrishna:

"The entire day has been spent joyfully listening to classical music and singing hymns of mystic union. Now that the sacred hour of twilight is approaching, suddenly the Great Swan (Paramahamsa) who has been swimming silently in the ocean of bliss for several hours, opens his eyes wide and begins to reveal rare gems from his treasury of secrets concerning the spiritual path – the path that not only leads to God but that unfolds entirely within God.

Ramakrishna: *When one awakens into Supreme Reality which is at once Absolute Being, Absolute Consciousness and Absolute Bliss – then all social and religious obligations disappear, not because one becomes insensitive or passive, but because all obligations are being spontaneously fulfilled by the living power of Truth, operating invisibly through the subtle body of the awakened person who becomes the perfect Divine Instrument. Deep absorption, called samadhi in the yogic tradition, is then experienced ceaselessly by every cell of the body, every strand of the awareness. This total samadhi need not be expressed through any particular trance state. It is sheer awakeness [Awareness].*

Nor need this realization be expressed through words, songs or ceremonial worship... Consider the honeybee, which at first buzzes loudly while circling a flower, but finally settles in silence deep within the core of the fragrant blossom. This is the portal to samadhi.

Yet the authentic practitioner [who really never practices] *never renounces prematurely the precious disciplines of his tradition – daily prayers, ceremonial worship, study and chanting of scriptures, silent meditation, and selfless service to fulfill the physical and spiritual needs of conscious beings. The genuine aspirant remains in a constant state of inward and outward pilgrimage until actually reaching the one goal of true pilgrims – complete God-consciousness, full awakening as Truth* [The Ultimate Understanding]. *After plunging irrevocably into that ocean of Being-Consciousness-Bliss – that shoreless sea of Sat-Chit-Ananda – the functions of clear philosophical reasoning and uncompromising spiritual discrimination do not disappear entirely. They become delight and compassion rather than doctrine or discipline. The honeybee sometimes becomes faint, even as it sits fully absorbed at the center of the lotus.*

Ecstatic love for God – heart and mind melted by passionate longing for Truth – is the one essential factor in the process of awakening. Divine Presence, however one may understand and experience it, exists in and through all conscious beings. And conscious beings exist solely in and through it. Who then deserves to be called a true lover? The one whose awareness dwells entirely upon God, awakens entirely within God. But such awakening is not possible so long as the mind is constantly distracted from Truth by remaining habitually egocentric, by instinctively seeking personal gratification. Divine Grace, the healing and illuminating energy that rains down ceaselessly upon the human mind, heart and soul, cannot be absorbed or assimilated by the high rocky hill of personal interest and personal importance. This precious life-giving water runs off the high ground of Ego, without ever penetrating its hard, barren soil. God is far, far away from the mind obsessed with conventionality. It is very difficult to gather the dispersed mind when it becomes identified with habitual egocentric structures [volition or sense of personal doership].

Obsessive self-awareness [self-consciousness], *whether collective or individual, is a mere machine, an automatic function. God is the only living presence within us, our only true bliss and freedom. Divine*

Nature, which alone is our ultimate being, has nothing to do with narrow self-interest or limited self-consciousness. Divine Nature can be realized and fully actualized in daily life by sincerely following any number of revealed paths. All the integral transmissions of sacred wisdom and contemplative practice that survive the test of time are true – true in the sense that they function authentically and bear the same fruit of sanctity.

The goal is to reach the flat roof of the house, which affords an unobstructed view of the entire countryside. You can reach this highest point by climbing stone stairs, wooden steps, bamboo slats or rope ladders. You can even scale a nearby tree and somehow clamber onto the roof along a large limb. Just get there. Then you will see clearly that the unimaginable variety of prayerful or meditative methods all lead to the same goal, to the same panoramic vision, to the same timeless awareness.

One certainly perceives errors of understanding and superstitious behavior in the various religious traditions as they are imperfectly practiced. So what? Every human approach inevitably contains error or partial understanding. Such distortions are, of course, most difficult to notice in our own approach, because each person stubbornly assumes his own watch tells the correct time. There is no way to purge your personal, social or religious content of every error, but if you persevere in sheer yearning for God, sheer love for Truth, these unavoidable limitations will gradually be dissolved. It will be sufficient simply to love for love's sake. Merged in motiveless love, one experiences every moment the tremendous natural attraction of Divine Presence. This presence is the inner guidance that we feel flowing through us as conscience, intellect, intuition, sense perception and longing. Divine Presence alone generates the yearning of our heart, the seeking of our mind, the ease of our body, the illumination of our soul. God sees everything because God constitutes everything and, therefore, everything seeks God... God is all-embracing Oneness – although the names, facets and appearances of this Oneness are beyond numbering [the magnificence and variety of God's creation].

Who are you? Who am I? It is the Great Mother who has become all this. Only so long as you fail to recognize Her Reality can you assert 'I act' or 'I am'. Absolutely nothing exists within you except Her Power, Her delight. She even manifests as the limited ego and its smallest desire.

The Master gazes at us, amused by our amazement, and laughs like a child."

It is an unfortunate fact that in day-to-day living man does not realize the extraordinary importance of relaxation. The very word brings images of some kind of discipline like yoga or something similar to be done at a particular time of the day. As a matter of fact, relaxation can be of three kinds: physical, mental and transcendental – and none of these would necessarily demand a system as such.

Thus, physical relaxation simply means deliberately, consciously releasing the tension that has somehow crept into the body. For instance, merely sitting in the dentist's chair causes tension. The dentist, therefore, has to tell the patient to relax. All that is really necessary in such a case is to make oneself consciously relax all the muscles in the body at one time. This is really the basis of the famous *shavasana*: you lie down and let all the muscles consciously let go of all tension. You are sometimes told to go gradually from one end of the body to the other, relaxing muscles in each part of the body. But it has been the experience of many that one clear command to the muscles in the entire body consciously to let go works very well. "Slack off" was what one dentist had to yell at his patient before the patient did relax.

The real benefit of physical relaxation is found not in doing the *shavasana* which needs you lying down, but at any time, whatever you are doing, to stop for an instant and consciously relax the whole body and then while you are so relaxed, to continue whatever you were doing. Or, you could take a minute or two between your tasks, and stay consciously relaxed. You will soon find that you get into the practice of doing your normal work without getting into any kind of tension, and only a gentle reminder to relax is all that is necessary.

There is an in-built mechanism for relaxation unique to the human being: the human being is the only animal who laughs and can laugh heartily. Laughter, even deliberately induced laughter, not only provides emotional satisfaction, but also significant physiological benefits and relaxation. The basis of laughter is a deep inhalation followed by rhythmic exhalation, especially using the diaphragm, the large muscle mass in the body that separates the abdominal and chest cavities. This helps equalize the pressures in both the cavities and apart from aiding venous drainage, also causes massage to the internal organs. There are four types of laughter described by health practitioners that can be beneficial (people with heart or lung problems or high blood pressure should use caution): *a)* 'Etiquette laughter' starts with a smile and extends to mild laughter, with no special attention to breathing. The tempo gradually builds up. *b)* In 'pigeon laughter', a deeper inhalation is done and, keeping the mouth shut, you produce laughter making the sounds like hums of pigeons. This is an internal laughter and has its own advantages. *c)* 'Soundless laughter' is the most difficult to learn, but very effective. Take a very deep in-breath, and then open the mouth and put the tongue out and let laughter out – but without making any sound! Also, after one inhalation you can exhale as long as possible, with rhythmic jerks to the diaphragm; this 'inner jogging' is vigorous and exhausting. *d)* 'Belly laughter' is similar to the soundless laughter, but you let go and laugh loudly – even rolling on the floor or doubling up. Repeated in-breaths are needed and this can last for as long as you like.

Mental relaxation is of an entirely different kind inasmuch as it means, in effect, an absence of thinking, of conscious physical relaxation. Such mental relaxation liberates you from conditioning. You can easily find out for yourself that there is a period of silence between the thoughts that is totally unrelated to the thinking process. In fact, that interval, that period of silence, being not related to time, brings an enormous amount of relaxation whenever you are consciously aware of it. In any position, it is possible to be focused upon these intervals, even for short periods, during one's day-to-day living. The meditation *gurus* may resent such focusing on the intervals between thoughts during one's day-to-day living being called 'meditation', but if you are able to do this focusing on the interval between thoughts during your working day, you will suddenly realize that at the end of the day, you are much less tired and that you have considerable amount of energy left for the rest of the evening.

What actually happens in those intervals between thoughts is that the mind has become 'silent': the mind has emptied itself of all its contents and is, therefore, 'vacant' or silent, intensely aware of What-Is in the moment. This silent mind is not unaware of the stream of thoughts flowing through the conscious mind, but *it does not participate in the thinking*: it does not discriminate between them, it does not make a judgment between them in terms of right or wrong or importance. The immediate effect of the silent mind in day-to-day living is that psychological problems do not seem to have any substance and many just evaporate. What could be more important is the fact that the silent mind gives full play to the creative and intuitive faculties, with the result that not only psychological problems disappear but, that even, intellectual problems and even practical problems may find their solutions.

There is another kind of relaxation – neither physical nor mental – which is not to be achieved but which can only happen as a result of the deepest possible understanding that the individual entity as the 'me', as opposed to the 'other', truly does not exist. It is understood that the billions of human beings have no individual volition or choice of decision and action and that they are only uniquely programmed instruments through which the Source or Primal Energy or Consciousness or God functions and brings about such happenings as are supposed to happen according to what might be called a Natural Law or a Cosmic Law. The total acceptance of this concept, which one can test in the fire of one's own experience, results in the total acceptance of What-Is as God's Will, which leads to the real relaxation of the body-mind organism leading to enlightenment or Self-realization: the fictitious ego-entity doer finds himself surrendering to the noumenal Source in its entirety. This is what might be called transcendental relaxation, the sheer Joy of Being.

*W*hatever you think
you should do at any moment
is precisely what God would
want you to think and do.

CHAPTER 11

SELF-REALIZATION
IN DAILY LIVING

In his day-to-day living, deep into himself, the human being finds an inexorable pull towards something Divine, far beyond any pleasures and pains of daily living. The saint Tukaram, who lived in Maharashtra in the mid-17th century, typifies the tortured human being entrapped in the ephemeral joys of this life and the searing miseries, which are inseparably bound with the fleeting pleasures as the very basis of life. Tukaram wrote nearly 5000 *abhangas* (verses), being the sincere and spontaneous outpouring of a tortured soul. In these *abhangas* he gave vent to his suffering. In one of these, he said: "How much have I suffered, O God! If all my suffering could be dropped on a hard stone, it would break into pieces." He was conscious of what he considered his vices and sins: "In body, speech and mind I have done many evil acts... Hatred, betrayal, arrogance, adultery and many more are my sins." He prayed to God not to abandon him. "Thou art an ocean of compassion", he said, and prayed to Him for guidance, and not to make him dependent on false *gurus* because, he wailed, he found "only arrogance in the houses of the learned".

Tukaram started with the sincere belief that it was possible for him as an individual to have a vision of God. He made every possible effort and tried various means towards that end, but all to no avail. He became more and more despondent, and at one stage decided to commit suicide. At last Tukaram's extreme agony bore fruit and, as in the case of many other mystics, the deep darkness of the soul was suddenly lifted by a great Self-illumination. In one particular *abhanga* he expressed the state of his Self-realization: "When I look at God's face, I am blessed with infinite ecstasy. My mind is fixed on the vision and my hands firmly grasp his feet as all the accumulated agony suddenly vanishes and gives way to great bliss."

He, however, soon realized that all visions are merely appearances in Consciousness and described his ultimate experience, when all separation between God and devotee disappeared totally: "I gave birth to myself and came out of my own womb. Tuka looks everywhere and sees nothing but Himself... God is the Giver and God is Himself the One who enjoys." The essence of *bhakti* is suddenly transformed into pure *jnana*.

Self-realization is the realization that the source of all happiness is the Source – the Self – within you, and not the external object that you think has given you the happiness. All that the external object has done is to take you for an instant back to the Self within and ignited the happiness of the moment. When this Self-realization happens, you do not have to depend upon any external objects for happiness. Then there is the realization that what the external object brings is merely a sense of pleasure that arises on the base of peace and equanimity that is the Self.

What the seeker seeks is a Master Key to the Ultimate Understanding. The Master Key is simply this: from the viewpoint of the illusory individual entity, problems never cease; from the viewpoint of the total phenomenal functioning, problems never arise. This is because Consciousness is all that exists, and everything else is merely an appearance, including the illusory individual entity with volition or sense of personal doership. True understanding is impersonal, noumenal: we can only BE the Understanding.

Houdini, the renowned magician, had an act that was believed to be his masterpiece: to be tied up in chains or sealed up in sackcloth, or imprisoned in other ways, and he would free himself in a matter of seconds. On one occasion, however, in Italy, he could not get out of a jail for several hours. When he was finally let out, utterly tired and frustrated, he was very angry and complained most bitterly: "Not fair, not fair at all. They fooled me. They tricked me. In spite of all my efforts all those hours, I could do absolutely nothing. And now I find that the door was never locked!"

The door to the Ultimate Understanding is never locked. The trouble is that the seeker is looking for a Master Key. During the process of the Ultimate Understanding – the Ultimate Understanding means the absence of all questions – the ultimate question that remains in day-to-day living is: if nothing really has happened and the phenomenal manifestation is merely a mirage or a sound that has appeared and will finally merge in its Source, how is one to live one's life in this world?

Life, Nisargadatta Maharaj mentioned repeatedly, is like a dream, like a stage play where the various actors play their respective roles while never being really unaware of their true identity. The expert actor playing the role of a king is never for a moment unaware of the fact that he is really in life a pauper. In day-to-day living, what we have to do is to live our roles naturally, and accept whatever life brings in its course according to the grand design of the Totality of phenomenal functioning.

All that one is expected to do – and all that one can do – is to live according to one's inherent nature, according to the programming in the psychosomatic apparatus, and let the deep understanding of our true nature bring about such changes as it considers necessary, without any sense of volition on one's part. Any attempt at controlling our inherent nature can only result in suppression and its adverse consequences.

All that is necessary in one's day-to-day living is the witnessing of whatever happens in life, including the thoughts and acts of the 'me' while being passively but continuously aware of our true identity. Then there would be no wanting to change the What-Is to what the 'me' thinks 'what-should-be' because the Ultimate Understanding reflects the realization that all the 'me's' and 'you's' concerned in life, devoid of the subject-object relationship, are together truly the eternal, subjective 'I' expressing Itself objectively as the phenomenal manifestation in its Totality.

The one seemingly insurmountable difficulty for the average spiritual seeker regarding Self-realization in his day-to-day living is the concept of 'separation'. He has heard it, time and time again, from different Masters, that Self-realization cannot happen so long as he harbors the notion that he is separate from other human beings. And he finds it obviously impossible to accept, even intellectually, that he himself as an entity, as a 'me' as the ego-doer, can ever possibly be not separate from every other ego-doer. And curiously enough, in the many teachings, various methods are prescribed for the seeker to practice, several disciplines to be followed, so that 'he' may accept that he is not a separate entity. The result is that there are hundreds of seekers who find themselves mired in frustration so deeply that some have even contemplated suicide. And the pity of it all is that the solution is truly astonishingly simple!

The question that arises at this stage is: if the solution is so simple, why are there so many deeply frustrated seekers? Perhaps the answer is that it is the very simplicity of the solution that evades the solution for many seekers. And the answer for this situation is to be found in what Lord Krishna said in the *Bhagavad Gita*: "Out of thousands of people hardly one seeks salvation; among those who do strive for salvation, hardly one knows me *in principle*." This is the situation that is supposed to prevail according to a conceptual Cosmic Law that no human intellect could possibly understand.

And what is this simple principle that a separate entity, living his day-to-day life, is supposed to know, which would make the separate human being accept that there is truly no separation between the billions of human beings? The principle is that every human being is a *separate* uniquely programmed instrument, through which the *same* Primal Energy (or the Source, or Consciousness or God or whatever other concept) functions and brings about whatever is supposed to happen through each human instrument, in the moment, according to a conceptual Cosmic Law. In other words, the separation as such, is only in regard to the outer appearance of the human instrument, and the functioning element is the same: the Source, or the Primal Energy, or Consciousness (as the Hindu *Upanishads* call 'It') or God. The Primal Energy functions through each uniquely programmed human gadget precisely as electricity, an aspect of the same energy, functions through each electrical gadget, producing precisely what each electrical gadget is designed to produce. This is the way 'separation' both exists and does not exist in our day-to-day living.

Even in the usual hurly-burly of daily living, it does happen in the core of some persons that there occurs a compulsive intense desire to find out 'how life works' – what functions – a desire to find out the meaning of life, that simply cannot be denied. Such a thing happened in the case of the Buddha. Dr. D. T. Suzuki made the following remarks at a conference held at Oxford in 1953:

"According to legend, the Buddha was tormented at an early age by the problem of life and death... The need to escape from this cycle of birth and death preoccupied the Buddha so completely that He was not able to pursue His usual life. He left His family and His palace and set off towards the forest at the foot of the Himalayas. First of all He made visits to the philosophers... But, although He had studied under the direction of the philosophers, the Buddha perceived at the end of several years that His problems were not still resolved...

He then directed Himself towards moral discipline and ascetic practices. He reduced His physical needs to the minimum. According to tradition He only ate a few grains of sesame each day. At the end of several years He became so feeble and so thin that He could no longer stand up. Seeing Himself in this state, He thought: 'If I die before having resolved the problem, I shall not have accomplished what I started. I must come back to the living, with good health and in full possession of my faculties.' He then started to take food again. Thus neither intellectual discipline nor moral discipline had enabled Him to resolve His problem... He did not envisage any other way. But the problem persisted...

Then He sat under the Bodhi tree and tried to find a solution... After having remained a week under this tree, so the *Sutras* say, His spirit was in extreme agitation. When He was studying philosophy, the intellectual pursuit of the problem had constituted a well-defined object; this object no longer existed. When He had followed moral and ascetic discipline, there had been an object; this object no longer existed either. There was nothing remaining. But the problem persisted and He was not able to be indifferent to it... He was unable to find the meaning of life and, without the meaning of life, why should He live? He was not able to die either, because death would not have resolved the question. He was not able to either live or die.

When the torment came to its height, the Buddha lost consciousness of subject and object and sank into unconsciousness... But when such a state is attained it is by no means the end of the process. There must be an awakening and this awakening is generally provoked by an excitation of the senses. The Buddha was in this state when His gaze rested on the morning star. The rays of the star penetrated His eyes and reached His brain. He was

awakened from unconsciousness and passed to the conscious state...
What the Buddhists call 'illumination' is this passage from
unconsciousness to consciousness."

This 'unconscious' state of the Buddha was not similar to inattentive
sleep; on the contrary, it has to be a state of 'super wakefulness', of total
awareness, of total attention without object, the total absence of a subject-
object relationship. Then, when this state of 'unconsciousness' was itself
surpassed, the mind which perceived the image of the morning star was
totally new, totally unattached, which was the perceiving essence of the
Mind itself. The dualism of the perceiving and the perceived was healed.
The problem was not 'solved' – the problem had been 'dissolved'. The
important point, however, is that it was a 'happening' and not an achieving
by the Buddha.

What does the ordinary person expect to get out of spiritual seeking
in his day-to-day living? It is really astonishing how vague the
misunderstanding is, how much the ordinary person expects to get in life
merely because he is a 'spiritual' or 'religious' person. This is what I found
in a letter I recently received: "My brother is well-educated and is healthy
but he is unemployed, at 37 years of age. He is somehow unable to keep a
steady job. So, most of the time he is home, eating, sleeping and watching
TV and seems quite happy about it. How does one deal with this situation?
What does one do?"

The only thing I could tell him was to do whatever he thought he
should do, without expecting any result, because he has no control over
the result, which is entirely dependent on his destiny, the Will of God,
according to a conceptual Cosmic Law. What could he do about a situation
in which a young friend or relation is suffering from cancer?

This is what a well-known Indian journalist wrote in his popular
column in a newspaper: "Spiritually we have been the No. 1 nation for over
two thousand years. And look where it has got us." What indeed did he
expect – the No. 1 nation spiritually, also to be the No. 1 nation materially?!

One is amazed at the amount of confusion that prevails over what
exactly is Self-realization and what precisely it is supposed to do for the
individual entity who considers himself a spiritual seeker. How many

would be prepared to accept the concept that Self-realization merely means the realization that, in the words of the Buddha: "Events happen, deeds are done, but there is no individual doer thereof?" How many can accept that Self-realization is the acceptance that noumenal Reality is the only Truth, everlasting without any change; that in the functioning of the phenomenal manifestation, which has emerged from the Reality (the Source), all happenings happen according to a Cosmic Law, as they are supposed to happen, through the human objects or instruments, each uniquely designed and programmed to produce exactly that which is supposed to happen at that time and place, through that particular human object, which, together with billions of other three-dimensional objects, constitutes the totality of manifestation?

This always brings up the question: if no one does anything and everything just happens, how is one to live one's life in a society which does not accept this concept? Let us look to the German mystic, Meister Eckhart, for the answer:

"Man ought to live as if he did not live, neither for himself, nor for the truth, nor for God... The man who is to achieve this poverty shall live as a man who does not even know that he lives, neither for himself, nor for the truth nor for God. More, he shall be quiet and empty of all knowledge, so that no knowledge of God exists in him... A man ought to be empty of his own knowledge, as he was when he did not exist, and let God achieve what He will and man be unfettered."

What Meister Eckhart obviously meant is that all intellectual knowledge can only be a concept – a concept that may be acceptable to some and not to others. In other words, live your life, apparently doing whatever you think you should do. And, whatever you think you should do at any moment is precisely what God would want you to think and do.

One might well wonder what precisely Meister Eckhart meant by the words, "man ought to live as if he did not live". One might get a very good idea of what Meister Eckhart meant when we see the expression in the context of what the artist, Kederick Franck, said about some of his subjects: "Albert Schweitzer became indignant when he noticed I was drawing him with his glasses on: 'Don't please, they make me look so old!' He was eighty-six. And a famous theologian demanded: 'Before you publish that drawing I want to approve it! I want to check it as I do all my interviews.' I respected his wishes; I never published it, not even for his obituary." And then there was the famous philosopher who did not want people to see that he was getting bald, and so he let the hair on the side of his head grow as long as possible and then combed it across his head to the other side to cover the bald patch in the middle.

Perhaps Meister Eckhart merely meant, 'live as if you are being lived'. Marat Safin, the Russian youngster who won the 2001 U.S. Open Tennis Championship in the final round against the world champion, Pete Sampras, knew precisely what Meister Eckhart meant. When he was asked how he managed to beat the world champion, he said that in the very beginning, even before the match started, he knew it was foolish to try to beat the champion – it was obviously a wholly unequal match – and he decided to forget the match, to forget that he was playing against the world champion, and only try to play each ball and return it across the net. And he did exactly that. He forgot about the match, and returned every ball, including the ones the champion thought were winners. And in the end, it was quite true that he was the winner but it was not he who had done the winning. The Russian lad played as if he were being played.

It is only a mind that is free from the restrictive preoccupation of doership and blame that can be receptive to peace and tranquility in the phenomenal day-to-day living. Also, it is only such a mind, not fragmented and limited by the sense of personal doership either for oneself or others, that can be receptive to the experience of expanded Consciousness in the inner space, generally known as a mystical experience. And it is only such a mind, totally devoid of a sense of personal doership, which is free from any sense of separation. And absence of separation means Love.

In our day-to-day living, what happens is that our education extends to knowledge about our society in such a way that we continue to be slaves of the mind rather than the Masters. We cater to the endless desires and demands of a turbulent psyche that seeks security in life through material gains and rewards. There is simply not enough emphasis on knowing about ourselves, about what it is that the human being ultimately wants: peace and harmony in life, which goes beyond material gains and achievements. Our outward seeking is rarely turned inward, except in those rare moments of grief or crisis. Even on such occasions, a genuine inward inquiry is not kindled, only a pervading sadness and self-pity remains. The key to this dilemma lies in education. Education has turned out to be the means to accumulate information and know-how to attain material gains and social and economic status. Etymologically, 'education' means 'bringing out the potential', and this basic aspect of the word is usually ignored.

In India, it is the deficiency of the human sensitivity, 'conscience' if you will, that is the root cause of our present problems. As one writer has put it: "It is the root cause of our degeneration and decadence, masquerading as amoral culture, and crass civilization fostering violence and vice versa all over the globe. The extortion, corruption and criminality of the powerful elite and the governing polity are traceable to the glaring deficiency of sensitivity."

A change can happen only when the human being realizes that material wealth and social status do not, by themselves, bring what the human being truly wants, deep down: to be anchored in peace and harmony, to be comfortable with oneself and comfortable with others, while facing life and accepting whatever the moment brings. It is a sad fact that spiritual seeking has not become an integral part of day-to-day living. It is generally considered that 'such activities' are meant only for those who have retired from active life: the younger people just do not have the time or the inclination for such fashionable and pulchritudinous activities. In actual fact, what is sought through spiritual search and practice is the most important thing in one's life, in one's day-to-day living: to be able to live, from day-to-day, whatever one's occupation, without mental stress and tension. It is because this basic fact is not appreciated that *Advaita* has become something meant only for the older people.

To repeat, my basic concept of *Advaita* is that the human beings are all not individual entities with volition and free will, but programmed body-mind instruments through which the Primal Energy functions. Therefore, there is truly no individual entity responsible for any action. All actions – and their results or consequences – happen according to God's Will. Therefore, no one need blame himself or anyone else for any consequences. Therefore, there is no load of guilt or shame, for one's own actions, nor any hatred and malice towards anyone else. This is what brings about relief from mental stress and tension.

It is in one's routine daily living that the human being feels stress and tension – the infamous 'bondage' that simply cannot be pin-pointed and removed. The normal human sensory system is geared to function within the usual environment. Each human body-mind organism is a uniquely programmed instrument, with its own genes and DNA, which has received its conditioning in its own social and geographical environment. The result is that each human body-mind organism reacts to an outside event according to its own programming, its own 'nature' to use the colloquial phrase. In such a reaction, a natural biological reaction in that human sensory system, the ego is not concerned and, therefore, there is no question of any 'bondage'. The bondage is always for the ego, not the sensory system.

The ego feels the bondage only because it reacts to the natural reaction in the sensory system. Anger or fear arises: there is no 'bondage' until the ego reacts and wishes that he or she did not get angry or afraid, and wants to do something about it! That is the bondage, the infamous 'human bondage' about which books and books have been written.

The seeking of freedom from so-called human bondage is based on a complete misconception. The misconception lies in the fact that the ego misconceives as his own reaction what is essentially a natural biological reaction in the human sensory system. The reaction in the sensory system to an outside event, which is certainly not in the control of the ego concerned, is an entirely natural or biological reaction as much to an outside event as to heat or cold. The ego mistakes this biological reaction for his own reaction: anger or fear arises as a biological reaction and the ego transforms it into his anger or his fear, and wants to change it. The ego, in other words, reacts to a biological reaction, and therein lies the bondage: wanting not to be angry, wanting not to be afraid, wanting always to be calm and collected, wanting always to be a brave man. This is truly the human bondage, from which freedom is sought. The freedom that is sought really consists in not being dependent on any tendency, inclination or circumstance. What does this freedom truly mean in day-to-day living? We could say in general terms that it means a state of mind, an awareness, which is not dependent on any knowledge (information) or any stimulus, or any conformity to any code of conduct. Freedom consists in being able to accept What-Is in the moment. In other words, it means peace, serenity, tranquility – perhaps 'love'.

Again, what does 'freedom' mean more precisely in day-to-day living? Could it not perhaps mean, in simple terms, being comfortable with ourselves, being comfortable with 'others', being comfortable with God? All this, of course, while living our lives in the modern world, accepting the pleasure or pain that is our destiny of the moment. No one can control What-Is in the moment. Freedom consists in being able to accept What-Is in the moment. This freedom can arise only if we can accept the basic premise, "Thy Will Be Done". Then there would be no need to blame anyone, neither ourselves nor others. Then, and only then, will there be the absence of the load of guilt and shame, hatred and malice, that the human being usually carries, the load that is indeed the human bondage.

Clearly, the bondage of the human being consists in the obvious fact that he reacts in a personal way to a natural or biological reaction in the body-mind organism to an outside event over which he has no control. The natural reaction is strictly according to the programming in the body-mind instrument (or computer) over which, again he has had no control, i.e. the genes and the unique DNA, plus the up-to-date conditioning (including all personal experiences and all the collected information) over which, too, he has had no control. The evidence of experiments with the effects of hypnosis and drugs clearly shows that this process of reacting by the ego to the natural, biological reaction in the programmed body-mind instrument can be temporarily suspended. The result of this temporary suspension of egoic activity is to expand the mind, the identified consciousness, to a sense of the wholeness of life and release it from the confines of the stagnant waters of the small pool. This is to be liberated from the bondage of the ego reacting to the biological reaction in the body-mind instrument. The final, total liberation, of course, depends on something that is not the temporary effect of hypnosis or drugs. That something is the Ultimate Understanding that there is no individual doer of any action or deed. And this can only happen.

With the Ultimate Understanding, how does the sage live his day-to-day life? The sage is the one who has truly understood the principle of non-duality which, in effect, means non-volition or non-doership. He, therefore, no longer 'acts' either positively by doing something or negatively by ceasing to do something. Chuang-Tzu describes the acts of such people as follows: "They are upright without being conscious of duty to their neighbors; they love one another without being conscious of chastity, they are true without being conscious of loyalty; they are honest without being conscious of good faith; they act freely in all things without recognizing obligations to anyone."

In short, what actually happens is that having understood the principle of non-doership very deeply, they truly let go of their individual sense of personal doership and merely witness the actions happening through all body-mind organisms as happenings and not the doing by someone, with the result that the question of blaming anyone for any action simply does not arise. In other words, they let the *dharma* of the individual psyche take over with such modifications as the intuitive understanding might have made. The essential point is that the deep understanding of non-volition pushes the individual sense of doership so far back into the psyche that an extraordinary sense of freedom comes about. When the identity with a single individual as the doer disappeared into the Universal Consciousness, the robber-murderer Valya Koli could turn instantaneously into the sage Valmiki.

A familiar complaint, prior to the happening of the Ultimate Understanding, is that the individual is able, on some rare occasions, to know his 'natural state' but that what he wants to achieve is to be in that natural state all the time. It is a misconception that there is something to be achieved. The fact of the matter is that the 'natural state' is indeed the natural state of the individual human being at any moment. It gets covered or hidden or forgotten whenever the individual ego gets himself involved in horizontal thinking or conceptualizing in duration. There is no question of anyone 'achieving' that natural state. It is our natural state that always exists whenever we do not stray away from it through getting involved in the hurly burly of life. Indeed, such involvement in which we get ourselves entangled is itself the 'hurly burly' of life! Life flows in its own way without any problems.

Life can happen only in the present moment. Anything that happened 10 years ago, or anything that will happen after 10 years, can only happen in the present moment. The involvement happens when we view what is happening in the present moment from the personal perspective, based on the memories of the dead past or the fears and hopes of the unborn future. It is the involvement based on the past and the future which creates the problems in the present moment. It is the thinking mind that gets us involved in horizontal time, away from the present moment.

If we deal with life as it happens, from moment to moment, making our decisions and taking our action as responsibly as we can, we would not get involved in horizontal time. It is only because we let the past and the future concerns, based on our personal considerations, affect our decisions in the present moment that life presents problems. Unfortunately, we do not face our problems in the present moment with total attention; if we did, we would get our solution, we would make our decision, with much greater ease and confidence. And, most importantly, we would still be in our natural state because we would not be involved in the horizontal past and future, while making decisions in the present moment.

The seeker of the natural state labors under a basic misunderstanding that he has lost that state every time he gets angry and becomes afraid, or has any thought or feeling. This is not so. It is not so easy to lose our natural state! This life situation that occurs almost all the time needs to be very clearly understood. Again, you have not strayed away from the natural state every time anger arises or a desire arises. The most important point to remember, in this situation, is that when one of the senses in the body comes into contact with its relevant object – when the eye sees something or the ear hears something – whatever arises, anger or fear or compassion or whatever, is a natural, biological or mechanical reaction in the body-mind instrument, according to its particular design or programming. Therefore, if this natural reaction is accepted as such, there is no involvement. The involvement that takes you out of the natural state happens only when you identify yourself with the reaction: 'I am angry or I am afraid, and I don't like it.' Unless this personal involvement happens, *the mere natural arising of the reaction does not take you out of the natural state.*

It would be a distinct step forward for the seeker to realize clearly that it is not that he glimpses 'his' natural state of peace and equanimity only in rare moments, but that he is always in the natural state – what other state could he be in?! He forgets it only on those occasions when he happens to wallow in the memories of the dead past, thinking of the many actions he did which he should not have done, or actions he should have done and did not do. When he is not thinking of the dead past, he finds himself conceptualizing about his fears and hopes in the unknown future, and unnecessarily imagines himself to be unhappy. Either way, he loses the tranquility of being at home in the natural state of the present moment by indulging in the illusory luxury of living in the past or the future. You are always in the natural state except on those occasions when you happen to stray away: the impersonal Awareness in the present moment – I AM.

Thus, we find the sage, who has been widely accepted as a man with the Ultimate Understanding, going through his daily living, being quite busy most of the time, exhibiting the same symptoms of daily living as the ordinary person from moment to moment: pleasure, pain, anger, fear, amusement, compassion, or whatever. And yet, he is seen to be anchored in the natural state – in peace, tranquility, humility, virtuosity. The natural reactions in the body-mind organism are seen only from moment to moment; there is no involvement in horizontal duration, through personal reaction to the natural reaction.

The ultimate result of the Ultimate Understanding, the total understanding of the principle of non-volition, is the acceptance of all events quite cheerfully as the Will of God. This means that the sage lives his day-to-day life, freed of affective attachments, without blaming anyone for any 'actions', in the "state of life to which it has pleased God to call us", playing his role in this dream-play called life, without taking anything too seriously, with a certain attitude of amusement at the apparent absurdity of it all!

In day-to-day living how does the understanding translate itself into action? The answer is: by being aware of life without consciously thinking about it, continuously but effortlessly, so that this 'being aware' keeps functioning even when there are thoughts. This is not unlike the same awareness of one's home and family being present continuously, even during the entire working day, without consciously having to think about them. True understanding accepts whatever life brings and responds to each experience whole-heartedly without any resistance or recoil, giving the mind freedom to think whatever it wants to think, including the freedom to worry. This is the reason behind the advice supposed to have been given by the very successful German General

Rommel to his troops before the start of the battle: "Do not worry about the fear you have. It is this very fear which will lead you to acts of incredible bravery."

It is the psychosomatic apparatus that reacts to an experience, according to its own programming. Differently programmed psychosomatic apparatuses will react differently, and the same apparatus may react differently in different circumstances according to the Will of God. In other words, the senses, feelings and thoughts must be allowed to operate in their natural way because any attempt to control them can only result in worsening the disturbance. To quote Lord Krishna again: "Even for a wise man (the sage) the energy within the body-mind organism produces actions according to the natural characteristics. What is the use of any external restraint?"

It would easily be the experience of many people in their day-to-day living that spontaneity, virtuality, does indeed work effectively. The question, however, would arise – perhaps a valid one – regarding the basis on which spontaneity works so effectively. The answer in one word would be 'humility', but not in the sense in which the word is generally used. What is generally known as 'humility' happens to be in fact nothing but inverted pride or negative pride, whereas the real basis of true humility is the utter absence of any entity, with the sense of personal doership, either to be proud or not to be proud. In other words, it is the absence of the sense of personal doership that prevents the arising of any pride for any action approved by the society, or guilt and shame for any action disapproved by the society.

Thus the sequence is clear: the deep and clear Understanding, far deeper than the intellectual comprehension at the linear level, of What-Is leads to true humility because of the annihilation of the volition or sense of personal doership in the ego-entity. The absence of volition leads to the absence of self-conscious personal effort, which means in effect the presence of natural and spontaneous action. This spontaneous action reflects the understanding that human intelligence, totally transcending the phenomenal intellect based on information and knowledge, is not anything of an outside agency implanted into the sentient being, but that it is indeed the inherent aspect of the whole organism of the phenomenal universe – the aspect that maintains the functional order in dynamic balance through the operation of the Consciousness that is the substratum of the entire phenomenal manifestation.

In other words, what produces the essential humility is the realization that the functional element operating through the individual human body-mind organism is not the puny individual intellect or volition but the Primal Energy or Consciousness, the very source of all phenomenal manifestation. This balance in the functioning of the manifestation – 'life' as we know it – is maintained through the natural mechanism of polarity between apparent opposites. The non-acceptance of the polarity between the apparent opposites leads the human ego to the conflict and unhappiness in life.

Most 'successful' men know in their heart of hearts that the most vital decisions in their lives have been intuitive or spontaneous – "from outside", as the great Albert Einstein readily admitted – but the conditioning over the years is so powerful that they cannot admit it in public. The fact of the matter is that as soon as a goal is conceived, spontaneity is at once destroyed and the self-conscious sense of volition takes over. The 'purposeful' life, ironically, misses the very purpose of life, which is to go with the flow of the river of life and enjoy the unity in the duality and multiplicity of life as we know it. When the floodlight of the true vision *happens*, there arises the sense of total freedom that allows life being enjoyed to the full, including everything that happens: good, not good and indifferent. Then, in the day-to-day living, spontaneous action, not being in conflict with the natural flow of events, enables the man of understanding to be fully receptive, through his senses, to the entirety of the world, free of all tension.

It is interesting to see how the Ultimate Understanding – and the spontaneous action that happens in day-to-day living – relates to the 'virtues' that almost every organized religion exhorts man to 'cultivate'. Let us take the case of the phenomenon of anger with which one is painfully familiar, and which one is supposed to control. Controlling anger is a virtue to be cultivated. It is debatable who is more susceptible to the ravages of tension: the one who freely gives vent to the anger and gets it out of the way, or the one who is conditioned to the necessity of controlling his anger and finds that every effort at such control only suppresses the tension until it explodes into a heart attack or a stroke or something similar.

The supposed controlling is to be done by the ego, the 'me' in the split-mind of dualism; and so long as the separation between the 'me' and the 'other' exists, based on the sense of doership, anger and the allied phenomena must occur.

On the other hand, what happens when there is true understanding, based on the annihilation of the sense of personal doership? So long as the body-mind organism exists, there must necessarily be a response, through the senses, to an outside stimulus in various ways, in varying degrees. When anger arises, the man of understanding does not think that he is angry and try to justify his anger against the 'other'. The anger is witnessed and there is no personal egoic involvement based on 'me' and the 'other'. What happens then is that the anger does not receive any sustenance from the ego and naturally gets annihilated, and this fact is also witnessed. In other words, thoughts, desires, emotions do arise as natural, biological reactions in the psychosomatic apparatus, but they are not pursued by the ego in the absence of the sense of personal doership.

A similar pattern can be seen in regard to the 'achievement' of virtues like tolerance, patience and compassion. There is hardly any extant religion in whose commandments these virtues do not take the pride of place. Such commandments have been made continuously over the last two thousand years or more, without the slightest improvement in human nature or conduct. Every 'me' is worried sick over the world situation, with the constant threat of a nuclear holocaust. And yet, every 'me' – individual, community or nation – continues to compete fiercely for the slightest material gain against every 'other', totally ignoring the good advice of the commandments.

There is a story that illustrates this point. The army chaplain at one Sunday service announced, "I am going to preach this morning on the serviceman's misuse of the word 'hell'." Then he proceeded to discuss at great length the absurdity and poverty of expression betrayed by such everyday expressions like "get the hell out of here" or "what the hell do you want?" He explained how easy it is to get out of this sickening habit by making only a little effort. It was a good sermon. Standing at the door after the benediction, greeting the worshippers as they emerged, the chaplain received this sincere compliment from a senior officer: "Chaplain, that was a hell of a good sermon. I hope the boys will keep it in mind."

When there is understanding, the concepts of tolerance, patience, and compassion take an altogether different hue. They lose their perversity of compulsion as commandments and become the natural, consequential aspects of the understanding itself. Understanding, based on the annihilation of the sense of personal doership in all human beings, presupposes the demolition of the separation between the 'me' and the 'other' because both are clearly seen as merely uniquely programmed instruments through which the Source, or Consciousness, or God functions and brings about actions, which are in fact only happenings and not something 'done' by anyone.

In day-to-day living, far too much importance is given to the 'who' than to the 'what'. Whatever is created in phenomenality – music, painting, sculpture, dance or scientific invention or whatever – the fact of the matter is that it is really a part of the totality of the phenomenal functioning. The 'who' connected with such creation is totally irrelevant because the apparent creator is relevant only insofar as an appropriately programmed apparatus was needed for the purpose. Albert Einstein declared with utter sincerity that the equation ($E=MC^2$) came to him "from outside".

There is an interesting anecdote about this point: the Truth is to be recognized on its own merit, and not on 'who' utters it.

A Tao Master one day read out for his monks a text not familiar to them. The monks were most impressed by the text, and one and all wanted to know who the author was. The Master replied: 'If I tell you that this text is written by the Buddha, you will venerate it and prostrate before it; if I tell you that this text is written by a patriarch, you will ponder it with great respect though not with the same veneration you would accord it if it were from the Buddha himself; if I tell you that it is written by an unknown monk, you will not know what attitude to take; and if I tell you that this text was written by our cook, you will laugh and mock at it.'

What exactly is day-to-day living for the sage who has to face the pains and pleasures of life, like any ordinary person, but seems to be anchored in peace and tranquility? Very simply, for the sage, it does not mean his living from day-to-day, but merely witnessing living that happens through his body-mind organism. It means that the sage has been able totally to accept that no one lives his life, but that living happens through every body-mind organism according to a conceptual Cosmic Law, or more simply, according to God's Will. In other words, the sage witnesses life happening while simultaneously being in stillness, anchored in peace and tranquility, and also at the same time being in movement: being in Consciousness-at-rest and in Consciousness-in-movement, with the Ultimate Understanding that Consciousness is all there is.

There was a scene on a TV program that showed baby seals on a Scandinavian beach being clubbed on the head and killed for their tender skins. This was being watched by two people in two different places, J. Krishnamurti, the famous philosopher-writer, and the famous actress Brigitte Bardot. Krishnamurti has gone on record to say that he could not bear to watch this scene and switched off the TV. Brigitte Bardot, on the other hand, could not forget the scene and spent a sleepless night. The next morning she decided to start a movement against the practice of the baby seals being killed. The movement gained strength rapidly and the nation concerned was forced to put a legal stop to the practice.

The ordinary person would interpret what happened as a good deed by the actress and indifference by the philosopher. The man of understanding would simply accept that whatever happened, through either of the two body-mind organisms, was precisely what was supposed to happen according to God's Will or according to a conceptual Cosmic Law: neither person concerned 'did' anything.

On 11 September, 2001, my wife and I were watching the news program on the television in the evening as usual. Suddenly, we saw one of the twin towers of the World Trade Center in New York engulfed in fire and the news anchorman telling us of a plane plowing into one of the higher floors and starting an explosion. As we watched the sight in horror and deep compassion for the people trapped in the building, we saw in abomination a plane plowing into a higher floor in the adjoining building at one end and an explosion at the other end of the floor. Very soon, both the buildings collapsed in a heap of smoke and rubble. As my wife and I looked at the sight for the next several hours, I could witness a thought arising: "First Pearl Harbor, then the atom bombs on Hiroshima and Nagasaki, now this horror, what next? Only God knows."

One of the simplest guidelines for peace and harmony in day-to-day living for the common man has been given nearly 400 years ago by the Maharashtrian saint Gora, a potter by profession, in a *bhajan* (translated from the original Marathi):

> *May Your form be in my heart and Your name constantly on my lips.*
>
> *The body is subject to the laws of phenomenality; let it naturally do the work that happens through it.*
>
> *Body-mind organisms can only function strictly according to the way they are programmed.*
>
> *Therefore, the individual human being can have no other duty by way of good conduct and particular behavior* [there is no list of do's and don'ts].
>
> *With the total faith that nothing can happen that is not Your will,*
>
> *I surrender my will* [sense of personal doership] *entirely at Your feet.*
>
> *May the 'I Am' in this body soar into the heavens, without any involvement* [attachment] *in the phenomenal universe* [illusion].
>
> *In the meantime, Gora recites Your name with great feeling, without the slightest expectation.*

What a bold statement for the time, and yet there could hardly be a more accurate statement for daily living in peace and harmony in any time or any place.

*This knowledge of
the Self is absolutely beyond
that knowledge which is
the counterpart of ignorance.*

CHAPTER 12

ADVICE
FROM THE SAGE
MUKUNDARAJ

It is only when day-to-day living loses all its charm in spite of all the excitement, or when some calamity brings a man to the very end of his patience and forbearance, that man feels compelled to inquire into the very nature of his being: Self-inquiry. At such times, the Source seems to lead him miraculously to a guide, the *Guru*. It is the *Guru* who guides the disciple in his inquiry into the nature of the Self because he knows the utter misery of the seeker, which he has himself gone through. This knowledge of the Self is absolutely beyond that knowledge which is the polaric counterpart of ignorance. It is the kind of knowledge which has existed intuitively from time immemorial, indeed since before time ever was: that knowledge is itself *Beingness* because it can happen only when everything other than Beingness is totally annihilated.

As the *Guru's* introductory advice to the disciple concerning the nature of Self-inquiry, it would be difficult to find anything more inspiring than that offered by Mukundaraj, one of the greatest sages of Maharashtra who lived in the 12th century. Mukundaraj addressed the disciple:

> *I shall now tell you how to be able to acquire that basic secret knowledge, without the apprehension of which there cannot be anything gained, in which one must keep one's mind concentrated, that knowledge in which the yogi keeps himself constantly immersed...*
>
> *I shall convey to you clearly the very essence of this knowledge like the nectar churned out of the ocean or butter from the milk so that you may give up the various practices that are based on mere untested*

concepts and which are, therefore, only an exercise in futility so long as there has not been a clear apprehension of the significance of the sublime pronouncements of the Mahavakyas...

Who can understand the extent of the seeker's misery so long as he has not clearly apprehended and experienced the true nature of the Absolute? Those poor souls who have accepted the shackles of physical penances and mental disciplines have in reality entangled themselves in doubt and indecision. How can they ever hope to cross the ocean of samsara? Worship, pilgrimages, charities, sacrifices, mantric and tantric practices can only provide time-bound results. Prayers and penances cannot bring about liberation unless there is Self-knowledge...

Pure Knowledge – Reality – cannot shine forth until the basic unity of the individual phenomenon and the Absolute Noumenon is clearly apperceived, and there is an unblemished understanding of the nature of maya, which is the cause of the apparent difference between the two. How can there be any question of liberation so long as the identification with the body as a separate entity-doer is not lost through a proper understanding of the terms 'Thou' and 'That' in the Mahavakya 'That Thou Art'?..

How can there be liberation unless there has been a) instruction on Vedanta from the lips of the Guru; b) meditation on the Guru's words; and c) total absorption in the Guru's teaching?..

Rules of conduct laid down by the Shastras are only meant for the smoother working of the social structure. The seeker should seek instruction from the Guru regarding the essence of Vedanta, whereby one would realize that state of liberation, which is prior to thought and word. And when, in that state of liberation there is the union of Jiva and Shiva, the state of duality disappears.

Mukundaraj, thereafter, proceeds to explain to the disciple the significance of the *Mahavakya*, 'That Thou Art':

When the Absolute Subject with the help of its Primordial Energy objectivizes Itself as the multi-faceted manifestation, the aspects of the creation, maintenance and dissolution of the manifested universe happen in Consciousness. Whatever has form and shape and is, therefore, perceptible to the senses is to be rejected, and that which is unseen and remains as the witness is to be recognized as the Reality. Know That to be the Reality, which is prior to the arising of Consciousness, which is termed the all-knowing, all-controlling principle.

That Reality is the witness of everything. It cannot be measured by any criterion, it has no specific place of abidance: it is all-pervading, limitless, unknowable. That Reality is what remains when everything that is illusory is rejected, and is Itself pure knowledge, pure joy, self-evident. That Reality is all by Itself, the original fullness of Potential, the Plenum, prior to witnessing of all that is created, maintained and dissolved. The Absolute Reality is totally apart from all aspects of manifestation: Brahma (the Creator), Vishnu (the One who maintains the universe), and Rudra (the destroyer) and the Primeval Power (Consciousness). It is pure Brahman. It is only in this perspective that Reality is to be apprehended – it will not be comprehensible by any other means and practices based on ignorance and duality...

The superficial meaning of the term 'Tvam' (Thou) is conveyed by that which is governed by maya, the physical form. The true meaning of the term 'Tat' (That) is pure Brahman, which cannot be apprehended except after due discrimination. A clear apperception of the true meaning of the term 'Tat' is indeed liberation itself. The same sight in both eyes, the same sound in both ears and the same word on both lips – similarly, when one sees the same meaning in both 'Tat' (That) and 'Tvam' (Thou), the state of Brahman is attained, which is beyond duality. Just as the difference between the space in a pot and the space in a house disappears when both are broken up, so also the duality disappears when both terms are superimposed. The apparent difference between the two is only because of the illusion of maya. As soon as the false is seen as false, only Reality remains...

The knowledge of the Self is Advaita, that is non-duality, but it is obviously to be acquired in apparent duality so that the duality disappears in due course when one remains firmly in that knowledge. Instead of looking ahead as one usually does, one must look back and seek the Source in order to realize one's true Beingness.

"Looking back" is to be interpreted in the sense that the eye can see the objects in front but it cannot see itself; if one wants to see one's own eyes, it can be done only by the mind, the mind can be seen only through intellect, and it is Consciousness that can witness the intellect. Mukundaraj continues:

What one sees from this transformed perspective is nothing tangible but an all-pervading Oneness, where there is an absence of maya and non-knowledge – something immeasurable which one can know only by experiencing it. That knowledge of Brahman is self-effulgent, like a solid mass of profound happiness, the realization of which comports the end of conceptualizing...

I shall tell you how to acquire that knowledge by which you shall have perpetual peace and contentment. But one must first find out precisely who or what it is that is doing the seeking. The only thing you know as a matter of certainty is the fact I AM, I exist. But you do not know who this 'I' is. My friend, why have you forgotten your Self? Who are you, and where have you come from? Indeed, have you really gone anywhere or come from anywhere? You have never even thought of considering this matter on these lines...

Are you the body, or is it you who have the body? You are the subject and the body is your object. It is you who have the knowledge of the body and indeed that you wear this body like a garment. Although you have acquired this body as a covering made of five elements, you have identified yourself with it and you strut about as an individual. Be clearly aware that this body is an object and that you are quite apart from it, and thus give up this mistaken identity with the body...

You are aware of the constitution of your body, that a) the hair, skin, veins, flesh and bones – the solid part of the body – represent the earth; b) saliva, urine, blood, marrow and semen – the five fluid materials – represent water; c) hunger, thirst, indolence, sleep and sex represent fire; d) movement, running, resisting, relaxing and contracting – the five kinds of activity – represent air, and e) desire, anger, grief, greed and fear – the five qualities – represent ether. The physical body, with these twenty-five parts, qualities, and activities has six natural changes: it is conceived, delivered, grows, matures, becomes old and finally dies. You know the color and the form of this body, and the name it has been given. How then can you identify your Beingness with the body that is something other than you. You, as the Beingness – or Consciousness – are formless, whereas you can see the form of the body. In the waking state it is Consciousness that acts through the body and has the various experiences through the senses. The feeling that you have a particular name and form belongs to the mind, and you as the knower of the body and the mind, are apart from both...

Although you are apparently seen as the manifestation of the psyche (antahkarana), mind, intellect, concentration and ego, nevertheless you exist prior to the manifestation of these five constituents of the subtle body. It is Consciousness that is there first – spontaneous, Self-effulgent.

The one who is aware of the rising passions and emotions is the mind, and it is the intellect which discriminates and decides; that which purposefully concentrates on the decisions of the intellect is the chitta or the operational center; and the one who accepts the doership of actions is the ego. It is you who are aware of this five-fold analysis of the psyche because you are the Self-awareness or witness or Atman. The thread is made out of cotton though it is different in appearance. Similarly, mind, intellect, discrimination and ego may appear to be different but all arise from the same Source – Beingness or Conscious Reality...

The breeze is the cause of the ripple on the water, and the twist in the cotton is the cause of the thread; similarly maya is the cause of the appearance of the subtle body. When the cause is removed, both the ripple and thread disappear; similarly, with the arising of Self-knowledge and the removal of ignorance, maya becomes exposed and disappears. When the ripple and the water, or the thread and the cotton, unite – the duality disappears. Similarly, when mind merges into Consciousness, the sense of duality disappears...

The psyche is the subtle body and the relevant condition is the dream state that is based on desire. Mind works through the senses, and such desires that remain dormant in the mind manifest themselves in the dream state as objects and desires that have been experienced earlier. The manifestation of the dream world occurs because of that very speck of Consciousness that illuminates the psyche, just as the heat that heats a metal in sunlight is the quality of the sun. It is this Consciousness that has made manifestation possible. If Consciousness were to disappear, there would be no manifestation to perceive, and you would be in your original state of the fullness of the Potential, the Plenum. If you are able to reject as illusion without any substance all that you see and experience in your Consciousness, then you will be immersed in what remains as Reality. Consciousness will remain merged within Itself without movement.

According to Mukundaraj, the physical form could be classified into four segments: *a)* the physical body associated with the waking state, *b)* the subtle body associated with the dream state, *c)* the causal body associated with the deep sleep state, and *d)* the super-causal body associated with the *Turiya* or super-conscious state. Having dissociated from the individual entity, the one that remains as the witness of the four types of the body and the relevant states is the pure *Brahman*. Having thus clearly shown to the disciple that he could not possibly be either the physical body or the subtle body, Mukundaraj then goes on just as relentlessly to show that the disciple is not even the causal or super-causal body. Now, he is, as it were, taking his disciple by the hand and guiding him towards the higher cliffs of *Advaita* or non-duality. He tells the disciple:

The shadow shows the shape, form and parts of the original body but is really without substance; similarly, the one who says 'I do not know' is an illusion. There is the prior one who knows or witnesses the other one who says 'I do not know'. The fact of the not-knowing was known not to ignorance but to knowledge. That knowledge to which the not-knowing was known is the Atman. Make no mistake about it. Even if one believes that one does not have Self-knowledge, this very fact could not have been known in the absence of knowledge: I know that I do not know. Therefore, ignorance as such is an illusion: if you know that you do not know why do you unnecessarily involve yourself in the concept of ignorance? This ignorance is itself the causal body of which the physical body and the subtle body are the instruments...

Listen now to the symptoms and the quality of deep sleep. Various concepts, based on the events in the waking state, arise in the mind and reflect themselves in the dream state. But when Consciousness, which is the substratum for both the waking state and the dream state, suspends its operation, then comes the state of deep sleep – total non-knowledge. This non-knowledge is true knowledge because it is the absence of both knowledge and ignorance, which are both polaric interrelated opposites. When Consciousness re-emerges into movement, the deep-sleep state forgets its true nature and again identifies itself with the individual entity and accepts the world as real. When, however, ignorance gets discarded, Reality shines just as gold remains in its purity when the impurities are destroyed in the fire. After ignorance has been demolished and Self-knowledge has come about, that which sees the physical, the subtle and causal bodies as a witness, is the supra-causal body – this is the Turiya state. When through Self-knowledge the working bodies and the causal body are demolished, the supra-causal body itself cannot survive: when the effect is destroyed, the cause cannot survive...

That changeless state where one is aware of one's self-existence is Parabrahman, Liberation, Reality. Meditation along these lines results gradually into firm conviction, and then one experiences the hollowness of the world. When both knowledge and non-knowledge disappear, then will dawn that Knowledge which is the Absolute Reality. One must recede into the Source whence springs all knowledge. That Source is Reality, the immeasurable Potential, the Plenum into which Consciousness ultimately merges itself.

Mukundaraj has thus brought the disciple to the stage where Consciousness merges into its Source, the stage where conceptualization ceases and duality ends, the stage where the basis of all duality, the polarity of interrelated opposites, gets demolished into what phenomenally would seem to be a void. Mukundaraj, therefore, proceeds to show to the disciple that what seems to be a void cannot be a void but the Plenum, the fullness of Potential. How can something know, itself, it is a void?

That Reality which is Self-effulgent is Subjectivity and, therefore, cannot have a seer to see it as an object. Reality, therefore, cannot be a void: it is neither Consciousness in movement nor manifestation nor ignorance but the fullness of pure knowledge, the limitless Potential, beyond comprehension. You are that Reality, the Absolute Plenum, the fullness of Potential that has gobbled up even the concept of the Void, that Self-effulgent Source of everything. It is this Reality that you should understand yourself to be: independent, pure, the witnessing principle whose clear image it is impossible to visualize...

You are that Reality where all that is illusory has been absorbed, where the duality of a 'Thou' cannot survive; and so the terms 'That' and 'Thou' have become superfluous.

Now that the disciple has lost his individuality how will he rest in his natural state? Mukundaraj inspires supreme confidence in the disciple by assuring him that if his advice is clearly apprehended and diligently followed, *"you will have a conviction about your real nature, you will apperceive Reality, and will thus be always calm and peaceful."* Mukundaraj tells the disciple:

First convince yourself about your true nature as has been expounded so far, and then adopt the regular practice as follows: find a quiet spot, sit quietly, calm and relaxed, and check the outward flow of thoughts. With an attitude of renunciation towards all that is manifest, the mind should be turned inwards, away from the sense objects, to the core of the heart. Then give up gradually your identification first with the gross physical body and then with the subtle body and the causal body, and let your mind be one with space. Release your attention, smoothly and effortlessly, from the gross senses and let it merge with the total Mind or Consciousness. Wherever the attention strays, it should again be brought back into the vacant mind smoothly and gradually, so that with patience the period of concentration (not tension) becomes longer and longer. Whatever object the mind gets attracted to, let your discrimination reject it as illusory and worthless. It is only in this manner that the mind will soon give up its flights of fancy and remain in quietude...

Until the mind naturally remains in Consciousness (having given up its affinity with material things), persistent but gentle persuasion is necessary to make it drop whatever it tends to get involved in, and return to its Source. As you keep watching your mind and discover yourself as the witness, nothing else can appear on the screen of your Consciousness: two things cannot occupy your mind at the same moment.

When you understand that anything with a shape and form is, by its very nature, a hollow shell without substance, and that what is real is formless – the light of Consciousness – you will be immersed in the depth of Reality. When the mind gets absorbed in Consciousness, all objects disappear from the mind.

Mukundaraj at this juncture issues a warning to the seeker that if one were to pursue Self-knowledge while being firmly identified with the body as a separate entity, without proper guidance from the *Guru*, there is the danger of losing one's mind (Self-knowledge cannot be 'achieved' by a sense of doership). Mukundaraj says:

Do not put yourself in the position of the person who suddenly wakes up in the deepest dark of the night and thinks he has become blind. Do not get yourself enveloped in the darkness of ignorance, see all manifest phenomena as an illusion, and remain peacefully in Reality. Delve within and find out where thoughts arise. Seek the source of all thought – it is this Source, the Consciousness, which must seek and acquire the Self-knowledge: it can only happen...

Imagine for a moment that everything that is now manifest, including one's own body, has suddenly disappeared. Where precisely is it that the resulting nothingness would be registered? All that remains is 'I'-Consciousness: inside and outside, there is nothing other than the nothingness of the Void, which is the fullness of Beingness, the Potential Plenum. That on which Consciousness has arisen must surely be prior to Consciousness. Understand beyond any doubt that it is this Source of Consciousness that you are in Reality. It is in Consciousness that everything appears including your sentience – the 'I Am' sense of presence and the psyche consisting of mind, intellect, discrimination and the ego. Once this fact is clearly apprehended, nothing can remain other than Self...

Whenever you think, it is the mind that does the thinking; when the 'me' is involved in the thinking, it is the ego; when you are quiet, the very quietude is in the Consciousness itself. Consider this: if you could have remained absolutely quiet, would any mnemonical recollection have ever sprouted? Would there have been any wish, any desire? If you could have remained absorbed in the Consciousness, would you have been troubled by thoughts? Would there have been any cause then to identify yourself with the body as a separate individual? Therefore, my friend, that wherein all ignorance disappears is in a totally different dimension. If there were not something called pure knowledge, the Totality of all Potential, where would the ego have arisen? This pure and perfect knowledge – neither knowledge nor non-knowledge – is not aware of itself. It becomes a witness only when a movement in Consciousness presents some manifestation to witness.

Mukundaraj winds up this subject by giving an admirable summary, at the same time re-emphasizing the nature of Reality, which all sentient beings *Are*. He expresses the central concept in one mind-shattering epigram: *"That you do not know is known to no one else but yourself – that is itself the Reality from which arose the knowledge that you do not know."* Can this Source, the Potential of all knowledge, from which arises the very knowingness – the animating Consciousness and the sentience of sentient beings – ever be non-knowledge or ignorance?

Mukundaraj gives his final advice to the disciple:
Giving up your identification with the body if you would remain quietly absorbed in the sense of the Totality – in the 'I Am' – without attachment, you will know all that is to be known. When you thus remain immersed in Consciousness, the personal, identified consciousness having lost the power of maya, will itself take you to its Source, which is what you Are – Reality. In that state, there is no duality of any kind, all interrelated opposites have been naturally superimposed into nothingness. All there is, is pure knowledge, pure Beingness, pure Subjectivity. One cannot hold it, one cannot drop it, one cannot say it is, one cannot say it isn't. Indeed, it cannot be something one can experience – it is only something that is nothing, to be apperceived, to be felt to BE and to remain in...

Hold on to the sense 'I Am' to the exclusion of everything else. The mind being thus silent, will shine with a new light and vibrate in the Totality. When you keep the 'I Am' feeling in the focus of awareness and watch yourself ceaselessly – when there is continuous witnessing of all movements in Consciousness – the conscious and the unconscious will for a time play the game of hide and seek ['flip-flops' will happen] *until finally the two become one and the one becomes the Totality. The individual then merges in the witness, the witness in awareness, in pure Being – who is there then to take a measure of that ecstasy?!*

*The basis of
Self-realization is that
   all actions are not the doing
by some individual entity –
   but are happenings,
      according to the Cosmic Law.*

CONCLUSION

What exactly is one's 'daily living'? It does not mean just carrying on one's physical existence, but means a series of relationships from the time of birth – as a baby to one's parents, then as a brother, then as a fellow-student at school, at college, then as a colleague in an office, then as a husband, father, grandfather, and so on. Apart from this series of relationships, one is also related to one's belongings, one's ideas, one's images, one's opinions and one's expectations.

One also realizes that one is caught in a daily grind, both outwardly and inwardly. One is caught in a daily grind outwardly: keeping to the same schedule, going to work in the morning, doing the same type of work every day – maybe with some modifications here and there – till the evening, and then starting all over again the next day. This happens day after day, month after month – with an occasional holiday to break the routine – year after year for 20, 30, 40 years. Then there is the inward grind also: one continues to live within a very limited and narrow field of one's consciousness, bound by one's desires, hopes, longings, expectations, day after day. In other words, life itself has become a routine with no real sense of deep spontaneity.

When one looks at this grind of life, the next thing one sees is that one's brain is under tremendous assault and pressure from all sides: the mass media, cable television, newspapers and magazines, political upheavals, overcrowding, competition, terrorism, the pressures of globalization, environmental degradation, and so on. One somehow manages to cope with all these, and when the pressure becomes severe, one's mind tends to break down into a depression.

Another thing one clearly sees in one's daily living is that it means living in a society that is extremely aggressive and acquisitive, a society where most of the relationships are formed, sustained and terminated by economic and financial considerations. When one looks around – when one does find the time to do so! – what one sees is a big rat race: more and more people spending the money (much of it not honestly earned), buying the things they really do not need, and trying to impress people who really do not care! And it is extraordinarily difficult to get out of this rat race.

And, at some point in this rat race, the thought might occur to someone: what is all this daily living about? Nothing more than a rat race ultimately ending in death? Once this kind of searching begins, it is possible to realize, with a certain amount of probing into one's own experience, that considering oneself as a separate entity as one has to, in life and living, means a psychological fragmentation – 'me' and the 'other' – that is consolidated, nourished and sustained by the search for security against the 'other'. This fragmentation has in effect been nothing less than a prison in which one is sentenced for life.

Analyzing one's daily living, it is possible for one to see clearly that one is deeply conditioned by many factors and it is from this conditioning that one responds to anything at any time, that one lives one's life anchored in the past or the future but very rarely in the immediate present moment, that there is incredible freedom on those rare occasions when one does remain in the present moment: freedom from the fragmentation of the 'me' and the 'other', incredible tranquility. One realizes, on those rare occasions, the basic fact that what one wants most in this life is extraordinarily simple: not to be uncomfortable with oneself and not to be uncomfortable with the 'other'. There is also the realization that this discomfort is based entirely on what 'me' and/or the 'other' has done in the past or fears about what might happen in the future. And such a realization, if and when it happens, makes one stop in one's mental tracks.

The probing into one's own past experience is likely to bring out another important fact: what makes one really uncomfortable with oneself is the memory of what one had done in the past, however recent or however far back. And the memory makes one often wonder: how could I possibly have done anything so stupid – or so horrible?! On the other hand, something similar could make one uncomfortable with someone else who had done something that he should not have done, or something he should have done and didn't do.

And then, if it is supposed to happen according to one's destiny – or according to a conceptual Cosmic Law – someone or something would draw one's attention to the Buddha's pronouncement: "Events happen, deeds are done, but there is no individual doer thereof." This could again stop you in the middle of your conceptual track. "No individual doer" – surely, if that were indeed so, the stupid or horrible thing that I thought I had done was not really something I did, but something that had happened as an event. If so, I surely need not any longer carry the load of guilt or shame for something I thought I had done or not done, nor the load of hatred and malice, jealousy and envy towards any 'other'. And the absence of these two monstrous loads would surely mean the presence of peace and harmony; it would mean being anchored in tranquility while facing the inevitable happening in life from moment to moment.

And then could arise the sneaking doubt: but is it really a fact that there is no individual doer in any deed? It is a lovely concept, but is it really so? The only way you can answer this question is when you test this concept in the fire of your own experience. Investigate any single action that you are convinced is your action: did I at any time decide to do that action, from out of the blue? And you will realize that the origin of that action was not your independent decision but, perhaps, a thought that had occurred to you just previous to your decision to do that action; in other words, if that thought, over which you had no control, had not happened, what you now consider your action would not have happened!

And when you come to that same conclusion – if I did not happen to see something, or hear something (over which I had no control) what I now consider my action would not have happened – every time you do the investigation of any action, at some point a sudden flash of total acceptance could happen: I cannot be the doer of any action – no one can be the doer of any action. The happening of this flash, of course, depends upon your destiny or the Cosmic Law.

The basis of Self-realization is the realization that all actions are not the doing by some individual entity – but are happenings, events according to the Cosmic Law. If this basic concept is not acceptable, the seeker could unfortunately get into an awful frustration of trying to achieve – and not succeeding – Self-realization. An instance is provided by the teaching of a world-famous Teacher who insisted that the individual seeker must himself achieve the understanding, and does not need a *Guru*, that "any insight must be your own." He said: "Throw the *Bhagavad Gita* into the Ganges."

His ardent follower confessed in a talk at the end of an annual gathering:
"During the course of my journey with the teachings, I traveled through these various phases... Having passed through those phases, where am I now?.. I seem to be caught in a paradox: I seem to see clearly and yet do not seem to see clearly... I see that I have taken a few steps, but what is required is a giant leap, and I am unable to take that leap. I have a vague sense of what he is hinting at, but at the same time I am not quite clear about what it means; and in that sense I am caught in a paradox."

Then again, the frustrated seeker continues:
"He has talked about the 'great denial'... I see that negation is not an act of the intellect or an outcome of my conflicts, that there cannot be any reconciliation, compromise in this great denial... For the great denial to happen, there has to be a radical shift in my consciousness... that would wash away all the content of my consciousness... I see that the great denial has not taken place. What has taken place are many great escapes from facts. What has taken place are small denials and peripheral renunciations."

He further goes on to say:
"The teachings have given me considerable strength, clarity, resilience and a capacity to tackle problems with a certain poise and confidence... But when I face the world with all its complexities, pressures and challenges, when the waves of life hit me hard, it is then that reality seeps in... I also see that these deep imprints, wounds, and the debris in my consciousness just won't disappear in a flash."

Finally, the poor, frustrated seeker confesses:

"I see him as an extraordinary seer who has gone into the most profound depths of human consciousness. But I also wonder whether he has dug the entire depths of human consciousness and has brought forth all the human insights possible. I wonder whether some other equally great teacher would descend into the world in the future, dig further, and bring forth newer insights... And in this long line of seers, is he a comma or a full stop? I have no answers to these questions."

The Teacher is supposed to have begun his journey by intending to set man unconditionally free. It seems such a pity that he could not accept (according to his destiny, of course) the concept of his contemporary, the great Ramana Maharshi, that God created the world and the human being should let Him take care of His creation, or even more so, that he could not have accepted the declaration of the Buddha: "Events happen, deeds are done, but there is no individual doer thereof."

Let us be grateful for the Grace that has been conferred on us.

July 9, 2002

Dear Bhagwan,

It is as if old age and illness were dammed for the past few years. That dam has suddenly burst and in its wake, it is sweeping this body away!

I have been ill now for just over 3 weeks. First week, the body sustained itself. Second week, fever, stomach pain, total lack of appetite and strength – has laid me flat in the bed.

I was flown to Dharamshala (where the Dalai Lama lives), with another cancer patient. We were there on the 4th and 5th July, to see a venerable, 84-year old Tibetan Monk, who specializes in treating blood cancers. I was happy to be sitting in his Presence. Thru Pulse Diagnosis, pills of Tibetan herbs have been prescribed, which I have been taking regularly.

I returned here on the 6th. The long journey exhausted me and was very low on the 7th. I have lost strength even to sit up and write. This morning, I have been able to do it.

Chemotherapy has been started. The best of specialists are looking after my body. Loving care at home by one and all helps me to pull thru each fresh day.

Yesterday's blood-reports, taken after a week's gap, show that the disease is progressing very rapidly. My hemoglobin has gone down, so they are arranging for a transfusion. The platelets are low, with the possibility of any sudden bleed.

All in all, from deeply within, I feel that this show can't last for more than a week or ten days. Everybody is expecting miracles. For me, the Miracle is the Unaffected – watching all of the happenings – inside and outside.

The body remains relaxed. Mind is quiet. Searching inside, I find no thoughts of either wanting to die or wanting to live. It is very strange.

All that was an intellectual Understanding is effortlessly getting transformed into actual living Reality of each moment:

"Under the wish-giving tree my imagination has faded away, worries have disappeared. Every day, (I sip) a cup of divine nectar. My heart is absorbed in paradise, which is (my) permanent abode now. My trials and tribulations, my shortcomings and sins have all ceased to be.

With the mystical revelation, my self is effaced, my illusion is diffused (has become threadbare, scattered) everywhere. The various earthen pots have fallen to pieces. The shackles are broken, my soul is freed from its ties.

This is the work of knowledge bestowed upon me by my preceptor."

– Last words of sage Jnaneshwar

If I feel the strength, I shall write again.

Yours,
Baburaya

(Dr. Phadnis, from Pune, attended satsang with Ramesh when possible for nearly 2 years, and on the occasion of his 75th birthday. Several weeks later Ramesh received this letter.

Baburaya Phadnis expired peacefully at home at 9:00 pm, Saturday, 3 August, 2002.)

INDEX

K

Kabir 228
Kant 108
karma 17
karma yoga 212
Katha Upanishad 58
Khayyam, Omar 40, 48, 135, 162, 207
King Janaka 58
Kipling, Rudyard 76
knowledge 173, 193, 203, 274, 277, 282
Krishna 63 (see also Lord Krishna)
Krishnamurti, J. 271

L

Lao-Tzu 142, 143, 198, 199, 226
Law of Indeterminacy 231
liberation 223
Libet, Benjamin 113
lila 58, 63, 145, 146, 188, 232
living-dream 36, 37
Lord Krishna 68, 119, 144, 164, 170, 256, 267
Love 260
love 115, 204, 215, 220, 262

M

Mach Principle 234
mahabhogi 80, 133, 145, 171
Mahakasyapa 60
mahavakya 186
manifest 38
manifestation 36, 37, 38, 39, 43, 57, 74, 130, 137, 139, 144, 150, 169, 186, 191, 232, 259
Manu 150
maya 112, 116, 139, 152, 170, 187, 190, 200, 276
'me' 26, 48, 49, 51, 61, 72, 74, 75, 79, 80, 85, 90, 92, 93, 132, 133, 140, 145, 155, 156, 167, 170, 183, 215, 218, 221, 223, 240, 251, 255, 269, 286
'me'-doer 49, 50, 51, 74

me-entity 84
meaning of life 164
meditation 59, 60, 73, 122, 123, 158, 245, 250
Meister Eckhart 126, 192, 259, 260
metanoesis 191
metaphysics 235
Mind 186, 281
mind 39, 40, 48, 49, 51, 52, 53, 56, 67, 68, 79, 93, 154, 187, 202, 238, 244, 266, 278, 282
mindfulness 85
'mine' 72
moksha 212
Monoimus 154
Mother Kali 130
Mukundaraj 274, 278, 279, 280, 281, 282
'myself' 67
mystic 116, 123, 126, 192, 193, 217, 231, 232, 234
mystical 234

N

Natural Law 200, 251
natural state 92, 264, 265, 266
nature 61, 66, 70, 73, 123, 164, 189, 200, 211, 212, 213, 262, 280
near-death 201
Neem Karoli Baba 138, 148, 172, 173
Newton 151
nirvana 145, 163
Nisargadatta Maharaj 164, 255
Nizamuddin Aulia 173
no-mind 79, 80, 85, 191
No-self 113
non-action 81
non-doership 52, 55, 127, 133, 154, 263, 264
Non-duality 137
non-duality 15, 137, 166, 180, 181, 203, 204, 263
non-volition 263, 264, 266
noumenal 38

For information on Ramesh Balsekar visit:
www.rameshbalsekar.com

For further details, contact:
Yogi Impressions Books Pvt. Ltd.
61, Anjali, Minoo Desai Road, Colaba,
Mumbai 400 005, India.
Website: www.yogiimpressions.com

Telephone: (022) 22842923/4/6
Fax: (022) 22046825
E-mail: yogi@yogiimpressions.com

Also visit:
www.indiayogi.com
Spiritual Resources from India

ALSO PUBLISHED BY YOGI IMPRESSIONS

Paperback

Stillness Speaks
by Eckhart Tolle

The essence of his teaching in short, simple pieces that everyone can understand. The book is arranged in ten chapters with subjects ranging from 'Beyond the Thinking Mind' to 'Suffering & the End of Suffering'. The result is a book filled with timely and powerful messages, and profoundly transformative when read as a whole.

Hardbound and
Paperback

The Power of Now
by Eckhart Tolle
(Hindi version – Shaktiman Vartaman)

To make the journey into 'The Power of Now', you will need to leave your analytical mind and its false created self, the ego, behind. The journey is challenging, yet Eckhart Tolle describes it simply in a question and answer format to guide us. It is here, in the Now, you can find your joy and embrace your true self.

Paperback

Practicing The Power of Now
by Eckhart Tolle

This handy companion book to Eckhart Tolle's internationally bestselling 'The Power of Now' extracts the essence of his spiritual teaching. Arranged in it are a set of meditations and exercises to actually help you lead a more liberated life, and discover the path to "a life of grace, ease and lightness."

Pocketbook

Little Book of Mind-Power
by Uri Geller

Every page will energise you with a new confidence and determination to develop and super-charge your own will to win. Uri Geller teaches us how we can tap into the hidden strengths each one of us possesses and explore our highest individual potential.

Paperback

Present Moment Awareness
by Shannon Duncan

'Present Moment Awareness' is filled with practical, down-to-earth advice for living in the present. With easy, accessible exercises, it shows readers how they can drop their emotional baggage, calm their worries about the future, and start enjoying the peace and happiness that can only be found in the present moment.